Social Security
in the Fifteen Member States
of the European Union

Social Security Law in the Fifteen Member States of the European Union

prof.dr. Danny PIETERS

in co-operation with

Dr. Gabriel Amitsis
Dr. Wolfgang Brodil
Prof. dr. Eberhard Eichenhofer
Mr. Thomas Erhag
Mr. Claude Ewen
Prof. dr. Bent Greve
Prof. dr. Francis Kessler
Mr. Matti Kari
Mr. Sebastião Nóbrega Pizarro
Prof. dr. Antonio Ojeda Avilés
Mrs. Maria B.C. Pacheco Turnes
Dr. Christina Sanchez-Rodas Navarro
Prof. Adrian Sinfield
Dr. Steven Vansteenkiste
Dr. Michaela Windisch-Graetz

MAKLU
Antwerpen-Apeldoorn

Danny Pieters (editor)
Social Security Law in the Fifteen Member States of the European Union
Antwerpen - Apeldoorn
MAKLU
1997

285 pag. - 24 cm x 15.5 cm
ISBN 90 6215 590 1
D/1997/1997/48
NUGI 695

Omslagontwerp: Danny Pieters
Gedrukt op chloor- en zuurvrij papier

© 1997   MAKLU-UITGEVERS n.v. en Danny Pieters

No part of this book may be reproduced in any form, by print, photoprint, microfilm or any other means, without written permission from the publisher

MAKLU-UITGEVERS n.v.
Somersstraat 13/15, 2018 Antwerpen (België), Tel. + 32(3)231 29 00
Koninginnelaan 96, 7315 EB Apeldoorn (Nederland), Tel. + 31(55)522 06 25

Table of contents

Table of contents 5

Preface 11

Chapter One. AUSTRIA 19
   1. Introduction: concept and sources of social security law 19
   2. Administrative organisation 20
   3. Personal scope of application 21
   4. Risks and benefits 23
      4.1. Old age 23
      4.2. Death 25
      4.3. Incapacity for work 26
      4.4. Unemployment 29
      4.5. Health and long-term care 29
      4.6. Family 31
      4.7. Need 32
   5. Financing 32
   6. Judicial review 33

Chapter Two. BELGIUM 35
   1. Introduction: concept and sources of social security law 35
   2. Administrative organisation 37
   3. Personal scope of application 40
   4. Risks and benefits 42
      4.1. Old age 43
      4.2. Death 44
      4.3. Incapacity for work 45
      4.4. Unemployment 45
      4.5. Health care 47
      4.6. Family 48
      4.7. Need 49
   5. Financing 50
   6. Judicial review 52

Table of Contents

Chapter Three. DENMARK ... 55
1. Introduction: concept and sources of social security law ... 55
2. Administrative organisation ... 57
3. Personal scope of application ... 58
4. Risks and benefits ... 61
    4.1. Old age ... 61
    4.2. Death ... 63
    4.3. Incapacity for work ... 64
    4.4. Unemployment ... 67
    4.5. Health care ... 68
    4.6. Family ... 69
    4.7. Need ... 69
5. Financing ... 71
6. Judicial review ... 72

Chapter Four. FINLAND ... 75
1. Introduction: concept and sources of social security law ... 75
2. Administrative organisation ... 76
3. Personal scope of application ... 77
4. Risks and benefits ... 78
    4.1. Old age ... 78
    4.2. Death ... 80
    4.3. Incapacity for work ... 81
    4.4. Unemployment ... 84
    4.5. Health care ... 85
    4.6. Family ... 86
    4.7. Need ... 87
5. Financing ... 88
6. Judicial review ... 89

Chapter Five. FRANCE ... 91
1. Introduction: concept and sources of social security law ... 91
2. Administrative organisation ... 94
3. Personal scope of application ... 96
4. Risks and benefits ... 97
    4.1. Old age ... 97
    4.2. Death ... 98
    4.3. Incapacity for work ... 100
    4.4. Unemployment ... 102
    4.5. Health care ... 103
    4.6. Family ... 105
    4.7. Need ... 107
5. Financing ... 108
6. Judicial review ... 109

Chapter Six. GERMANY 111

1. Introduction: concept and sources of social security law 111
2. Administrative organisation 113
3. Personal scope of application 115
4. Risks and benefits 117
    4.1. Old age 117
    4.2. Death 118
    4.3. Incapacity for work 120
    4.4. Unemployment 123
    4.5. Health and long-term care 124
    4.6. Family 126
    4.7. Need 126
5. Financing 127
6. Judicial review 128

Chapter Seven. GREAT BRITAIN 131

1. Introduction: concept and sources of social security law 131
2. Administrative organisation 132
3. Personal scope of application 133
4. Risks and benefits 134
    4.1. Old age 136
    4.2. Death 137
    4.3. Incapacity for work 138
    4.4. Unemployment 139
    4.5. Health care 140
    4.6. Family 141
    4.7. Need 142
5. Financing 143
6. Judicial review 144

Chapter Eight. GREECE 147

1. Introduction: concept and sources of social security law 147
2. Administrative organisation 150
3. Personal scope of application 152
4. Risks and benefits 155
    4.1. Old age 155
    4.2. Death 158
    4.3. Incapacity for work 160
    4.4. Unemployment 162
    4.5. Health care 163
    4.6. Family 164
    4.7. Need 165
5. Financing 166
6. Judicial review 168

Table of Contents

Chapter Nine. IRELAND 171

1. Introduction: concept and sources of social security law 171
2. Administrative organisation 172
3. Personal scope of application..173
4. Risks and benefits 175
   4.1. Old Age 176
   4.2. Death 177
   4.3. Incapacity for work 178
   4.4. Unemployment 179
   4.5. Health care 180
   4.6. Family 181
   4.7. Need 182
5. Financing 183
6. Judicial review 183

Chapter Ten. ITALY 185

1. Introduction: concept and sources of social security law 185
2. Administrative organisation 187
3. Personal scope of application..188
4. Risks and benefits 189
   4.1. Old age 189
   4.2. Death 191
   4.3. Incapacity for work 192
   4.4. Unemployment 194
   4.5. Health care 195
   4.6. Family 196
   4.7. Need 196
5. Financing 197
6. Judicial review 198

Chapter Eleven. LUXEMBOURG 199

1. Introduction: concept and sources of social security law 199
2. Administrative organisation 201
3. Personal scope of application..204
4. Risks and benefits 206
   4.1. Old age 206
   4.2. Death 207
   4.3. Incapacity for work 209
   4.4. Unemployment 211
   4.5. Health care 212
   4.6. Family 213
   4.7. Need 214
5. Financing 215
6. Judicial review 217

Chapter Twelve. THE NETHERLANDS 219

1. Introduction: concept and sources of social security law 219
2. Administrative organisation 221
3. Personal scope of application 224
4. Risks and benefits 227
    4.1. Old age 228
    4.2. Death 228
    4.3. Incapacity for work 230
    4.4. Unemployment 231
    4.5. Health care 232
    4.6. Family 233
    4.7. Need 234
5. Financing 235
6. Judicial review 236

Chapter Thirteen. PORTUGAL 239

1. Introduction: concept and sources of social security law 239
2. Administrative organisation 241
3. Personal scope of application 242
4. Risks and benefits 244
    4.1. Old age 244
    4.2. Death 244
    4.3. Incapacity for work 247
    4.4. Unemployment 250
    4.5. Health care 251
    4.6. Family 252
    4.7. Need 253
5. Financing 253
6. Judicial review 254

Chapter Fourteen. SPAIN 255

1. Introduction: concept and sources of social security law 255
2. Administrative organisation 258
3. Personal scope of application 259
4. Risks and benefits 261
    4.1. Old age 261
    4.2. Death 262
    4.3. Incapacity for work 264
    4.4. Unemployment 266
    4.5. Health care 268
    4.6. Family 268
5. Financing 269
6. Judicial review 270

Chapter Fifteen. SWEDEN 273

    1. Concept and sources..273
    2. Administrative system..274
    3. Personal scope of application...275
    4. Risks and benefits 276
        4.1. Old age 276
        4.2. Death 278
        4.3. Incapacity for work 279
        4.4. Unemployment...280
        4.5. Health care 281
        4.6. Family 282
        4.7. Need 283
    5. Financing 283
    6. Judicial review 284

Preface

In each Member State of the European Union, the policy makers and the people responsible for the administration of social security are paying more and more attention to the social security systems of other Member States. Various explanations can be given for this ever growing attention. Since the latter half of the seventies, due to the economic crisis, the national social security systems of nearly all the Member States have been under severe pressure; indeed, the systems, which have often been in existence for decades, appear to be incompatible with newly arisen social circumstances. This led to research into ways of reorganising and, as far as possible, qualitatively improving social protection; and since the grass is always greener on the other side of the fence... Ever since the full integration of the internal market, and especially since the emergence of the European Union (Maastricht) and the progression towards the European Monetary Union, the interest in foreign social security systems has gained momentum. A central and recurrent question which appears in this context relates to whether it is possible, desirable and practical to harmonise the national social security systems. An improvement of the co-ordination regulations, which are designed to protect the rights of intra-community migrants, has also been called for. However, before methods of greater harmonisation and means of improving the instruments for co-ordination can be contemplated, some insight is needed into the specificities of the systems which are to be harmonised or co-ordinated. Apart from all that, even the public opinion has shown interest in foreign social security systems: do we not often hear or read in the media (of all the Member States!) how much a country's own system compares poorly with that of its partners within the European Union. Figures are often supplied which can support such views and propositions.

Confronted with such a growing interest in the social security systems existing within the European Union, we were surprised seven years ago to find out that no clearly structured key to these systems was available. There were only the so called 'Comparative Tables': "MISSOC. Social Protection in the Member States of the Union". These are published approximately every two years by the Commission of the European Community. In these comparative tables it is attempted to place similar (sometimes small) aspects of the social security schemes of the Member States alongside each other. Without throwing doubt upon the value of the tables, it must be agreed that they are not suitable for deriving a general insight into the structure of the social security systems. Then there are of course numerous works about comparative social security law, as well as publications on specific themes. In introductory chapters these sometimes give a brief, general overview of the systems in the light of the specific theme of the comparison; but generally, these too are inappropriate for providing an overview of the social security systems compared therein.

In short, seven years ago we became convinced of the necessity to write an introduction to the social security systems of all the Member States, written in a simple, straight forward style and within the "unreasonably" brief space of a few hundred pages. The book was given the title "Introduction into the Social Security Law of the Member States of the European Community". After having produced a revised second edition in 1993, we decided in 1997 to rewrite the compendium and to include within it new chapters about the social security systems of the three newest Member States, Austria, Finland and Sweden. The title has also been adapted to encompass the concept of the European Union.

The present book will offer the social security expert, who has some comparative experience, the opportunity to place his knowledge of (aspects of) foreign social security systems within the broader national context of these systems; for others, this book will simplify their first ventures into the field of comparative social security law. It constitutes, therefore, a real introduction and does not pretend to provide an exhaustive description of all the aspects of social security within each of the Member States. Thus, on the basis of this introduction, the reader can decide for himself which foreign social security systems deserve attention for his/her area of comparison, without necessarily being confined to a study of the larger and/or linguistically accessible states. The reader will not be able to rely upon this work for the purpose of a true comparison of specific themes, e.g. the role of the means-test in social security; nevertheless, he can use it as a guide which tells him from where he could best start his further research.

Although the fundamental aim was to offer a brief overview of the national social security systems of the fifteen Member States, we also wanted to facilitate the broader comparison of these systems. As a matter of fact, even for the purpose of obtaining a good understanding of the social security system in a single country, it often makes sense to structure that system in the same way as the systems of the other countries that are studied. For this reason, our description of the social security systems of each of the fifteen Member States is based upon a uniform structure, subdivided in the following chapters:

1. Introduction: concept and sources of social security law;
2. Administrative organisation;
3. Personal scope of application;
4. Risks and benefits;
5. Financing;
6. Judicial review.

This structure follows that presented in our general introductory work: "Introduction into the Basic Principles of Social Security" edited by Kluwer (Deventer/Boston) in 1993 (ISBN 90 6544 787 3). In the latter work, each of these chapters are developed and the basic terminology is explained fully.

Before summarising the main topics of interest we discussed under the above mentioned headings, a short remark must be made. We wanted to offer a legal introduction into the social security systems of the fifteen Member States. Information with regard to the demographic situation in which the social security system of a country operates, with regard to the economics of social security, or with regard to sociological questions, will not be found within the present work. This book describes the normative, legal state of social security. Only if the legal norms blatantly conflict with the reality of the social security system within a Member State, are the above subjects dealt with.

The description of social security law within each European Union country starts with an introductory section devoted to the concept of national social security and to the national sources of social security law.

An introduction to social security law in a particular country must include a clear description of what is understood by social security within that country. There is no such thing as an international or E.U. definition of social security. In international or E.U. instruments which relate to social security, the material scope of application is determined differently for each instrument, so the definition of social security varies from one legal norm to another, which means that there is no uniformity. Nevertheless, the enumeration of risks as laid down in I.L.O. Convention no. 102 containing minimum standards of social security, exercises considerable influence: medical care, sickness, unemployment, old age, employment injury, family, maternity, invalidity and death. The material scope of application of the important regulation (EEC) no. 1408/71 concurs with this. It is now of interest to find out whether the concept of social security in a specific national context includes, exhaustively, all benefits schemes for the coverage of one or more of the risks listed above and whether it excludes the schemes for the coverage of other risks. Of course, to a large extent, the national social security concept will conform with the concept of the above international instruments, but there are exceptions. Sometimes, a specific branch of social security, e.g. unemployment benefit, is not considered to be a part of the national social security system, whereas it may equally be the case that the coverage of a non-social risk branch, e.g. study costs, is included within the concept of social security. Sometimes, social assistance and (other) schemes providing minimum means of subsistence are included within the social security concept and sometimes they are not. From his own experience the reader will know that even within his own system there is no general consensus of opinion with regard to the definition of social security. However, we do not concern ourselves too much with problems of definition. Our starting point is the concept of social security which has gained the highest degree of national consensus. For the purpose of the subsequent description of national social security law we then depart from the national concept of social security and consider the schemes which, although not deemed to be within the national definition, cover one of the social risks contained in the above international instruments. As a rule, social assistance (covering the risk of need) is also included.

The sources of national social security law are dealt with in the next part of the first section. Special attention is paid to constitutional provisions which are relevant for social security, especially clauses concerning fundamental rights, provisions with regard to the organisation of social security and the possible division of powers between central government and federal states. Furthermore, it is discussed which source must be considered to be the most important for the main body of social security rules; formal statutes, administrative regulations, self-administration of social security institutions, or collective agree-

Preface

ments? Social security schemes, which derive their source from collective labour agreements, or contracts under private law are mentioned, but generally they are not taken into consideration in the subsequent chapters.
Finally, it must be mentioned that in line with the objective of this study, international law which applies for or within the Member States is not taken into consideration, even if this grants directly enforceable rights to citizens in particular Member States.

Before we continue with the description of the contents of the various chapters, first a remark of a more general nature must be made. Various social security systems often co-exist within the national borders of the Community countries. It was not always possible to map out all of them. Due to the limited scope of this work, attention could only be paid to the most important schemes; and so the "general schemes" have been discussed, as well as the schemes which apply for employees in general. The systems for self-employed persons have also been discussed to the extent that this coincided with the national social security traditions. Due to the large variance which exists in the Member States between, on the one hand, schemes for civil servants and, on the other hand, schemes for those who carry out other occupational activities, and because the social coverage of civil servants is often closely connected with administrative law, it was decided in principle not to discuss the social security schemes which apply for this category of people. It goes without saying that schemes of a universal nature, i.e. applying to all residents have been included.

The administrative structure is highlighted in the second section of the country reports. It is perhaps surprising that we concentrated first upon the administrative structure of social security and only after that upon its actual contents (e.g. benefits, financing). However, it is often the case that the understanding of the organisation of administration, management and supervision is necessary in order to appreciate the material aspects of social security law. As mentioned above, there is no country within the European Union which has only one social security system; there are always a number of parallel systems, sometimes even more than a hundred social security schemes co-existing within the borders of a single country. Often there appears to be as many social security schemes as there are corresponding administrative bodies, rather than perhaps more logically, the opposite. In any case, the experience of drafting the brief descriptions of social security for each country gradually taught the authors that is was preferential to start with the administrative organisation. Thereby attention has been paid to, among other things, the competent ministers, the (other) bodies charged with supervision, advice and/or policy development and the institutions in charge of the actual administration of the social security schemes.

The personal scope of application is discussed in the third section of the reports. For each scheme it is considered which people are potentially eligible for benefit. Here attention has been paid to the usual distinctions, such as those between universal insurance schemes and employee insurance schemes, or between obligatory and voluntary insurance. Furthermore, attention has been paid to the question of whether entitlement to benefits exists upon an individual basis or upon a family basis. In this section the effect of international and E.U.

law upon social security and the delimitation of the personal scope of application of the national schemes, is in principle being disregarded.

The fourth section of the reports deals with the social risks which are covered and the benefits payable upon the materialisation of these risks. First of all, when this was considered to be useful, some general remarks were made which are relevant for a number of, or for all the risks and/or benefits within a country. Thereafter the following risks are dealt with consecutively: old age, death, incapacity for work (short term and long term), unemployment, health care (and long term care, where this is recognised as a separate branch), family and need. In principle, the coverage of professional risks is discussed under the heading of the risk which is actually covered (regardless of the professional origins), i.e. incapacity for work, death or medical care. Benefit levels are not included, but attention has been paid to the question of whether or not there is a mechanism for the adjustment of the benefit levels to increases in prices and/or to increases in the general wage level.
In this section we were sometimes confronted with the problem of classifying certain rather hermaphroditic benefit schemes under a particular risk, e.g. the difficulty of classifying 'pre-pension' benefits either as unemployment benefits or as old age benefits. Where such a problem arose, we dealt with the scheme in question within the framework of the most appropriate risk, taking into account national traditions of classification.
Obviously, the entitlement conditions of the various benefit schemes could only be roughly described. Specific regulations which are designed to prevent overlapping of benefits were generally not discussed.

The legal framework for the financing of social security is dealt with in the fifth section. The complex "ins and outs" of the actual financing of social security as such has not been described, instead we have limited ourselves to mapping out the most important legal provisions which exist in this area. As such the structure of the financing is only sketched.

Judicial review is the subject of the sixth and final section. It is not sufficient to simply grant rights to citizens (or to specific groups); there must also be certain ways for the citizens to realise these rights. Here, attention is paid to legal procedures, as well as to some "extra legal" procedures which are of importance in a country. In view of the legal nature of this study, no attention is paid to possible factual obstacles which prevent the citizen from obtaining access to justice.

In editing this work, the reports were not only uniformly divided into sections, but also the description of each national system within the separate sections was kept as uniform as possible. Yet, the specificity of each system sometimes required special attention and thus sacrificing some of the uniformity within each chapter.

As far as possible, the names of systems, benefit schemes and institutions are mostly referred to in the (or a) language of the country studied. A personal, rather literal, English translation is given whenever a name is mentioned for the first time.

Preface

In principle, this description of the national social security systems was concluded in the Summer of 1997. In full accordance with the aims of this book as described above, an overview is given of the law as it applied at that time. Thus, as a rule, attention is neither paid to historical developments, nor to future expectations with regard to the systems studied. On the same grounds, temporary transitory schemes are generally not discussed.

The present book has been written in observance of the strictest methodological principles that remained feasible. It describes the national social security systems of the fifteen Member States in a uniform way, but does not compare them. It is therefore not really a comparative work; for the methodology of social security (law) comparison, we would like to refer to our 'Socialezekerheidsrechtsvergelijking ten dienste van Europa' edited by Kluwer (Deventer, 1992) (ISBN 90 268 23428) and of which an English summary will be published in 1998 in our contribution to the Liber Amicorum for the 65th anniversary of prof.dr.dr.h.c. Hans F. Zacher.

We took the final responsibility for the final text of all the country reports. However, the present work builds further on the earlier versions of the 'Introduction into the Social Security Law of the Member States of the European Community' as well as on an intensive collaboration with our foreign colleagues. The way of operating when writing this book was the following. On the basis of the earlier country reports of the 'Introduction' (except of course for the three new countries) an up to date version was made either by ourselves or by our corresponding colleagues. If the country reports were first made by ourselves, the text was sent for further comments to our foreign colleagues and subsequently adapted by ourselves. The first draft of the Austrian and Swedish country reports were made by our foreign colleagues and then adapted by ourselves to fit with the over-all structure of this book.

Our foreign colleagues and correspondents thus played a very crucial role in the realisation of the country reports and therefore are to be thanked in the first place: Dr. Gabriel Amitsis for Greece; Dr. Wolfgang Brodil and Dr. Michaela Windisch-Graetz for Austria; Prof. dr. Eberhard Eichenhofer for Germany; Mr. Thomas Erhag for Sweden; Mr. Claude Ewen for Luxembourg; Prof. dr. Bent Greve for Denmark; Prof. dr. Francis Kessler for France; Mr. Matti Kari for Finland; Mr Sebastião Nóbrega Pizarro, Prof. dr. Antonio Ojeda Avilés, Mrs Maria B.C. Pacheco Turnes and Dr. Christina Sanchez-Rodas Navarro for Spain; Prof. Adrian Sinfield for the United Kingdom; and Dr. Steven Vansteenkiste for the Netherlands. Mr. Tim Callan provided us with valuable information about Ireland. Mr. Floris Goyers screened the changes which have occurred in the social security systems of the Member States during the last few years and deserves all our gratitude; also thanks to Mr. Jason Nickless for revising the English text and to Mr. Jan Spooren for taking care of the communication lines between all the persons involved.

However, as was mentioned above, we also built further on the earlier 'Introductions': and must therefore thank again all persons who played a role in the realisation of these previous editions.

Preface

One category of critical readers of the earlier 'Introductions' deserve a special word of thanks: various generations of students of the ERASMUS and TEMPUS Programme Social Security in Europe have used these to penetrate the jungle of Europe's social security systems and have helped us improving the country reports and the general set-up of the work.

It was not always easy to include sufficient and correct information within the restricted space of some fifteen pages per country. Generalisation and simplification should of course not result in incorrect statements. Sometimes collecting relevant material was a problem. If readers consider that any of the country reports contain unexpected mistakes or flaws, we shall be pleased to hear about this. However, in our view, the above way in which each report was drafted and the exceptional care that our correspondents have given to the realisation of this introduction guarantee the quality of the information contained. Nonetheless, comments which we may receive could further improve this quality.

prof. dr. Danny PIETERS
Leuven, October 13th, 1997

Chapter One

AUSTRIA

1. Introduction: concept and sources of social security law

The help organised by the State in favour of an individual who is confronted by the emergence of certain every day social risks, is regulated by 'social law' (*Sozialrecht*); there is no real concept of 'social security' corresponding to this branch of law. However, within 'social law' a distinction is made between three forms of social security: social insurance (*Sozialversicherung*), compensation schemes (*Versorgungssysteme*) and assistance schemes (*Fürsorgesysteme*).

The social insurance schemes are characterised by their compulsory nature; by their coverage of all the members of the same category of professionally active people who are confronted with a particular social risk and by their financing, in principle, out of contributions by the concerned persons. Today, the social insurances cover the risks of sickness, maternity, labour accident and professional disease, work incapacity, old age, unemployment and death of the bread winner. These risks are not covered by one single social insurance system; persons are rather grouped according to their professional activity and submitted to separate social insurance systems. We can distinguish between the social insurance system of the wage earners (regulated by the *Allgemeines SozialVersicherungsGesetz ASVG*), of the self-employed (regulated by the *Gewerblich SelbständigenVersicherungsGesetz GSVG*), of the farmers (regulated by the *Bauern SozialVersicherungsGesetz BSVG*), of the free professions (regulated by the *Freiberufler Sozial Versicherungs Gesetz FSVG*) and of the civil servants (regulated by the *Bundes-Kranken-und UnfallVerischerungsGesetz B-KUVG*). Within each of these systems there are separate branches for 'sickness insurance', 'accident insurance' and 'pension insurance'. The unemployment insurance (regulated by the *ArbeitslosenVersicherungsGesetz AlVG*) is treated separately because it is intimately linked to the labour market management.
Self-employed persons and farmers are not covered by the unemployment insurance. Neither are the self-employed compulsorily insured for incapacity for work, they can, however, join this insurance on a voluntary basis.

The compensation schemes or the *Versorgungssysteme* provide benefits which are not granted under social insurance for a specific professional group, but guaranteed by the state and financed out of the general budget (taxation), without being dependent upon the need of the beneficiaries. Compensation schemes exist for war and army victims and victims of crime, as well as for family allowances. The pensions of the civil servants are also linked to this category of social security, although the compensation character of these pensions has been broken by the imposition upon the civil servants of the obligation to pay pension contributions. The typical *Versorgung*-schemes, like those for war and army victims and victims of crime, provide cash benefits compensating persons who have made a special sacrifice for society or who have performed special services.

Unlike the two preceding categories, the third category of social security schemes is characterised by means testing. Only persons who are needy, i.e. only those who cannot meet the necessities of daily life with their income from work or their patrimony or alimonies paid to them by others, qualify for social assistance according to the principle of subsidiarity. The *Fürsorge* is also financed out of the general budget (taxation).

The Austrian constitution does not contain fundamental social rights, but specifies the federal (and state) competencies in the area of social security. In article 10 we read that
"(1) The Federation has powers of legislation and execution in the following matters: (...)
11. labour legislation in so far as it does not fall under Article 12; social and private insurance; (...)
12. public health (...), but only sanitary supervision with respect to hospitals, nursing homes, health resorts and natural curative resources; (...)
17. population policy in so far as it concerns the grant of children's allowances and the organisation of the equalisation of family charges (...)"
In article 12 we read that:
"(1) In the following matters, framework legislation is the competence of the Federation, the issue of implementing laws and execution is the competence of the States:
1. social welfare; population policy in so far as it does not fall under Article 10; public social and welfare establishments; maternity, infant, and adolescent welfare; hospitals and nursing homes; requirements to be imposed for health reasons on health resorts, sanatoria, and health establishments; natural curative resources;(...)
6. labour legislation and the protection of workers and employees in so far as it is a matter of workers and employees engaged in agriculture and forestry.(...)".

Federal and state statutes lay down the basic rules of Austrian social security. The social insurance institutions and their association, the *Hauptverband der Sozialversicherungsträger*, are competent to issue binding regulations (called 'Richtlinien', 'Satzungen' or 'Krankenordnungen').

2. *Administrative organisation*

The over all policy responsibility lies with the Federal Minister of Labour and Social Affairs, except for the family benefits, which are the competence of the Federal Minister for Youth and Family Affairs.

In total 28 social insurance institutions administer the social insurance schemes; they are grouped in one association, the *Hauptverband der Sozialver-*

sicherungsträger. The social insurance institutions are set up according to the appropriate branch of social insurance (e.g. the General Accident Insurance Institute), the region (e.g. the regional sickness funds *Gebietskrankenkassen*) and/or the group of insured persons (e.g. the Insurance Fund for the civil servants). There is no choice concerning the Institute or Fund to which one has to become affiliated.

The pension insurance branch is managed by the Pension Insurance Institute for Blue Collar Workers and the Pension Insurance Institute for White Collar Workers.
The sickness insurance branch is administered (both in the collecting and distributing function) by 9 regional sickness insurance funds and 10 company sickness insurance funds. These sickness insurance funds also collect the contributions for the two other branches of social insurance and for the unemployment insurance.
The accident insurance branch is managed both for wage earners and the self-employed by the General Accident Insurance Institute.
The Social Insurance Institute for Trade and Industry manages the sickness insurance and pension insurance branches of the insurance system for the self-employed.
The Insurance Fund for Civil Servants runs the accident and sickness insurance branches of the system applicable to the civil servants.
The Social Insurance Fund for Farmers runs the three traditional insurance branches of the farmers social insurance system.

The social insurance institutions are public law bodies subject to self-government, with the Minister of Labour and Social Affairs only exercising a controlling authority, making sure that the law is respected and that the administration is efficient.

The administration of the unemployment insurance lies with the Labour Market Service (*ArbeitsMarktSecrvice Österreich AMS*), a service enterprise of public law without self-government. There are one federal, 9 provincial and about 100 local agencies. Each of them is directed by a board, half of which is composed of representatives of the public authorities, the other half contains representatives of the trade unions and employer organisations. The first task of the *AMS* is the labour mediation of the unemployed; but it also grants the unemployment benefits.

Austrian social assistance is organised on the level of the nine *Länder*.

3. *Personal scope of application*

The wage earner social insurance system (*ASVG*) covers all those professionally active people who are not self-employed, i.e. everyone who is working for remuneration in a relationship of professional and economic dependency upon their employer. However, employed persons whose monthly wage does not exceed a certain limit (the '*geringfügig Beschäftigte*') are excluded from the

ASVG. Some persons who commit themselves to similar activities, though in personal independence, such as accountants, members of the controlling board of companies etc. are also insured under the *ASVG*. The *ASVG* only covers those who commit themselves for either a determined or undetermined period of time, as opposed to those who work toward a specified result. If the person is concerned with achieving a set goal then they are not covered by the *ASVG*. Wage earners insured under the *ASVG* are also covered by the unemployment insurance.

Many of the latter category of self-employed people are covered by the social insurance system of the self-employed (*GSVG*). Insurance under the *GSVG* is conditional upon running an enterprise and consequently to being affiliated with the chamber of commerce. Farmers, whose estimated income out of the agricultural or forestal exploitation of their grounds exceeds a certain amount, are insured under the farmers social insurance system of the *BSVG*. Other self-employed persons are partially covered by the social insurances of the liberal professions (*FSVG*) but they remain partially uninsured and are thus dependent to some extent upon private insurance. The latter is the case for self-employed physio-and psychotherapists.

Civil servants are covered for the branches of 'sickness' and 'accidents' under the social insurance system of the civil servants (*B-KUVG*), whereas their pensions are part of the *Versorgungssystem*.

When a person has made contributions to a social insurance scheme in good faith for at least six months but he does not officially qualify according to the personal scope of this system, he will benefit from what is called 'formal insurance' (*Formalversicherung*). Once formally insured he will enjoy the same rights as a person who does belong to the scope of application of the concerned system.

If persons exercise several professional activities which are covered by different professional social insurances, they will be insured under each of the relevant social insurances for each corresponding activity.

The social insurances do not only confer benefits upon the socially insured persons themselves, but may also benefit their family members.

The (compulsory) social insurance starts and ends according to the relevant statutory provisions, in other words, it is independent of the registration of the socially insured person. However, the socially insured person (or his employer) is under an administrative obligation to report to the relevant social insurance institutions.

The statutory social insurance schemes are in essence compulsory. However, next to compulsory insurance, different voluntary insurances have been created within the statutory social insurance schemes in order give those persons who are not covered by compulsory insurance, an option to participate in the public social insurance system.

Unlike the other benefits, the 'emergency assistance' granted to unemployed people who have exhausted their unemployment benefits, is in principle only granted to Austrian nationals. This restriction has, however, been held contrary to the equality principle of the European Convention of Human Rights and Fundamental Freedoms, by the European Court of Human Rights of Strasbourg.

When social assistance is awarded on a provincial level, it depends upon the concerned *Land* whether or not a nationality condition is imposed upon the receipt of social assistance. Residence within the *Land* is, however, always required.

4. Risks and benefits

The social insurance benefits normally relate to the income upon which social insurance contributions have been paid. However, the social insurance schemes only take into account the professional income up to a maximum level (*Höchstbemessungsgrundlage*). Not only are contributions only paid up to this maximum base of calculation but also the benefits are calculated on the basis of an income not exceeding this maximum amount.

As we shall hereafter meet the benefits of the accident insurance under various headings, let us define here what is understood by labour accident and professional disease.
A labour accident occurs whenever the event that damages the claimant's health is locally, temporary and causally related to the insured activity. This definition extends to include accidents suffered, whilst travelling between home and work, whilst on the way to and from a medical doctor, whilst on a journey that is related to one's professional interests or representations (trade unions) and whilst travelling once a month to the bank in order to cash one's wage. Self-employed individuals and farmers are insured for the activities which, according to objective criteria, are directly related to the maintenance, promotion or realisation of their self-employed activities.
The law enumerates a catalogue of recognised professional diseases and determines in which enterprises, which diseases may lead to benefit under the professional disease insurance. It is also necessary here to establish a causal relationship between the insured activity and the emergence of the health damage; a high degree of probability is deemed to be sufficient for the establishment of a causal link.

4.1. Old age

Within the social insurance schemes it is possible to distinguish between the following pensions related to reaching a certain age after having worked: the normal old age pension, the early old age pension in case of a long insurance record, the early old age pension in case of unemployment, the early old age pension in case of reduced work capacity (to be dealt with sub 4.3) and the partial pension (*'Gleitpension'*).

Men having reached the age of 65 and women having reached the age of 60 qualify for the normal old age pension. The Constitutional Court has declared the difference in pensionable age contrary to the principle of equality and has held that the distinction is void. However, a long transitory period has been provided over which to equalise the pensionable ages for men and women; only until 2024 will the pensionable age for women be gradually increased to reach the same age as men. In order to obtain the normal old age pension, the insured person has to show evidence of 180 insured months (or about 15 years) during the last 30 years. The normal old age pension is still paid when the pensioner goes on working; however, if the income from such professional activity exceeds a given limit, the pension is reduced to 85% of its amount.

Men who are 60 years old and women who are 55 years old, may qualify for the early old age pension if they have a long insurance record. They will have to show a record of at least 450 insurance months (or about 37,5 years). The beneficiary of this early pension is not entitled to exercise any professional activity, be it as wage earner or as a self-employed person. The pension is stopped when the pensioner takes up a professional activity with earnings above the insurance limit (*Geringfügigkeitsgrenze*). When reaching the age of 65 (men) or 60 (women) the early old age pension is converted into a normal old age pension.

Men having reached the age of 60 and women having reached the age of 55 years, who have received cash benefits from the unemployment insurance for at least 52 weeks within the last 15 months before the age of 60 (men) or 55 (women), qualify for the remaining period of their unemployment, i.e. until reaching the normal pensionable age, this is known as an early pension in case of unemployment. The concerned pensioner is not allowed to exercise any professional activity when receiving this early old age pension.

The partial pension (*'Gleitpension'*) offers the possibility to men having reached the age of 60 and women having reached the age of 55 years, to gradually become a pensioner by reducing their working time whilst simultaneously receiving part of their pension. Before gaining access to this partial pension the claimant must have been insured for at least 37,5 years. The individual's working time has to be reduced by at least half in order to entitle the partial pensioner to 70% of his pension; when the working time is reduced by 30% the partial pension amounts to 50% of the normal pension. As the amount of the partial pension depends upon the reduction in working time, the insured person has to make a declaration about the amount of his working time during the past year and has to provide proof of an agreement with his employer about the intended reduction of working time. If this intended amount is later found not to correspond with reality, the partial pension amount is reduced or increased accordingly. The partial pension is stopped as soon as the insured person takes up any self-employed activity. A partial pension cannot be applied for without the agreement of the employer, as the change in working time implies a change in the labour contract. In fact the partial pension is not very popular.

To qualify for any of the above mentioned pensions it is not only required that the applicant has reached a certain age; he also needs to fulfil a certain 'waiting period', i.e. he has to show a number of insurance months have been built up within a certain period before the start of the pension. These insurance months may consist of contribution periods during which the concerned person has effectively worked and thus paid contributions, or *'Ersatz'*-periods which are equalised to contribution periods although no work was actually performed and no contributions paid during this period. *'Ersatz'*-periods include time during which sickness benefits or unemployment benefits were being received, or periods during which one was a prisoner of war or performed military or civil service, as well as the periods spent educating one's children (maximally 4 years per child). If the applicant also wishes to bring into account his periods of higher or professional education, he can do so by paying in the contributions set for this by the government.

The level of the pensions depends upon the level of the insured professional income, which serves (up to a maximum) as the calculation base for both contributions and benefits. Today the pension is calculated upon the best 15 years of contribution.

The pension amount also depends upon the duration of the insurance as the number of insurance years determines the percentage applied to the calculation base; the maximum percentage being 80%. If the pension, when calculated in this way, does not reach a certain minimum, the pensioner may apply for an 'adaptation allocation' (*'Ausgleichszulage'*). This allocation is based upon the recipient's need and is granted after testing the income and other means of the beneficiary. The alimony the concerned person can claim from his (former) spouse is also taken into account.

Pensions are adapted every year by government according to the increase of the net professional incomes (as reflected by the evolution of the average contribution basis over the last year).

The pensions of the civil servants are not governed by the social insurance principle, but reflect a *'Versorgungs'*-logic: the employer of the civil servant, the *Land*, continues to pay its employees even after they become pensioners. The civil servant's pension amounts to 80% of his (unlimited) previous wage. The pensionable age is the same for both men and women, 65 years.

4.2. Death

Both the pension and the accident insurances provide cash benefits for widows, widowers and orphans.

The insured person having at least 60 insurance months in the last 10 years before his death opens entitlement to a widow's or widower's pension. If the insured person was already receiving a pension, no insurance record requirements have to be fulfilled. Further conditions of entitlement relate to the difference in age between the spouses and the duration of the marriage, except when children were born out of the wedlock. In simple terms, this means that the longer the marriage lasted and the smaller the difference in age between husband and wife, the easier it is to obtain a widow/widower's pension.

The beneficiary is not only the actual spouse of the deceased insured person, but also the former spouse as well, provided that the insured person was paying alimony to his ex-spouse at the time of his death. The pension amount varies between 40% and 60 % of the pension the deceased received or would have received. The precise amount depends upon the total family income before the death. In case of remarriage the widow/widower's pension stops; a termination benefit is then paid which is equal to 35 times the monthly widow/widower's pension. Eventually, the widow/widower's pensions are to be supplemented by the need based 'adaptation allocation' (*'Ausgleichszulage'*).

Children of the deceased insured person qualify for an orphan's pension until the age of 18 or until the age of 27 if the child is attending school or professional education; persons handicapped before the age of 18 years maintain their classification of beneficiary orphan for an unlimited duration. The orphan of one parent receives 40% of the pension amount, the orphan of both parents is given 60% of the pension amount the deceased was receiving or would have received.

If the death is due to a labour accident or professional disease, the widow(er) or in absence of a surviving spouse, the orphans, get a benefit from the accident insurance amounting to 20% of the calculation basis.

4.3. Incapacity for work

The incapacity for work is covered by the sickness benefit (*Krankengeld*) of the sickness insurance and then by the invalidity pension (*Invaliditätspension*) of the pension insurance; the accident insurance also includes a damaged person's benefit (*Versehrtenrente*).

When an insured person is no longer able to exercise the professional activity he was exercising just before the health damage, he qualifies for the sickness benefit. The beginning and the end of the claimant's incapacity are determined either by the recipient's personal physician or by a doctor who is appointed by the sickness fund.

The sickness benefit is paid for maximally 26 weeks; this maximum duration being doubled when the concerned person was insured for at least 6 months over the last year. The benefit amounts to 50% of the calculation basis; and as from the 43rd day, 60% of the calculation basis. The competent sickness insurance institution has the option to prolong the maximum duration of the benefit to one and a half years and to raise the benefit to 75% of the calculation basis. The payment of the benefit is suspended during periods in which the employee can claim continuation of his pay from his employer or remains outside the country without permission.

The sickness insurance also pays a 'monthly benefit' (*'Wochengeld'*) in case of maternity. This benefit is paid during the eight weeks before the presumed day of confinement and eight weeks after confinement. When the concerned worker is not allowed to work for a longer period, the monthly benefit is continued for that period. The 'monthly benefit' equals the average wage of the insured person in the last 13 weeks before the start of the payment of the benefit. The 'monthly benefit' is equally suspended if the employer has to continue payment of the wage.

The pension insurance guarantees a benefit to socially insured persons who are unable to perform sufficient amounts of paid work due to a long term reduction of working capacity. In contrast with the old age pensions, the pensions for long term incapacity for work distinguish between white and blue collar workers, and inside the latter group between the skilled and the unskilled workers. The pensions for blue collar workers are called 'invalidity pensions' (*'Invaliditätspension'*), those for white collar workers are known as 'professional incapacity pensions' (*'Berufsunfähigkeitspension'*). They are paid from the first day following the contingency or the application; the pension is first granted for a period of two years, which can then be extended.

The reduction of working capacity relates to a certain professional reference area (*'Verweisungsfeld'*) for each of the above mentioned groups of insured persons, it determines the professions the insured person can be expected to exercise. If the insured person can still exercise some professional activity, he will not qualify for a pension if he can still earn at least half of the corresponding average professional income in this field.

The blue collar worker qualifies for invalidity pension when the invalidity may be expected to last at least 6 months and the insured person has collected at least 60 insurance months during the last 10 years. The skilled worker will be considered to be invalid if he cannot earn half of the professional income in his own profession. The category of "skilled worker" includes: workers who have learned the profession in a recognised educational programme or have acquired the corresponding professional skills by practising the profession. A non-skilled worker does not enjoy a similar protection of his profession: his professional reference area corresponds to the entire labour market.

The evaluation of the presence of the invalidity is done according to abstract standards. The health expert establishes which activities the insured person can still exercise. Case law requires that the insured person should be able to exercise his reference profession without limitation, i.e. like a healthy person. However, the insured person is required to collaborate; he is required to submit himself to health treatment or operations to recover his working capacity. This treatment is only compulsory when no special risk or extraordinary pain is involved and the treatment or operation can be expected to be successful. This forms the general principle of 'first rehabilitation, then compensation', under which an application for a pension is automatically considered to constitute an application for rehabilitation measures. The pension is only granted when suitable rehabilitation measures do not allow the recipient to re-integrate into professional life.

The professional incapacity pension of the white collar workers is granted under similar conditions as the invalidity pension of the blue collar workers, only the white collar workers enjoy the protection of their profession. They can be referred only to professional activities requiring a similar education or similar knowledge and skills.

Elderly wage earners of which the capacity to work was reduced due to health reasons, have an eased access to the old age pension. The age limit is in such case reduced to 57 years for men and 55 years for women. The insured persons may not be able to exercise anymore professional activities similar to the ones exercised in the last 15 years.

Farmers and the self-employed (except free professionals) do not enjoy the protection of their profession. They will only be considered to be invalids if they are completely incapable of exercising any regular professional activity. The professional reference area includes activities both as a wage earner and as a self-employed person. However, when the self-employed individual (but not the farmer) reaches the age of 50, he will also enjoy the protection of his profession.

The victim of a labour accident or professional disease, whose working capacity has been permanently reduced, qualifies for a damaged person's benefit from the accident insurance. The level of the benefit depends upon the earlier professional income (the calculation basis) and the degree of work incapacity. The damaged person's benefit is paid as soon as the reduction of work capacity over a period of three months amounts to at least 20%. In the case of full incapacity to work the benefit amounts to 2/3 of the calculation basis; in the case of partial incapacity the benefit equals the percentage of work incapacity applied to the benefit amount in case of full incapacity. Special supplements can also be awarded for cases of severe handicap.

The reduction of the capacity to work is established according to abstract standards, relating the earnings capacity before the accident or disease to the remaining work capacity. It is without relevance whether the socially insured person continues his or any other professional activity. Thus, even when continuing his former professional activity without loss of income, the victim may still qualify for the damaged person's benefit. The benefit may also be cumulated with a professional incapacity or invalidity pensions.

The accident insurance also grants a one-off 'integrity compensation' benefit ('*Integritätsabgeltung*') when the health damage was caused by gross negligence in observing the legislation for the protection of the workers.

4.4. Unemployment

The unemployment insurance distinguishes between unemployment benefit (*'Arbeitslosengeld'*) and 'emergency assistance' (*'Notstandshilfe'*). Both are monthly cash benefits.

To qualify for unemployment benefit the person who becomes unemployed for the first time, must have been insured under the unemployment insurance for at least 52 weeks within the last 24 months; for every subsequent case of unemployment, he has to show evidence of 26 insurance weeks during the last year. The claimant is considered to be unemployed if he has no professional income or his professional income falls below the insurance limit (*'Geringfügigkeitsgrenze'*). He gets unemployment benefit when he remains available for the labour exchange, is willing to accept any suitable job and is not incapable of work. The unemployment benefit is paid for a maximum of 20 weeks, which is extended to 30 weeks if the beneficiary has an insurance record of at least 156 weeks. Elderly unemployed people enjoy longer periods of benefit. The amount of the unemployment benefit depends upon the level of the previously earned wages; the benefit being equal to 40% to 60% of this earlier wage. Where appropriate, family supplements are added to the unemployment benefit if the unemployed person is the head of a dependent family.

If the insured person has exhausted his unemployment benefits, he may claim 'emergency assistance' in cases of real urgency. The amount of the assistance is in function of the amount of the previously received unemployment benefit (normally 92% of the latter). The duration of 'emergency assistance' is subject to no time limits. It is only granted after testing the income of the concerned unemployed person and of his spouse; the income which may be cumulated with the 'emergency assistance' depends upon the number of persons to whose maintenance the claimant mainly contributes.

4.5. Health and long-term care

The sickness insurance grants in kind benefits to cover the need for health care of the socially insured persons and their dependants. The insured person's spouse, children, foster children and grandchildren , are all considered to be co-insured dependants. These people only benefit under the insured person's scheme if they live in his common household.

The guaranteed health care includes the services of medical doctors, health institutions, dentists, the services of midwives, home care, preventive examinations etc.
The health care is due when the insured person is working under a labour contract. When the social insurance period stops, the concerned person will continue to benefit from health care, if his illness started when he was still insured. In certain cases, health care will even be provided when the need for care emerges after the termination of the insurance period. Health care is also avail-

able when the illness existed even before the beginning of the insurance (work).

The sickness insurance distinguishes between illness (*'Krankheit'*) and 'human defect' (*'Gebrechen'*). Every irregular corporal or mental state, necessitating health care is considered to be an 'illness'. The health care is then aimed at treating, ameliorating or consolidating the illness and restoring the patient to a state of good health and his full working capacity or the ability to perform fulfil his own personal needs. Health care is necessary when useful for these purposes. Furthermore, the mere reduction of pain is considered to be included in the health care concept. When the health of a person cannot be improved any further, his condition is classified as a 'human defect'. The health insurance does not cover 'human defects': here we are in the realm of the federal and provincial care allowances and of social assistance. Health care is granted to organ donors who donate without lucrative aims.

Medical care can be provided by a conventioned medical doctor (*'Vertragsärzte'*), free doctors (*'Wahlärzte'*) or in the policlinics of the insurance institutions (*'Ambulatorien'*).

A conventioned medical doctor works on the basis of an agreement with the social insurance administration. When the patient visits this doctor he only has to pay the user's charge. The free doctors have no contract with social insurance institutions. The patient visiting him has to pay him the full honorary and is given a reimbursement a of 80% of what a conventioned medical doctor would have received from the social insurance fund.

The services of psychotherapists, clinical psychologists, physiotherapists, logopedists and ergotherapists are also included in the medical care concept. All these services, except those of the psychotherapists, are only covered when prescribed by a medical doctor. The medical care also includes the medicine and other appliances for combating the illness or for securing good health. Prostheses such as optical glasses, orthopaedic appliances etc. are also provided, albeit after the payment of a personal contribution. The medical care provided should be sufficient and efficient and must not exceed what is necessary. The efficiency is not questioned for traditional medical practice, but is to be checked case by case for alternative medical methods such as homeopathy.

Medicine can only be prescribed if it is listed; some other medicine may be prescribed under the authorisation of a chief medical doctor. If the patient needs medicines which are not available under the two arrangements mentioned above but which is still necessary and efficient, he is entitled to it. The patient has to pay a user's charge on all the drugs he is prescribed.

Socially insured patients who cannot be expected to go to the medical doctor, but can be treated at home, qualify for home health care. This care is provided by qualified nursing personnel on the request of a medical doctor. It is often impossible to call upon sufficient ambulatory nursing personnel. If the latter is the case, the insured person is to be granted care in a provincial hospital which is financed per case for this purpose by the social insurance fund. This care has to be distinguished from stays in a care institution for the chronically ill, in a rehabilitation centre or in a health centre, which are not covered by social insurance. Care in a private hospital is reimbursed by social insurance at the level of what would have to be paid by social insurance to the public hospital in such a case.

The victim of a professional disease or a labour accident will be granted treatment, rehabilitation and health appliances by the accident insurance.

As from 1993 all pensioners may qualify for care allowance (*'Pflegegeld'*) when they are in need of care. The care allowance is not an insurance, but a *'Versorgung'*-benefit.
The care allowance is designed to cover the costs related to the need of constant care and help. The cause of the need for care is irrelevant; it is only required that the need for care lasts at least six months, this in order to exclude mere temporary problems.
The extent of the recipient's need for care has been graduated into seven levels of care beginning with level 1 which corresponds to a need for care of at least 50 hours per month and ending with level 7 which involves a need for care of at least 180 hours per month. For each level there is a given amount of care allowance.

4.6. Family

The State guarantees a form of *'Versorgung'* family allowances, which are awarded irrespective of the means of the recipient and this is done via the Family Charges Compensation Fund (*'Familienlastenausgleichsfonds FLAF*). The benefit is paid for each child in education and its amount depends upon the age of the child. The *FLAF* also supports the equipment of Austrian schools with free school books, free transportation for school attendance etc.

There are also benefits aiming at the compensation for the care of children.
Closely linked to the unemployment insurance is the parental benefit (*'Karenzgeld'*). This benefit is awarded to the mother or father of a new-born or adopted child, which uses his/her right under labour law to stay away from work without pay. The same insurance contribution conditions must be met as those valid for obtaining unemployment benefit. The parental benefit is a lump sum benefit which is paid for a maximum duration of one and a half years from the birth of the child; it is paid for a maximum of two years if both parents take up the benefit.

Lone parents get a supplement to the parent allowance, the amount of which equals about half of the amount of the allowance. This supplement is to be paid back by the other parent within 15 years and at a maximum interest rate of 15%.

Parallel to the emergency assistance, parents may qualify for exceptional emergency assistance (*'Sondernotstandshilfe'*) after having exhausted the parental benefit or they may qualify for 'part time allowance' (*'Teilzeitbeihilfe'*) which is for insured persons who did not qualify for parental benefit because they lack the required insurance record. The part time allowance amounts to half the parental benefit. A monthly income exceeding the insurance limit (*'Geringfügigkeitsgrenze'*) is contrary to the allowance of the benefit.

4.7. Need

The social assistance, which is organised on provincial basis, constitutes the last safety net for needy persons. Normally there is a recognised right to social assistance for the maintenance of the needy (covering costs of medical care, food, housing etc.). While the benefits in cash are most prominent, there are also some assistance benefits provided in kind and assistance in special circumstances (natural disasters, creation of homes for the elderly etc.).
In principle, there are no special age limits set. Persons who are capable of work and willing to perform any reasonable job, except when they are older than 65 years (men) or 60 years (women) or are involved in care obligations or current training, are entitled to social assistance. Any personal income and entitlements to other social benefits or to alimony payments from other people must be exhausted before the claimant can receive social assistance. The amounts and conditions of social assistance for maintenance differ from one *Land* to another.

5. *Financing*

The social insurances are primarily financed out of contributions of the insured persons (and their employers).

Let us remember here that the contributions are calculated upon the real professional income but only up to an upper limit (*Höchstbemessungsgrundlage*).
The contributions to the sickness insurance and the unemployment insurance for wage earners are split in two equal parts, employer's contribution and employee's contribution; this is nearly also the case for the contributions for the pension insurance (slightly higher employer contribution). The accident insurance is only covered by employer's contributions.

The farmers' social insurances are (partially) financed out of a contribution from the farmers calculated in function of the size of their lands.

If the contributions are insufficient to cover the expenses of the pension branch, the State will have to cover the deficit.
The federal budget subsidises the sickness insurance and, to a rather considerable extent, the social insurances of the farmers and of the self-employed.

The social insurances are also fed by the revenue of its patrimony.

All social insurance benefits are financed on a pay-as-you-go basis.

Benefits belonging to the *Versorgungs-* and *Fürsorge*-systems are financed out of general taxation.

The three branches of social insurance contribute to the financing of the hospitals. The sickness insurance pays the provincial funds for hospitals, whereas the accident and pension insurances contribute to the in-patient care through their accident hospitals, rehabilitation centres and special hospitals.

6. Judicial review

As to the procedure to be followed, the distinction has to be made between benefit cases and administrative cases. Benefit cases are those related to the entitlement to a benefit; administrative cases concern the determination of the insurance obligation and contribution matters. Benefit cases are the competence of the ordinary courts, whereas administrative cases are the competence of the administrative authorities. In both cases the process of review begins with a procedure within the social insurance institution that took the decision.

First of all we shall address the procedure in benefit cases. Once the insured person receives a negative decision concerning a benefit entitlement, he has the option to go to the provincial tribunals (*'Landesgerichte'*) which act as labour and social courts; Vienna has its own labour and social tribunal. There is a possibility to appeal against their decision in the first instance to the superior provincial courts (*'Oberlandesgericht'*) and the further to the superior court (*'Oberster Gerichtshof'*). The provincial tribunals decide labour and social cases in chambers consisting of one professional judge and two lay judges, appointed by the representative organisations of employers and employees.
In administrative cases, appeal is possible to the head of the *Land*, and under certain conditions further to the Federal Social Minister. After this administrative procedure, there is still the possibility to go to the administrative court.

Chapter Two

BELGIUM

1. Introduction: concept and sources of social security law

There are two different kinds of schemes in Belgian social security law, social insurance and social assistance. The social insurance system is of a professional character, that is to say there exist different schemes for various professional groups. In particular, there are separate insurance schemes for employees and for self-employed people. Whereas we shall deal with both hereafter, we shall not comment upon the specific schemes of the various categories of civil servants.

The social insurance schemes include benefits supplementing income, which cover the costs associated with children and with medical care. They also include income maintenance benefits in respect of incapacity for work due to illness, invalidity and industrial injuries or occupational diseases, as well as unemployment, old age and the death of a person who guaranteed the livelihood of his other partner or child. The above benefits supplementing income exist for employees as well as for self-employed people and are not related to income or wage; yet their extent may differ for the various professional groups. Wage-related income maintenance benefits exist for all employees in respect of all the contingencies mentioned above. Self-employed people only obtain income maintenance benefits in cases of sickness and invalidity (flat-rate) and upon the attainment of pensionable age (mixed, partly wage-related and partly flat-rate).

Assistance schemes ensure that child benefits are payable in respect of children for whom there is no right to child benefit within the professional scheme (guaranteed family allowance)(*gewaarborgde gezinsbijslag*). A minimum income is guaranteed to the handicapped (*inkomensvervangende tegemoetkoming aan gehandicapten*), to the elderly (*gewaarborgd inkomen voor bejaarden*) and finally, to all citizens (subsistence level) (*bestaansminimum*). Furthermore, handicapped people who are deemed to be incapable of self-help, or whose capacity for self-help is reduced, are eligible for an integration allowance. Apart from these minimum income schemes, the possibility to apply for material and non material social welfare services from the municipal public centre for social welfare is also provided (individualised assistance).

So far we have only dealt with statutory social security. The extra legal social security benefit schemes mainly consist of additional sickness costs insurance schemes (of special importance for self-employed people) and funds which, on the grounds of collective labour agreements, provide extra benefits for workers in specific sectors (building, docking, diamonds) on top of the benefits paid under social insurance schemes for employees. Furthermore, there are industrial and occupational pension funds, as well as group insurance schemes to guarantee additional (extra-legal) pensions. Materially, these are not regulated, except where it concerns solvency guarantees and fiscal treatment.

Since 1995, the Belgian Constitution guarantees a set of fundamental social rights as well as a right to free access to education until the end of mandatory schooling. Indeed, the new Article 23 reads as follows:
"(1) Everyone has the right to lead a life in conformity with human dignity.
(2) To this end, the laws, decrees, and rulings alluded to in Article 134 guarantee, taking into account corresponding obligations, economic, social, and cultural rights, and determine the conditions for exercising them.
(3) These rights include notably:
1) the right to employment and to the free choice of a professional activity in the framework of a general employment policy, aimed among others at ensuring a level of employment that is as stable and high as possible, the right to fair terms of employment and to fair remuneration, as well as the right to information, consultation and collective negotiation;
2) the right to social security, to health care and to social, medical, and legal aid;
3) the right to have decent accommodation;
4) the right to enjoy the protection of a healthy environment:
5) the right to enjoy cultural and social fulfilment."
The legal impact these provisions might have on day to day social security is very much debated. It is too early to make decisive conclusions in this respect.
A law of 1981, containing general principles on social security for employees, in which *inter alia*, a number of fundamental principles concerning social security rights are enumerated, never entered into force as far as these principles were concerned and it is unlikely they will ever do so.

On the grounds of the Belgian Constitution some powers in the area of vocational training, health care and social assistance to people and families were, attributed to the Communities (Flemish, French and German speaking), while other powers, in areas like housing or employment policy, were attributed to the Regions (Flanders, Walonia, Brussels).
However, these powers are not concerned with the social security benefit schemes as described above, but rather with various sorts of social services. Therefore, the social security system applies to the whole of Belgium. Nowadays, this unitary character of Belgian social security is being increasingly challenged; the Flemish make claims for splitting up the system, especially the health care scheme.

The professional social insurance schemes, as well as the social assistance schemes, all find their basis in statutes, albeit that sometimes the statutory provisions may be very minimal (for example, with regard to unemployment benefits, there is only one article from a (decree) statute of 1944!).

Here we also have to note that important parts of the existing social security schemes are not the work of parliament but of the government ("The King"), who for that purpose was temporarily given "special powers" by formal statute to take decisions, which in their legal effect are principally equal to those of a formal statute. In this way, delicate interventions in the area of social security could be realised and executed without subsequent parliamentary approval.

In principle, the formal statute offers the framework of social security schemes; the statutes must therefore be read together with the Royal and Ministerial decrees. Sometimes, if a statute is frequently modified and supplemented, the statutory texts are co-ordinated by Royal Decree. This is done for reasons of clarity.

Social security is one of the very few areas of the Belgium law where national, independent governmental bodies have been granted powers to enact binding regulations. With regard to social security, such powers were attributed to the managerial committee of the National Institute for Employment Services (*de Rijksdienst voor Arbeidsvoorziening, (R.V.A.)*) and to that of the Benefits Service of the National Institute for Sickness and Invalidity Insurance (*Rijksinstituut voor ziekte- en invaliditeitsverzekering, R.I.Z.I.V.*). Until now, the independent governmental bodies have made very limited use of these regulating powers, of which the constitutional status is uncertain.

2. *Administrative organisation*

We shall successively discuss the administrative organisation of the insurance schemes for employees, the insurance schemes for self-employed people and the social assistance schemes.

The social security schemes for employees come under the authority of the Minister of Social Affairs and, in respect of unemployment benefits, the Minister of Labour and Employment. The corresponding ministers determine the policy and exercise administrative control over the social security institutions, as described below.

Other aspects of the administration of social security for employees, except for the industrial injuries insurance scheme, are functionally decentralised to 'parastatal' organisations, public institutions of social security which may be assisted by various co-operating institutions under private law. The administration of the industrial injuries insurance scheme is entrusted to private insurance companies and mutual insurance funds; all employers are affiliated to one of these bodies. The Fund for Industrial Injuries (*Fonds voor Arbeidsongevallen, F.A.O.*) controls these insurers, compensates for the disadvantages which are typical of private insurance, and takes responsibility, whenever necessary, for the affiliation ex officio of non-compliant employers.

For all other employee insurance schemes the National Institute for Social Security (*Rijksdienst voor Sociale Zekerheid, R.S.Z.*) is charged with the collection of contributions, as well as the distribution of contributions over the various branches of social security for employees. The Institute also takes care of the comprehensive financial management of social security. The payment of benefits on the grounds of these insurance schemes is entrusted to other public social security institutions, i.e. the National Institute for Sickness and Invalidity Insurance (*Rijksinstituut voor ziekte- en invaliditeitsverzekering, R.I.Z.I.V.*), the National Institute for Employment Services (*Rijksdienst voor arbeidsvoorziening, R.V.A.*), the National Institute for Pensions (*Rijksdienst voor pensioenen, R.V.P.*), the National Institute for Child Allowances for Employees (*Rijksdienst voor kinderbijslag voor werknemers, R.K.W.*) and the fund for occupational diseases (*Fonds voor de beroepsziekten, F.B.Z.*).

These public institutions are set up by the government, they are legal persons and enjoy administrative autonomy. Nevertheless, they are subject to the administrative control of a competent minister. The latter is represented in the 'parastatal' bodies by a governmental commissioner whose task is to exercise permanent control over the decisions and the action of these bodies.
The management of the institutions is entrusted to a managerial committee, which is composed of an equal number of representatives from the respective employer and employee organisations under an independent chairman, who, like the other members, is appointed by the King. Within the managerial bodies of the National Institute for Sickness and Invalidity Insurance (*R.I.Z.I.V.*) representatives of the sickness funds also take part in decision making and within the management of the National Institute for Child Allowances for Employees (*R.K.W.*) there are also representatives of family organisations.

In the field of the administration of the employee insurance schemes, some tasks are often attributed to certain co-operating bodies under private law; these are often the successors of the first free social insurance associations. They are mostly responsible for the direct contact with the beneficiary. Socially insured persons have the free choice between such co-operating bodies. Thus, within the sector of sickness and invalidity, approved sickness funds and their (national) unions often co-operate in the administration; the insured persons who do not wish to be affiliated to an (ideologically orientated) sickness fund, can join a public institution: the auxiliary fund for sickness and invalidity insurance, coming under the *R.I.V.I.Z.* As far as the unemployment insurance is concerned, unemployment funds set up by three trade unions act as co-operating bodies. For those who do not want to affiliate to one of these trade union run funds, there is the auxiliary fund for unemployment benefits of the *R.V.A.* In its activities the *R.K.W.* not only enjoys co-operation from the public compensation funds, but also from the recognised free child allowance funds set up by the employers. The government lays down rules, which the co-operating bodies must satisfy, and exercises control, usually through the above mentioned parastatal bodies.

The National Labour Council (*Nationale Arbeidsraad*) carries out an important advisory function. It is composed of an equal number of representatives of the most representative employee's and employer's organisations.

The social protection of the self-employed falls under the political responsibility of the Minister of Agriculture and Small Trade, except where the sickness and invalidity insurance scheme is concerned. The latter is the responsibility of the Minister of Social Affairs.

The sickness and invalidity insurance scheme of the self-employed is entirely structured as an extension of the scope of insured people under the sickness and invalidity insurance scheme for employees. Hence, it has the same administrative structure as described above, with the exception of the collection and distribution of contributions which, as is the case for all other social insurance schemes for self-employed persons, is charged to the National Institute for Social Insurance of the Self-Employed (*Rijksinstituut voor de Sociale Verzekeringen der zelfstandigen, R.S.V.Z.*). This public institution is a legal person and is subject to the control of the Minister of Agriculture and Small Trade. The *R.S.V.Z.* is also charged with granting benefits from the pensions branch and child allowances branch for the self-employed. The *R.S.V.Z.* is governed by a board of directors, within which a management committee is formed; the members of the board of directors are appointed by the King on the recommendation of the various representative organisations for self-employed persons. The *R.S.V.Z.* orders the *R.V.P.* to pay retirement and widow(er)'s pensions. The latter also carries out this task in the area of the employee insurance schemes.

For the collection and distribution of contributions, the payment of a so called unconditional pension and child allowances, the *R.S.V.Z.* makes use of the co-operation of the free social insurance funds for self-employed persons. Self-employed persons who do not wish to join such a fund may join the National Auxiliary Fund for Social Insurance of the Self-Employed (of the *R.S.V.Z.*) (*Nationale Hulpkas voor de sociale verzekeringen der zelfstandigen*).

The High Council for small trade, in which the organisations of the self-employed are represented, advises the competent ministers.

The assistance schemes are managed by public bodies.

The (financial) allowances for the handicapped are administered and managed directly by a special service of the Ministry of Social Affairs.

The guaranteed family allowances and the guaranteed income for the elderly are administered by the respective administrative bodies of the scheme for employees, i.e. the *R.K.W.* and the *R.V.P.*

The Public Centres for Social Welfare are charged with the administration of the minimum subsistence legislation, as well as the granting of social services directly on grounds of the *O.C.M.W.* Act. Each municipality has a Public Centre for Social Welfare (*O.C.M.W.*). This is an autonomous institution under public law, governed by a (politically composed) council for social welfare, appointed by the municipal council. The Minister of National Health is politically responsible in respect of the subsistence minimum legislation.

In order to simplify the social security administration and to facilitate the computerisation of social security with full guarantees for the respect of privacy, the "Cross-roads Bank of Social Security" has been created (*Kruispuntbank der Sociale Zekerheid*). This data bank does not centralise all information necessary for the execution of the various social security schemes, but links the various social security institutions, each of them keeping (exclusively) that data which is most relevant for them.

Finally, we mention that some benefits (for example pensions, allowances for handicapped persons) must be claimed from the municipal government. The municipality and its government, which as such cannot be labelled as administrative social security bodies, pass the claim on to the competent institutions.

A statute of 1995 introduced the 'Charter of the socially insured person', to promote the protection of all beneficiaries in front of social security administrations and judiciary. It formulates a series of duties of the social security administration, such as the duty to inform (in principle within 30 days) and to counsel the socially insured persons. It also stipulates that the social security administration has to decide benefit claims, in principle, within 90 working days, and that subsequently benefits have to be effectively paid out within 90 days.

3. *Personal scope of application*

The division in professional social security schemes is based upon the differences between the potential beneficiaries. Therefore, we will firstly discuss the two professional schemes.

Employees, within the meaning of the employee insurance schemes, are those who are bound to their employers by a contract of employment, as well as certain categories of people who are treated as such. *Ratione loci*, in principle, a double link with Belgian territory is required; i.e. the place of labour and the location of the employer's business must be in Belgium. Nevertheless, there are exceptions to this rule; in respect of workers who work abroad for a Belgian undertaking, in respect of mariners, in respect of the child allowance legislation, and on the grounds of public international law. A contract of employment is a contract whereby an employee agrees to perform work under the authority of an employer in return for a wage. Subjection to the authority of the employer is sufficient proof of the existence of a contract of employment, regardless of the special nature of the work which is performed (e.g. professional football trainers, hostesses).

Next to the employees in the classical sense of labour law, other categories of people are explicitly included within the personal scope of application, in respect of all or some of the insurance schemes for employees. Thus, the coverage for all employee insurance schemes is extended to, amongst others, apprentices, handicapped persons in occupational retraining, working students, domestic workers, paid musicians and actors, paid governors and the mandatories of non-profit making organisations.

Some groups of employees are only submitted to a limited number of employee insurance schemes, for example, professional sportsmen (only health care, pensions, industrial accidents and child allowance; for professional cyclists also unemployment and incapacity to work benefits).

On the other hand, some employees are excluded, such as e.g. domestic servants who work less than four hours a day for the same employer or less than 24 hours a week for one or more persons.

There is the possibility for those working abroad, who find insufficient social security coverage there, to join the "overseas social security", which includes retirement and widow(er)'s pensions, an industrial injuries insurance scheme, a scheme for health care and benefits in respect of severe illness or injury.

The scope of beneficiaries under the family allowance scheme for employees is extended considerably (for example to retired employees, the orphans of an employee, students younger than twenty five years of age, etc.).
Those who are unemployed and have stopped their studies and who are, in principle, younger than thirty years of age, may be eligible for unemployment benefit, provided they are the head of a family. If not, they may be eligible for a flat-rate waiting benefit.

Every natural person who carries out a professional activity within Belgium, on the basis of which he is neither bound by a contract of employment nor by the status of a civil servant, is self-employed within the meaning of the scheme for the self-employed. The concrete meaning of this is that the social security provisions for the self-employed constitute the residual scheme of the professional social security system and as such it covers a very heterogeneous group of people (industrialists and traders, free professions, farmers) who are engaged in employment other than as an employee or civil servant. Affiliation takes place on the grounds of a professional activity, regardless of whether or not an income is obtained from this activity. Not only the self-employed person, who carries out a certain occupational activity, is affiliated, but also his helper, the latter being the person who assists or replaces the self-employed person in his work, without being bound by a contract of employment.

The following persons are, however, explicitly excluded from the insurance scheme for the self-employed:
- writers (for example journalists) who have another main profession;
- spouse/helpers, unmarried helpers under twenty years of age and occasional helpers (that is to say those who occasionally act as helpers during a period of not more than ninety days per year).

The sickness and invalidity insurance schemes, notably the medical care branch, not only provide benefits for the beneficiary himself (the employee or self-employed person), but also for benefits in respect of the persons who are dependent upon him. The main category of dependent persons consists of spouses and children. Also treated as such are ascendants of the beneficiary or of his spouse, provided they are older than fifty five years of age or incapable of work, have an annual income from labour or from social security which does not exceed a certain amount, and have been registered as a family member of the beneficiary for at least six months. In principle, children remain dependent as long as they continue to entitle to family allowance, or as long as they are younger than twenty five years of age and are living at home.

We shall now deal with the personal scope of application of the assistance schemes.

Income maintenance is payable to handicapped persons who are of age but younger than 65 years, in respect of whom it is determined that their physical or mental state has reduced their earning capacity by one third or less of that which a healthy person can earn through an occupation in the general labour market. Integration allowances are payable to handicapped persons if damage to, or a reduction of, their independence is established.
Every resident who is either of age, or married, or unmarried with at least one dependent child, may be eligible for minimum subsistence.

All men of sixty five years or older and all woman of sixty years or older, may be eligible for the guaranteed income for the elderly.

Dependent children of residents of Belgium, who are also living in Belgium, create a right to a guaranteed family allowance, provided that no family allowance is payable on the grounds of any other scheme.

All the above mentioned assistance schemes are open to Belgians, citizens of other EC-countries, stateless people and political refugees. They all require the claimants to be really residing in Belgium. People of other nationalities will have to fulfil additional conditions in order to qualify for these assistance benefits.

Finally we should mention that, in principle, everyone can apply for the social services offered by the Public Centres of Social Welfare.

4. Risks and benefits

Before going on we must mention that the level of social security benefits is linked to the index of consumer prices, in other words to price increases. Furthermore, many social security acts provide for a supplementary adjustment of the benefits to the standard of living. However, in practice this adjustment is no longer made.

As we have chosen for a risk by risk overview of the social security systems, we shall define here the concepts of labour accident and professional disease, which are being used for schemes covering more than one risk.

A labour accident is any accident a wage earner is the victim of during and because of the exercise of his duties under a labour contract and which actually causes physical damage. To ease the burden of proving the occurrence of a labour accident, the accident will be presumed to be in the course of the fulfilment of the labour contract if any actual physical damage is caused by a sudden event during working time. Proving that there has been physical damage and then showing that a sudden event also took place will be enough to prove a causal link between the physical damage and the sudden event. An accident between home and the place of work is also considered as a labour accident.

The professional disease insurance approach in Belgium is of the mixed type: the list of professional diseases is of the greatest importance, but it is also possible to prove that a disease is due to professional activity even if it does not feature upon the list.

4.1. Old age

Under the social insurance schemes for employees as well as for self-employed people, a retirement pension is payable to insured persons who have attained a certain age and stopped working. The pensionable age is sixty five for men; for women it is being gradually raised from sixty (1997) to sixty five (2009). Correspondingly the age until which women are entitled to benefits under other social security schemes will also gradually be equalised.

Both men and women can take an anticipated pension from the age of sixty onwards under the condition they show a career of at least twenty years (at the earliest as from 1997), the latter number of years gradually being increased to reach thirty five years in 2005 at the earliest. Self employed people loose 5% of their pension amount per year of anticipation.

Those claiming retirement pension must cease their professional activities and may only perform a limited amount of permitted work.

The retirement pension of the employee amounts to 75% or 60% of the average wage (fictitious or real) over the period between twenty years of age and the normal pension age, depending upon whether the insured person is married and provided that his partner has neither income from work nor income maintenance ("family pension"), or does not belong to this group ("single person's pensions").

Pensions for self-employed people are determined in a double way. Since 1984 one year of a career as a self-employed person gives rise to the same retirement pension as for employees, albeit that instead of the earned wages, about half of the business income of the self-employed person is taken into account. In fact, sometimes more than half of the business income is taken into account up to the income ceiling for the calculation of wage earner's pensions; and sometimes less than half of the amount above that upper limit. For the years prior to 1984, pensions are based upon a low, flat rate business income per year. Furthermore, in respect of limited and partial periods of self-employment, this flat rate part of the pension may be subject to a means test.

Belgium

A half time pension possibility has been introduced for wage earners.

Under conditions established by law, wage earners may be entitled to a minimum pension, the amount of which relates to the number of years worked.

The industrial and occupational pension funds, the group insurance schemes for employees and the supplementary pensions for self-employed persons guarantee a supplementary pension to their members.

Men having reached the age of 65 and women aged 60 or more, who have no sufficient means of existence, qualify for the guaranteed income for the elderly.

4.2. Death

The spouse of a deceased, insured employee or self-employed person is entitled to widow(er)'s pension at the level of 80% of the (effective or fictitiously calculated) retirement pension of the deceased insured person, subject to the condition that the widow(er) is over 45 years of age or has a dependent child, or is 66% incapable of work. Entitlement ends upon remarriage.

If the conditions for widow(er)'s pension are no longer satisfied, the pension continues to be paid for one year; if the surviving spouse is less than forty five years of age, ceases to have dependent children or to be incapable of work, the period until the attainment of forty five years of age is bridged by payments on a minimum level. As for permitted labour, the same rules apply as those in respect of retirement pension.

No survivor's pension is payable to the 'pseudo widow'. However, in the schemes for employees and self-employed persons the divorced spouse is granted a personal and individual right to a pension for the years during which he or she was married to an employee or self-employed person. The divorced spouse is then treated as if he or she has carried out an activity as an employee or self-employed person during the period of the marriage. The level of pension is based upon an income which in principle is equal to 62.5% of the income which would be used as a basis of calculation for the ex-spouse's pension. The retirement pension of the ex-spouse is not dependent upon the claim to pension of the other spouse. It is fully independent and payable when the claimant attains the age of 65 (men) or 60 (women).

No orphan's pension is payable, but the orphan does receive an increased child allowance, subject to the condition that the surviving parent has not remarried nor formed a household with a partner.
On the death of an employee due to an industrial injury or an occupational disease, benefits are provided on the grounds of the employee's insurance scheme to the surviving members of the family. These are calculated as a percentage of the basic wage of the person concerned: 30% for the widowed spouse and 15% for each orphan (with a maximum of 45%; increased to 20%, *c.q.* 60% when both parents are deceased). Also parents, grandparents, grandchildren, brothers

and sisters can be entitled to such benefits (usually at a level of 15%) if they can prove that they have been dependent upon the wage of the deceased person.

4.3. Incapacity for work

The sickness and invalidity insurance scheme for employees guarantees benefits to the employee who is incapable of work and who has not attained the normal pension age, this is on the condition that he has ceased all activities due to a disease or an injury which is recognised by a specially appointed doctor. Furthermore, benefit is subject to the condition that the incapacity for work was directly followed by a decrease in the earning capacity of at least 66% of that which a comparable person could earn. For the first six months this condition is gauged upon the occupation of the claimant. Thereafter, (or earlier if no recovery can be expected), it is gauged upon his entire occupational category or against any occupation which the person involved could have carried out in view of his education. There is a presumption of incapability of work when there is entry into hospital. During the first period of one year (primary incapacity for work) benefit normally consists of 60% of the wage which gives rise to contribution liability. This percentage is reduced to 55% when the recipient of the benefit lives together with a person who has their own professional income. From the second year of incapacity for work (period of invalidity) people who are at the head of a household obtain 65%. Otherwise, this percentage is 45 or 40% of the previously earned wages (depending upon whether or not the lost income was their only income). Benefit is subject to minimum and maximum amounts; these amounts may be close to each other.

On a benefit level, the sickness and invalidity insurance scheme for the self-employed is substantially different from that for employees. The self-employed person (who has not attained pensionable age) is incapable of work if, due to an illness or an injury, he has to cease his self-employed activities. The first three months of incapacity for work are not compensated, but the following months are. The self-employed person who is incapable of work receives (low) flat-rate benefits, the level of which rises slightly after one year of incapacity for work and is higher for people who are at the head of a household than for single people. The amounts hover around the level of the minimum subsistence benefit.

If the incapacity for work of an employee is due to an industrial injury or an occupational disease, the victim will receive a percentage of his wage from the previous year that is equal to his degree of incapacity for work. However, if this percentage amounts to less than 10%, benefit is calculated on the basis of a lower percentage; if the claimant needs the constant attendance of another person, the benefit is increased.

4.4. Unemployment

Only the scheme for employees provides coverage in case of unemployment. In order to be entitled to benefit, the employee must be younger than the normal pensionable age, and must either have worked as an employee for a number of days during the period of reference relevant for his age (the required number of days and the period of reference increase with the age of the beneficiary; between 312 and 624 days), or have stopped his studies, not being thirty years of age and be registered as looking for work (or have performed work) during a number of days (155 to 310) depending on his age. The latter group of young job seekers, however, are only eligible for benefit if they are at the head of a household; if this is not the case they are merely entitled to the less favourable waiting benefits.

Unemployment benefit is subject to a number of entitlement conditions, i.e. one must be unemployed without a wage, be involuntarily unemployed, be registered as looking for work, be willing to accept suitable employment, be capable of work, and subject oneself to periodical control.

Benefits on the grounds of the insurance scheme for employees are divided into unemployment benefits (*werkloosheidsuitkering*), waiting benefits (*wachtgeld*) and bridging benefits (*overbruggingsuitkeringen*), early retirement pensions (*brugpensioenen*) and interruption benefits (*onderbrekingsuitkeringen*).

Under the Belgian unemployment insurance, benefits are in principle granted to the unemployed person without limit in time, be it that they can be excluded from the benefit as a sanction, when the duration of their unemployment appears to be abnormally long.
Cohabitees with dependants receive 60% of their (limited) earlier wage; single persons receive the same amount during the first year of their unemployment and 42% from the second year onwards. Cohabitees without dependants get 55% of their (limited) earlier wage the first year and 35% for a fixed number of months thereafter; after which they will be entitled to a lump sum allowance. However, unemployed persons who have worked for at least 20 years before becoming unemployed, or who are at least 33% incapable of work, continue to receive the wage related benefit without limit in time.
Young, first-time job seekers, who are not at the head of a household receive a low flat-rate waiting benefit (in respect of unemployed people who are obliged to follow part-time education this is referred to as "bridging benefit"). If the young graduate is at the head of a household, the minimum wage is used as a basis of calculation for unemployment benefit. A half time bridging pension has been introduced allowing the wage earner to partially leave the labour market.

At the present time, the 'bridging pension' or 'pre-pension' refers to benefits enjoyed by employees who were discharged after their 58th (sometimes their 55th) year and who receive from their employer a supplement on top of their unemployment benefit at a level of half the difference between unemployment benefit and their net wage. The unemployment benefit upon which the supplement is payable is not reduced after one year of unemployment.

Finally, we can mention the possibility for employees to interrupt their employment full-time or part-time for a limited number of months. The wage earners do not have a statutory right to interrupt their career; the employer has to agree with such interruption. The interruption benefit is low and flat-rate. The person receiving the benefit is entitled, after exhaustion of these benefits, to re-integrate into his former work place.

The same benefit is payable to the unemployed person who decides to step out of the labour market because of social or family reasons; the benefit can then last up to 5 years.

Long term unemployed people are obliged, and other job seekers have the option, to register for work with the local employment agencies. These agencies may provide them with jobs which are not usually associated with the regular labour market (e.g. household related services, gardening, ...) The unemployed person performing such tasks gets a supplement on top of his unemployment benefit.

Self employed people do not qualify for unemployment benefit. In 1997, however, a specific bankruptcy insurance was created. In case of bankruptcy, the self employed person, by virtue of this insurance, maintains his rights to health care and family benefits for a maximum period of one year, he will also receive a lump sum benefit for a maximum of two months, the amount of which varies depending upon whether he has dependants or not.

4.5. Health care

Insured employees and people dependent upon them enjoy financial compensation for the costs of medical care, this is borne by the health care branch of the sickness and invalidity insurance scheme.

The insured person pays for medical services himself and obtains a certificate stating the help that was given, after that he receives reimbursement from his sickness fund, minus a personal contribution (*remgeld*). Reimbursement is done on the basis of the amount which may be charged according to the official scale of tariffs for such medical services (the real amount paid may be higher than the official amount). The official scale of fees is fixed by agreement between the sickness funds and the health care providers, or failing this, laid down by government. In a certain number of situations, such as hospitalisation, the "third payer" rule is applied: in that case the provider of care will send his bill directly to the sickness fund and the patient only pays the personal contribution.

The personal contributions for the costs of medical services and pharmaceutical products are meant to restrict medical consumption; the amount of contribution is calculated as a certain percentage (for example 25% for general medical care; 50% for physiotherapy; 0, 25, 50 or 100% for specialist treatment or drugs) or as a flat-rate payment (for example for visits to the doctor, preventive dental care for those under twelve years of age, medicine prepared by the pharmacist and stays in hospital). For widow(er)'s, invalids, handicapped persons, retired persons and orphans with a modest income (*WIGW's*), the conditions are considerably more favourable (no or very low personal contributions).

The personal contributions paid under the heath care branch of the sickness and invalidity insurance scheme, will no longer be due as soon as their total over one year exceeds a fixed amount (which is itself determined in function of the concerned person's taxable income, the amount being minimal for WIGW's).

For self-employed people, the sickness and invalidity insurance scheme is limited to the so called 'major risks', such as admission into hospital, major surgery, delivery and specialist care. These are covered in the same fashion as for employees, as described above. 'Minor risks', for example normal doctor visits, dental care and medicine do not fall under the compulsory insurance for self-employed persons. However, many self-employed people take out an additional sickness insurance against minor risks on a voluntary basis. Such additional insurance is offered by the same sickness funds that run the compulsory basic insurance.

If medical care is necessary for employees due to an industrial injury or occupational disease, the relevant insurance schemes will ensure that the victim does not have to pay any personal contributions. Furthermore, the Fund for Occupational Diseases will sometimes compensate preventive care. If the private employer of the victim of an industrial injury has a recognised medical service, the employee concerned must be cared for by this medical service (cost free).

4.6. Family

Female employees enjoying their 15 weeks maternity leave, are granted a maternity allowance. The benefit is similar to the sickness benefit, except that the maternity allowance for women who are actually employed amounts to 82% of the (unlimited) wage during the first 30 days of the maternity leave. After the first 30 days the benefit amounts to 75% of the (limited) wage. If the woman was not effectively employed at the moment when she qualifies for the benefit, she will only get 79,5% of the limited wage during the first 30 days.

For self-employed women the maternity insurance is less generous: it provides a lump sum payment, which is intended to cover the three weeks after confinement.

Family allowance is payable in respect of the claimant's own children. Children of the spouse or ex-spouse or of the unmarried partner, grandchildren belonging to the family or brothers and sisters (if the latter are not entitled to family allowances in any other way) and families with children under state care may also qualify for this benefit.

Normally, family allowance is payable over the years in which school is obligatory (up to 18 years of age), albeit that this period is extended to twenty one or twenty five years of age in respect of various students. Handicapped children or children who are 66% incapable of work give rise to the entitlement to child allowance up to the age of twenty five years. If they are fully incapable of carrying out any kind of occupation or work in a sheltered work shop, they

give rise to a lifelong right to benefit. Unemployed young job seekers who are not entitled to benefits under the unemployment insurance, enjoy continued entitlement to child allowance.
Family allowances include the following benefits:
- flat-rate maternity pay (per birth);
- normal child allowance, in respect of which the amount for the second child is almost double that for the first and the amount for the third and following children almost threefold that of the amount for the first child.

Children of a handicapped claimant give rise to a slightly higher allowance. Orphans give rise to entitlement to a higher allowance provided that the surviving parent does not start a new family.

For handicapped children, in addition to the usual child allowance, a considerable supplement is paid up to the age of twenty five.

Furthermore, there is an age allowance for all children (groups between six and twelve, twelve and sixteen and from sixteen years; the allowance increases per age group).

The professional family allowance schemes are almost identical. The main deviation in the scheme for self-employed people is the significantly lower amount of child allowance for the first child (not one third of that for children of employees).

The guaranteed family allowances almost entirely coincide with those of the scheme for employees, although of course the right to this guaranteed family allowance only exists when the means of subsistence of the person concerned do not rise above a certain level.

4.7. Need

The income maintenance allowances for handicapped people guarantee the handicapped person a benefit amounting to at least the minimum subsistence level which is relevant for him. The (flat-rate) integration allowances are payable to handicapped people for whom damage to or a reduction of their capacity for self-help has been determined. The amount of both allowances is reduced by the amount of income in excess of certain limits, of the handicapped person, his spouse or the person with whom he forms a household. These limits may vary for both allowances, they may rely upon whether there are people who are dependent upon the beneficiary, whether the beneficiary is single or cohabiting and upon whether or not the beneficiary enjoys a pension.

Every Belgian or person treated as such, who is of age, with a real place of residence in Belgium, who has inadequate means of subsistence (means test), and who cannot earn such means through his own efforts or in some other manner, is entitled to the subsistence minimum (also called the '*minimex*'). The level of the subsistence minimum varies for cohabiting spouses, single people (about 3/4 of the amount for the former) or someone living with one or more than one person (1/2 the amount for spouses).

On the grounds of the legislation on the Public Centres for Social Welfare every person has the right to social services which are necessary for their human dignity. The administrative bodies have rather a wide margin of policy discretion with respect to the suitable form of assistance (cash or other), as well as in respect of the amount, and the conditions for, the granting of municipal services in cash.

5. Financing

The financing of social security for employees consists of contributions from employees and/or employers, state subsidies and other resources.

The basis of calculation for contributions is the gross wage of the employees. The contribution percentages are fixed by law (about 2/3 employer and 1/3 employee contribution). In some cases special rules apply, for example in the form of a reduced contribution rate for specific types of employers or employment; or by fixing special contributions for all kinds of non-employees to whom the insurance schemes for employees have been extended.

The employer deposits his own contribution as well as the contributions from the wages of his employees with the R.S.Z. The contributions, after deductions for administrative fees according to the budget, are divided between the R.I.Z.I.V. (both branches) the R.K.W. the R.V.P., the R.V.A., the F.A.O. and the F.B.Z. Recently the Fund for the Financial Balance of social security has been created in order to allocate the revenues of social security to the different schemes according to their needs, and no longer, as was the case before, exclusively according to the statutorily fixed percentages.
Also recently a new semi-social, semi-fiscal contribution was introduced, levied on the comprehensive taxable income of the wage earners (if this exceeds a certain minimum). A provisional payment of this contribution is withheld from the employee's salary by the employer, the remaining part being levied at the same time as the personal income tax by the tax authorities and than directly transferred to the Fund for the Financial Balance of social security.

Contributions are also paid on some social security benefits i.e. on industrial injuries and occupational diseases benefits, (the same percentages as on wage), on the invalidity benefits and early retirement pensions (which is 3.5% to the extent that benefits exceed a certain amount; contributions for the insurance scheme in respect of retirement and survivor's pensions), on all pensions, including occupational pensions (3,55% to the extent that the pension exceeds a certain amount).

State subsidies automatically cover the differences between income from contributions and the expenditure (benefits) of the unemployment insurance scheme (also of invalidity pensions for miners). In respect of the other branches of social security for employees, the statute defines the way in which the state subsidies are fixed, that is to say at:
- 20% of the expenditure for retirement and survivor's pensions

- 80% of the expenditure for sickness and invalidity insurance, branch medical care, in so far as this payment is made for *WIGW's* (Widows, invalids, pensioners and orphans);
- 50%, 75% or 95% respectively of the expenditure for the sickness and invalidity insurance scheme, benefit branches, applicable from the second, third or fourth year of invalidity; funeral costs are fully subsidised by the state.

In principle there are no state subsidies in the area of family allowances.

The employee insurance schemes are also financed from other (para-fiscal) sources, such as:
- a special lump sum contribution to be paid by the pharmaceutical industry per product they commercialise as well as a percentage of their turnover to be paid by the same (benefits the *R.I.Z.I.V.*);
- a part of the indirect tabacco taxes (these "health taxes" are collected by the normal tax service and supposed to be passed on to the *R.I.Z.I.V.*); and
- a supplementary premium of 10% of the usual insurance schemes premium for vehicle taxes (also for the *R.I.Z.I.V.*).

The last two taxes not only help to cover the costs of the *R.I.Z.I.V.* for the scheme of employees but also the costs for the other professional categories.

The financing of social security for the self-employed persons consists of contributions from self-employed people and of state subsidies.
The social security contributions of the self-employed are calculated on the business income i.e. on the basis of their income declaration for tax purposes. There are various contribution rates for people whose main activities are in self-employment, people with a self-employed secondary occupation and self-employed people who have attained pensionable age, yet who continue to work (for the two latter groups there are lower contribution rates than for people who are self-employed in their main profession). There are three income levels in the contributions scheme; if the business income falls below the minimum level, then a minimum contribution is still levied on the amount of this minimum level (also when no real income or even a loss was entered); if the business income falls above the middle level then a lower percentage applies than that which is applicable for an income below this middle level; all income above the maximum level is free from contribution charges. Thus the system of contributions in this case is digressive.

For both sickness and invalidity insurance state subsidies are determined in the same manner as in the employees scheme. In the annual budget, state supplements are set for pensions and family allowances

The social security system for self-employed is also financed by a low flat-rate contribution paid by every enterprise.

The guaranteed income for the elderly, the guaranteed child allowance and allowances for handicapped people are financed entirely out of general taxation.

In contrast, the subsistence minimum is in principle financed for one half by the local Public Centres for Social Welfare and for the other half by the central government. The Public Centres for Social Welfare also bear the costs for their social welfare services. The State bears the full costs of assistance to political refugees.

For the sake of completeness, it needs to be observed that since 1995 the sickness funds are progressively bearing a (small) part of financial responsibility for the costs of health care: in case they obtain a bonus (i.e. when their revenue calculated in function of the number and sort of their members exceeds their actual expenditures), they get part of this bonus for their reserves; in case of a malus they still have to cover a part of it out of their reserve or by raising the amount of the membership fee.

6. *Judicial review*

Disputes between insured employees or self-employed people and the administrative organisations are referred to the authority of the labour courts (*arbeidsrechtbanken*) (in first instance) and that of the higher labour courts (*arbeidshoven*) (upon further appeal). This is also the case for disputes concerning the assistance schemes. Cassation is possible on points of law to the Court of Cassation (*Hof van Cassatie*). In principle, appeal to labour court has to be entered within 3 months after the litigious decision.

The labour courts are fully autonomous legal institutions integrated within the judiciary. Besides social security cases, they also deal with labour law cases. They are composed of one professional magistrate who is appointed for life and of two laymen. Unless otherwise provided, one of the laymen is appointed on the nomination of the most representative unions, the other one on the nomination of the most representative employer's organisations. In disputes concerning handicapped persons allowances one of the laymen is appointed on the nomination of one of the professional organisations, the other on the nomination of the unions. In respect of disputes concerning the self-employed there are two professional magistrates and one layman appointed on the nomination of the professional organisations for the self-employed.

The application of the law by the labour courts is similar to that of ordinary courts; mostly the principles of the civil procedure are applied, albeit in a simplified way and tempered by the principles of inquisitorial procedure, inter alia as a result of the actions of a specific public ministry in social affairs. Like the civil court, the labour court can call upon medical and other expertise (for example in order to give evidence of incapacity for work).

The decisions of the labour courts are in principle subject to full appeal to the higher labour courts.

The Court of Cassation receives appeals of all judicial decisions taken in last instance, also of those of the labour courts, against which there is an alleged infringement of the law (or a violation of substantial procedural requirement). The Court does not decide on factual questions.

Only some of the matters dealing with social security fall outside the jurisdiction of the labour courts, e.g. the normal (criminal) jurisdiction is competent for the application of penal provisions of social security acts (the labour courts being competent to deal with administrative sanctions).

In the social security litigation the costs of the administration of justice are in principle borne by the involved administration of social security, even if the latter wins the case.

Chapter Three

DENMARK

1. Introduction: concept and sources of social security law

The concept of social security does not refer to a clearly defined body of social benefits and services. Yet there is a clear-cut distinction between social insurance and social assistance, with each one under the control of a different directorate of the Ministry of Social Affairs.

Thus, the social insurance schemes comprise of: social and part-time pensions, daily benefits in respect of sickness, maternity and child benefits; and, furthermore, (in a broader sense of the word) the benefits on the grounds of occupational damage insurance (industrial injuries and occupational diseases), additional labour market pensions, unemployment insurance, as well as health care services. Next to that, in various forms, exists social assistance.

Until 1970 there were no family benefits in Denmark. When they were introduced, they were considered to be part of the domain of social security and administered as such. Since 1.7.1987 benefits for children in general, i.e. child benefits (thus excluding the specific child allowances) have been removed from the competence of the administrative bodies for social security (Ministry of Social Affairs) and attributed to the national taxation service. As from that moment these benefits are no longer dealt with in social security literature. However, below we shall discuss all family benefits governed by public law.

In the seventies, Danish social security law was subject to a major simplification as a result of the introduction of a number of acts replacing numerous previous statutes, i.e.
- the act concerning social administration (*lov om styrelse af sociale og visse sundhedsmaessige anliggender*);
- the act concerning public health insurance (*lov om offentlig sygesikring*);
- the daily benefits act (*lov om dagpenge ved sygdom eller fødsel*);
- the act concerning social administrative adjudication (*lov om den sociale ankestyrelse*)
- the social assistance act (*lov om social bistand*).

The reform was based upon the principle that the citizen should have optimal access to one service for his social security and assistance, and this should be closely situated to his place of residence. The realisation of this principle implied a major harmonisation of the numerous acts previously in existence, as well as a decentralisation of the administration to local communities (*kommune*).

Section 75 of the Danish Constitution (latest version: 1953) deals with social security (lato sensu). Section 75(1) lays down the principle that, in the interests of general welfare, each able bodied citizen should have the opportunity to perform work of his own choice which enables him to provide for his own subsistence. Section 75(2) gives the right to assistance from the state to each person who cannot provide for his own subsistence or that of his dependants, and in respect of whom no person carries a maintenance liability. On the grounds of the latter provision, the beneficiary of state assistance may be restricted in the enjoyment of civil and political rights. Indeed, in the last century such restrictions were linked to the granting of the poor relief. However, at the present time they have entirely disappeared from Danish social security law.

Section 75 Constitution has not had any impact upon the creation of Danish social law. It was almost entirely ignored, both in legal doctrine and in case law. At the most the following principles may be derived from Section 75(2):
- there must be a system of social assistance under public law which guarantees every person a certain subsistence level;
- social assistance is a right, not a charity; those who satisfy the legal requirements are entitled to it;
- the primary duty to grant subsistence does not rest (necessarily) upon the state but upon other individuals. The government is constitutionally entitled to recover the granted aid from those who are liable for the maintenance of the recipient.

In accordance with the general scheme of this work, we shall not deal with the social security law of the Faroes and Greenland.

Social benefits and services all rest upon a formal statutory basis. Sometimes parliament empowers the Minister or an administrative body to enact further rules which are binding upon administrative bodies and citizens; the *Bekendtgørelser,* which are issued on the basis of such authorisations, are published in the same way as statutes. They are quite important for social security law.
Guidelines and other administrative tools, which are issued by the competent ministers and administrative organisations, are not binding upon the citizen but do, nonetheless, play an important role in social security law. Depending on the case, the administrative guidelines are or are not legally binding upon the administrative bodies.

For questions of interpretation, one can often successfully consult the parliamentary preparation of acts (the *Betaenkning* which are formulated in respect of new material legislation) and even political policy guidelines concerning (social security) problem areas (the *Redegørelser*).

Unemployment funds have their own regulations. A supplementary pension has been introduced by collective labour agreement which covers more than two thirds of Denmark's employees.

2. Administrative organisation

The administration of almost all social security schemes is strongly territorially decentralised. As was said before, the system is based upon the principle that each citizen should have access to social security in his local community or, as the case may be, in larger communities, or parts thereof.

Within each local community council (periodically elected by the inhabitants of the *Kommune*) a commission (*det sociale udvalg*) is in charge of administering the social security schemes. The actual administration of social security takes place under the supervision of the *sociale udvalg* by an unique local community social service to which a person has access, for among others, his (daily) benefits in respect of incapacity for work, social and part-time pensions, family benefits, social assistance (in cash or in kind), as well as a number of other social services. Associations of *Kommuner (KLF)* and of *sociale udvalg (Sammenslutning af sociale udvalg)* operate at a national level.

Danish territory is subdivided into 14 districts, the so called *amtskommuner*. Each *kommune* is part of an *amtskommune*. However, this is not the case for København and the neighbouring Frederiksberg. In fact, for these towns the *kommune* and the *amtskommune* have been merged; this gives rise to special administrative regulations which we shall not consider here. The *amtskommune* is governed by an elected council which also appoints a social commission (*social og-sundhedsudvalg*). The council leaves the routine administration of the social security and health schemes to the social and health administration (including the social centre) of the *amtskommune*. Most of the secondary health services are offered on this district level; also the formation of hospital policy and specific medical and social services (such as rehabilitation centres) can be situated on this level. If they are confronted with specific complex questions, the *sociale udvalg* of the local communities may rely upon the expert aid of the social centre of the *amtskommune*.

On a district level, the *sociale brugerraad* gives advice with regard to social policy affairs. This council of clients consists of seven members and a chairman; three persons represent the Association of organisations of the handicapped, two represent the parents of children in day care institutions and boarding establishments and one person represents the inhabitants of the institutions of the *amtskommune*; furthermore, one more representative of other client groups of the district may be added.
On a national level, most social security affairs fall under the authority of the *Socialministerium*. However, sometimes the Health Minister or the Ministry of Labour is competent. The *Socialministerium* consists of politically independent civil servants; only the Minister himself bears political responsibility. The personnel of the *Socialministerium* operates as the secretariat of the Minister and deals mainly with policy questions and the preparation of statutes.

Furthermore, on a central level there is also a *Centrale handicapraad*, which advises on matters of policy with regard to the handicapped. The council consists of 11 members, five of whom represent the co-operating organisations of the handicapped (*samvirkende Invalideorganisationer*); the other members represent various levels of the administration.

There are a number of important exceptions to the decentralised system of administration as described above.
For example, as from 1987, child benefit for children younger than 18 years of age is awarded by the national taxation service; in case of problems, a person may still contact the *sociale udvalg* which, however, merely operates as an intermediary between citizens and the competent tax services.
Furthermore, the unemployment insurance scheme, which is still optional, is traditionally administered by the unemployment funds (*Arbejdsløshedskasser*) set up by the trade unions, and organised on an industrial branch level (or with respect to two funds, linked to the main organisations for the self employed). From the point of view of book-keeping and administration, unemployment funds are independent from the related trade unions; union membership is not a prerequisite for membership to a fund; however, such a link is often established in the reverse case. In order to be able to operate as an administrative body of the unemployment insurance scheme, the funds must receive recognition by the competent minister; for such recognition a minimum number of members is required; the minister can withhold recognition if there already exists a fund for the industrial branch concerned. Most of the funds have local offices which can be contacted by the insured persons. The *Direktorat* for *Arbejdsløshedsforsikring* of the Ministry of Labour supervises the unemployment funds. The funds are mutually associated in the *Arbejdsløshedskassernes Samvirke*.
A central body, which is governed by the employer and employee organisations on a parity basis, administers the additional labour market pensions *(Arbejdsmarkedets Tillaegspension/A.T.P.)*.

The industrial damage insurance scheme (industrial injuries and occupational diseases insurance) is set up by the employers with private insurance companies. The *Arbejdsskadestyrelsen* is empowered to award benefits; furthermore, it controls the insurance companies.

3. *Personal scope of application*

Every person living in Denmark is entitled to social assistance. The entitlement to assistance in cash which is expected to have a long term character (in the terms of the present administrative practice: an expected duration of more than one year) is restricted to Danish citizens, political refugees and citizens of states with which Denmark has concluded a reciprocal arrangement relating to this matter. Those who are not entitled to such social assistance benefits, but who are nevertheless in need of them, may be expelled from Danish territory. Danish citizens who are abroad may, under certain circumstances, claim a right to subsistence. This is, for example, the case for Danish citizens who stay abroad for a longer period due to illness and who cannot be expected to return home.

Every person living in Denmark is equally entitled to medical care.

In order to be eligible for a social pension, two conditions must be fulfilled:
a) the claimant must satisfy certain conditions relating to citizenship, these are met by those who:
   - have Danish nationality; or
   - have had a permanent and legal residence in Denmark for a period of at least 10 years between the ages of 15 and 67; furthermore, of these 10 years at least 5 must immediately precede the moment that entitlement to pension arises; or
   - are political refugees; or
   - are citizens of an EC state or a state with which Denmark has signed an international agreement; and
b) the applicant must have a permanent address in Denmark

Furthermore, it is required that people who are not Danish citizens must have lived in Denmark for a period of at least 30 years between the ages of 15 and 67.

Once entitlement to a social pension is recognised, a person may continue to receive benefit if he emigrates to another country; he should then satisfy the condition that he has had his permanent residence in Denmark for at least 30 years after the age of 15, as well as immediately preceding the moment that entitlement to benefit arose. Temporary residence abroad does not affect entitlement to a pension, at least when the pensioner maintains his real and actual residence in Denmark.

It should already be noted at this stage, that for the right to the full amount of social old age pension a period of 40 years of residence in Denmark (between the age limits mentioned above) is required; if this condition is not satisfied, the amount of old age pension is reduced pro rata temporis. With regard to the other social pensions, the right to the full amount of pension is made dependent upon the condition that a person must have lived in Denmark during a period of at least 4/5 of the years between the age of 15 and the moment that entitlement to a pension arises.

Only those who are employed in Denmark (including civil servants and unemployed persons receiving unemployment benefit) for at least 9 hours a week or 39 hours a month (between the ages of 16 and 66) are compulsorily affiliated to the additional labour market pension insurance (*A.T.P.*). Members of an unemployment fund receiving part-time pension or *efterløn* can take up a voluntary *A.T.P.*-insurance.

In order to be eligible for a part-time pension (*delpension*), it is required that one:
- is an employee (or recipient of *efterløn*) or self-employed person in Denmark;
- has a permanent residence in Denmark;
- is between the age of 60 and 67; and

- if one is an employee, one must have paid *A.T.P.* contributions for the last 20 years for a total equivalent to 10 years full time contribution; and have worked at least 9 out of the past 12 months; or
- if one is self-employed, one must have been self-employed in Denmark for a period of at least 4 out of the last 5 years; have been occupied full-time for a period of at least 5 years; and in the last year have had an income from self-employment which is higher than half the maximum amount of daily benefits in respect of sickness.

All employees are compulsorily insured for income maintenance in respect of sickness and maternity. Self-employed entrepreneurs and their spouses who are engaged in the same activity are equally insured, but only for the income maintenance as from the fourth week of incapacity for work; however, they can insure themselves on a voluntary basis in respect of the first three weeks. Voluntary insurance also exists for those who carry out domestic activities at home for at least one person other than themselves. In principle, all these persons must be subject to income tax liability in Denmark.

Employees (as well as self-employed fishermen, people who act in order to prevent accidents or to save human lives and some other categories) enjoy a special protection on the grounds of the industrial injuries and occupational diseases insurance scheme.

Child allowances and child benefits are only granted on the condition that the child or one of his parents is a Danish citizen; that the child is permanently resident in Denmark; that he is not maintained outside the family nor by public funds; and he is not yet married. The legislation specifically provides that the child allowance is a right of the child.

Every person who lives in Denmark, who is between 16 and 65 years of age, and has the status of an employee or a self employed person (or as a person doing his military service) can become a member of the unemployment fund. Pensioners only have limited rights and those who become 67 years of age lose their membership altogether. About 80% of the employees in Denmark and 1/3 of the self-employed are members of a fund for (optional) unemployment insurance.

In order to be eligible for *efterløn* one has to satisfy the additional requirement that one lives in Denmark; one has been a member of an unemployment fund for at least 20 years in the last 25 years and one is older than 60 years of age but has not yet attained the age of 67 years.

Approximately half of all the wage earners in Denmark work under collective labour agreements containing a 'social chapter'.

4. Risks and benefits

By the first of January of each year the amounts of the social benefits are increased in accordance with the evolution of the yearly income of the workers in the private sector during the preceding calendar year.

4.1. Old age

There are various schemes in Danish social security law which insure income maintenance for the elderly. Thus, we can make a distinction between: the social old age pension (*folkepension*), the additional labour market (old age) pension (*A.T.P.*) and the part-time pension (*delpension*). Furthermore, many employees and civil servants have joined pension funds, which often take the shape of a collective life or pension insurance.

The social old age pension is payable to those who belong to the group of people insured for social pension and who have reached the age of 67. The full amount of pension is payable to those who have lived in Denmark for 40 years between the ages of 15 and 67.
The social old age pension consists of a basic amount and a pension supplement. In addition there may be a whole range of special supplements. The basic amount is flat-rate; it is paid to insured persons who are 67 years of age or older. The basic amount of old age pension is reduced by 60% of the income from of work (exceeding an earnings limit).

The pension supplement is means tested; both the income of the person himself and that of his spouse are taken into account. Of the further supplements which are payable on the grounds of the legislation concerning the social pension, the personal supplement is the most important. This supplement is subject to a means test and payable to pensioners who find themselves in particularly difficult economic circumstances; a supplement is granted as a payment towards the costs of heating, although the pensioner himself is liable to pay a certain contribution for the heating costs. Furthermore, in exceptional situations, a personal supplement may be granted to meet certain other costs (e.g. for the coverage of medical expenses), yet only if the person finds himself in particularly difficult economic circumstances. The *kommune* has a general budget for the financing of personal supplements. Special rules apply for those who stay in institutions.

The part-time pension creates the possibility for those aged between 60 and 67 years of age to retire gradually from the labour market by reducing their work without fully ceasing it. For employees and the self-employed the entitlement conditions for part-time pensions differ.

The employee who is eligible for a part-time pension must reduce his weekly hours of work by either 1/4, or 7 hours per week (based upon a 37 hour maximum working week, as a starting point for the method of calculation). After the reduction of the regular working hours the employee must continue to work for a minimum of 12 hours and a maximum of 30 hours per week. The part-time pension is calculated by multiplying a uniform rate by the average number of reduced weekly working hours. Thus, the amount of benefit payable corresponds to the maximum amount of daily sickness benefit which would have been payable over the same period. Finally, it must be mentioned that legislation does not grant the employee a right to change to part-time employment with his employer, although arrangements to this effect are often adopted in collective labour agreements.

The self-employed who are covered by the part-time pension scheme must have enjoyed an income of at least half the above mentioned maximum in the year preceding partial retirement. A self-employed person must reduce his professional activities by at least 18,5 hours a week, leaving a working week of 18,5 hours. Thus, for the self-employed there is only one possible amount of part-time pension, i.e. 18,5 times the uniform rate. The scheme is not means-tested but the part-time pension may not exceed 90% of the difference of income from work before and after the moment of partial retirement.

After 2,5 year of *efterløn*, the part-time pension amounts are reduced to 82% of the previous amount. Again two years later the beneficiary only receives 70% of the original part-time pension. If the concerned person first starts to receive *efterløn* at the age of 63, he will continue to receive the same amount for the whole period.

Entitlement to *A.T.P.* old age pensions exists from the age of 67. It is built up with reference to each year of employment between the ages of 16 and 66. Those who started to participate in the *A.T.P.* scheme after the moment of its introduction (1.4.1965) are granted a set amount for each pensionable year of service. For those who have participated in the *A.T.P.* scheme from the moment of its introduction, there are age-related flat-rate amounts in respect of the preceding years.
When a person postpones the take up of his pension, the pension amount is increased by 5% per half year of postponement from the age of 67 onwards, up to a maximum bonus of 30%.

The amount differs for people employed in the public and those employed in the private sector.

The pension depends upon the number of years one has paid contributions. The additional labour market pension, however, provides higher amounts, as these are augmented with a bonus (the bonus may not exceed 50% of the amount of the original pension). This bonus follows from the profits made by the scheme, that is to say: from the difference between the income on the one hand, and the legally prescribed expenditures and benefits on the other. Indeed, the legislative provisions concerning the *A.T.P.* pensions are determined in such a way as to guarantee a profit of 4,5% of the contributions; if the interest rate appears to be generally higher, a surplus arises which then flows back to the beneficiaries in the form of a bonus.

4.2. Death

Survival pensions, as such, no longer exist under Danish social security law. The function of these pensions has been taken over, but only to a very small extent, by the early social pension (see section 4.3).

The beneficiary of a social old age pension, continues to receive the pension for a period of three more months after the death of the spouse.

The additional labour market pension for survivors (*A.T.P.*-survivor pension) is payable to the surviving spouse of an *A.T.P.* insured person from the age of 62 onwards. The deceased must have worked for a period corresponding to at least 10 pensionable years and the marriage must also have lasted for at least 10 years. The *A.T.P.* survivor's pension provides 50% of the *A.T.P.* old age pension plus a bonus which the deceased received or would have received at the age of 67 on grounds of the number of years that he worked under the *A.T.P.* scheme. If the surviving spouse satisfies the entitlement conditions for an *A.T.P.* old age pension himself, he receives the highest of the two *A.T.P.* pension amounts. Entitlement to *A.T.P.* survivor pension ends with a new marriage, but may revive at its termination.

Under the insurance scheme for occupational damage a lump sum is payable in respect of the costs which arise from the death of a victim of a professional risk. Normally, this sum is paid to the surviving spouse or partner. Also the surviving spouse or partner may be compensated for the death of the breadwinner, taking into account the possibility of the survivor to provide for his own subsistence, considering his age, health, education, activities, etc. Compensation is payable for a maximum period of 10 years and the annual amount consists of 30% of the yearly wage (subject to a ceiling similar to the one which applies in respect of the compensation for a loss of earning capacity); as an exception, this period may be extended, albeit maximally, to the age of 67. Sometimes the benefit is capitalised. The benefit does not end in case of a new marriage, but it does end if a person reaches his 67th year of age. In that case the beneficiary receives a lump sum, the amount of which corresponds to two years of the benefit.
For each child of the victim younger than 18 years of age (or, in case of education, 21) 10% of the yearly wage (subject to an upper wage limit), or 20% in respect of a child without any parents, is payable. Maximally, the total of all these benefits to children may add up to 40% of the yearly wage mentioned above (or 50% if the deceased was the only person financially responsible for the children).

If the total amount of benefits to the spouse and to the children does not exceed 70% of the yearly wage, a lump sum or an annuity may be granted to another survivor. For all the persons mentioned above it is required that they were maintained by the deceased or that their financial position deteriorated as a result of his death.

On grounds of the health care insurance scheme there is a right to a funeral benefit (*begravelseshjaelp*). Additional benefits in respect of death or a funeral are also often granted by, among others, the providers of collective pensions schemes and trade unions.

4.3. Incapacity for work

A person who does not work as a result of sickness, injury, birth or adoption of a child and thus has lost his income from labour, is entitled to an income maintenance benefit (daily benefit) for as long as he can be expected to return to work. If the incapacity for work is no longer considered as temporary, but permanent, the entitlement to daily benefit ends and it may then be considered whether the person is eligible for a social pension.

For daily benefits in respect of incapacity for work as a result of injury or sickness (*sygedagpenge*) a distinction must be made between two periods of compensation: the period during which daily benefit is payable by the employer and the period during which the daily benefit is payable by the *sociale udvalg*. The duration of the private employer's period is two weeks; the other period lasts as long as the duration of the temporary incapacity for work, yet no longer than 52 weeks.
In order to be entitled to daily benefit from the employer, it is required that the insured employee has been employed for at least 120 hours in the last 13 weeks and that he is not entitled to a continuation of wage payments. The daily benefit is calculated on the basis of the average weekly income during the last four weeks preceding the illness.
The amount of daily benefit is equal to the lost income from labour and in any case not more than a legally set upper level. Together with other possible compensation payments in respect of illness, the amount of daily benefit may never exceed the normal income from labour. If daily benefit amounts to less than 10% of the maximum amount of daily benefit, benefit is not payable by the *sociale udvalg*, except when daily benefit is due on grounds of voluntary insurance. In cases of partial incapacity for work, daily benefits are paid according to special rules.
Self-employed persons can get sickness benefit from their first day after a three week waiting period. It is possible to insure oneself for the first three weeks. It is a further condition that the activity as a self-employed has been significant (at least half of the income of an employed person in the specific sector) for at least 6 months before the sickness. The amount payable is calculated in the same way as for employed people.

During the last four weeks of pregnancy, employees, self-employed entrepreneurs and their spouses, who are engaged in the same activity, may receive daily benefit from the *sociale udvalg*. After a birth (or adoption), daily benefit continues to be payable during a period of 24 weeks, the last ten of which may be claimed by the father of the child. The father is also entitled to two weeks of daily benefit immediately after the birth of the child or at the moment that the newly born child returns home. It is required for entitlement to these daily benefits that professional activities are ceased during the relevant period. Daily benefit can only be received by one of the spouses during the same period.

We shall now discuss the benefits in respect of permanent incapacity for work. These constitute a part of the scheme for early social pensions (*førtidspensioner*). Although early social pensions do not consist exclusively of benefits in respect of invalidity, for the sake of clarity we have chosen to present here a comprehensive overview of all the social pensions concerned.

The act concerning social pensions distinguishes between high, middle, increased general and general early pensions. These benefits will be briefly discussed, each time with reference to the person who is eligible as well as the different parts which constitute the benefits. All benefits are flat-rate, generally a distinction being made between whether one is married to another social pensioner or not.

The highest early pension may be awarded to persons between 18 and 59 years of age, who, due to health reasons, have entirely or almost entirely lost their working capacity. The highest early pension consists of a basic amount, a pension supplement, an invalidity amount and an earning incapacity amount; both of these last mentioned amounts are free of tax liability. The pension is paid till the beneficiary is 67 years of age. From that moment on an old age pension will be paid.

The middle early pension is awarded to those who:
- are between 60 and 66 years old and satisfy the entitlement conditions for the highest early pension or
- are between 18 and 59 years old, and whose working capacity has, for reasons of health, not been reduced entirely, but by 2/3.

The middle early pension consists of a basic amount, a pension supplement and early invalidity amounts (not subject to tax liability), depending on the question of whether one belongs to the first or the second group of people eligible for a middle early pension.

The increased general early pension is payable to those who:
- are between 18 and 59 years of age, and whose earning capacity has been reduced by reasons of health by at least 50%;
- are between 18 and 59 years of age, and whose working capacity has been reduced as a result of medical and social reasons by at least 50%;
- are between 50 and 59 years of age, and in respect of whom the granting of a pension is justified on the grounds of social or health reasons; in the latter case a reduction of working capacity is not required.

The increased general early pension consists of a basic amount, a pension supplement and an early payment which is free of tax liability.

The general early pension is payable to those who:
- are between, 60 and 66 years of age, and whose working capacity has been reduced for reasons of health by at least 50%;

- between 60 and 66 years of age, and in respect of whom the granting of a pension is justified on grounds of social and health reasons or only social reasons; a reduction of the earning capacity is not required.

The general early pension consists of a basic amount and a pension supplement. The pensions for social reasons are not awarded if the income exceeds the maximum unemployment benefit for a couple or 2/3 of this benefit for a single person.

Under certain circumstances widowhood with dependent children, of a person who has never had any ties with the labour market, is accepted as a purely social reason for granting an early pension. Thus, the early social pension granted on grounds of purely social criteria offers some compensation (in cases of severe hardship) for the abolition of the social survivor pension.

Finally, we mention that there is a possibility of granting a personal, an assistance or a treatment supplement. The personal supplement has already been dealt with in the discussion of the social old age pension. An assistance supplement is payable to an invalid who regularly requires the aid of another person, as well as to the severely visually handicapped. If a person requires continuous care and attendance, he is entitled to a care supplement. Neither are liable to taxation; the supplements cannot be cumulated.

A person for whom a plan has been established as to how to be able to manage his own life, is entitled to a rehabilitation benefit instead of a pension. The plan shall include educational measures and vocational training in order to bring the concerned person back to the labour market. The rehabilitation benefit can be received for up to 5 years; its amount equals that of the unemployment benefit, except for people younger than 23 years of age for whom it equals half the amount of the unemployment benefit.

If the insured person is the victim of an occupational risk, entitlement to benefit can arise on the grounds of the insurance scheme for occupational damage.
Those whose earning capacity has been affected by more than 15% as a result of an occupational risk are, in case of full incapacity for work, entitled to an annuity of 4/5 of their yearly wage, subject to an upper wage limit. For the determination of the percentage of incapacity for work, both social-economic and labour market factors are taken into account. However, purely medical facts, which do not impede the claimant's ability to work, are not taken into consideration. In cases of partial incapacity for work, a percentage of the full annuity is paid; this percentage corresponds to the degree of incapacity for work. The annuity is payable until a person reaches his 67th year of age; at that time he will receive a lump sum equal to the amount of two years annuity payments. Incapacity for work of less than 50% does not result in entitlement to an annuity, but to the payment of a lump sum.
Finally, compensation is payable in respect of permanent purely medical damage, such as scarring. In accordance with medical scales percentages have been determined which express the discomforts experienced as a result of health damage. Thus, the amount of benefit can be determined, related to a flat-rate basis of calculation. Normally the amount is paid as a lump sum on the basis of

the life expectancy of a person and his age, but with medical damage of 50% or more payment of a periodical monthly benefit is also a possibility.

4.4. Unemployment

A person who has been a member of an unemployment fund for at least one year and who has worked in insured employment for at least 52 weeks within the last three years, is entitled to unemployment benefit (*arbejdsløshedsdagpenge*). Normally, the entitlement lasts for a maximum of two years in a three year period. After the elapse of this period, the insured person is entitled to be offered suitable employment or vocational training, for a duration of three years within a four year period. Employers obtain a premium in order to make extra jobs available; those who cannot be offered a job in the private sector must be given employment in the public sector.
The unemployment must be involuntary. The unemployed beneficiary is under a duty to register with the labour exchanges and to accept suitable employment. The level of unemployment benefit in relation to previously earned wages is determined by each of the unemployment funds; benefit may not exceed 90% of previously earned wages, subject to an upper wage limit. Those who have been allowed membership of an unemployment fund without having had any previous work experience (people carrying out their obligatory military service or having taken an education of at least 18 months) receive a flat-rate weekly amount. If the unemployed person has fully exhausted offers of employment and training, which normally will take 6 to 7 years, then the person will be eligible for social assistance.
The unemployment fund cannot pay benefit when unemployment is due to a strike or a lock-out.

The *efterløn* scheme constitutes an important addition to the unemployment insurance. Members of an unemployment fund who are at least 60 years of age and who have been members of the fund for a period of at least 20 years within the last 25 years may make use of this scheme. Furthermore, they must be capable for work. During the first five weeks of *efterløn* all employment is prohibited; subsequently 200 hours of employment per year is allowed (subject to an upper earnings limit). The beneficiary may not receive a social pension.
During the first 2 years (to be determined from the moment that employment ceased, thus possibly from the start of the unemployment), *efterløn* is equal to unemployment benefit; in the subsequent years it is 82% of this amount. *Efterløn* is payable up to the age of 67.

In recent years, alternative ways other than cash benefits have been emphasised in order to activate and train the unemployed. Thus, even persons who are not covered by the unemployment insurance can benefit from some of the measures taken, such as job offers or training. A new development has led to the partial reimbursement of the costs for moving if the employee has accepted a job in another area. For the long-term unemployed and the young unemployed persons over 25 the possibility to commission an 'individual plan of action' for their future career has been developed.

4.5. Health care

All residents are compulsorily insured; the insured population may make a choice between two classes of insurance. The greatest majority chose class 1 whilst less than 3% have opted for class 2 insurance.

Those who are insured in class 1 enjoy free care by a medical practitioner, yet they may only change their (personal) practitioner once a year; specialist care is also free, albeit on the condition of a reference by their personal practitioner.

Those who are insured in class 2 are completely free in the choice of their personal practitioner, but they only get reimbursed amount which corresponds to the tariffs for class 1, which have been negotiated between the organisations representing the practitioners and the state.

The income of the medical practitioners is dependent upon the number of medical operations carried out (one payment for each medical operation). Specialists are also fully paid on the basis of their medical achievements. Dental treatment, as specified in a list, is in principle for 40 to 45% financed by the (class 1) patient himself; the rest is covered by social insurance; class 2 patients are reimbursed an amount which is equivalent to the part of the costs of the same dental treatment which is not borne by the class 1 patients themselves.

Regardless of the class, hospital care (in principle in a hospital of one's own *amtskommune*) and obstetric care are free of charge (except for extra services, for example, a private room). With the consent of the *amtskommune*, it is possible to receive treatment in a private hospital; the costs of such treatment are reimbursed to the patient.

Under certain conditions ambulance services are (partly or totally) free of charge. If required, free interpreter services may also be provided. However, the treatment of a chiropractor is subject to a personal contribution. On prescription a patient may receive free care by a nurse at home.

The insured person must pay a personal contribution towards medicine equal to a certain percentage of the cost price, depending upon whether the purchased medicine is registered in list A or list B. Medicine, which has not been registered in either of these lists, must be paid for in full, unless in an individual case it is decided that a remission should particularly be granted. Ear and eye prosthesis are subject to a partial reimbursement.

A pregnant woman is entitled to five free preventive check-ups by a medical practitioner. Also birth assistance is free of charge. Abortion and sterilisation costs are also free of charge.

In cases of illness or industrial injury due to an occupational risk, the cost of medical care provided by a practitioner or dentist, of hospital care and of medical aids and rehabilitation services are borne by the occupational damage insurance scheme.

People who are financially incapable of paying their own charges for medical care, medicine, etc. may apply for assistance on the grounds of the social assistance legislation. There is also the opportunity of taking out private insurance for (a part of the costs) of the personal charges.

4.6. Family

As the result of several changes during the last decade, we can now distinguish the following family benefits:
- a flat-rate family child benefit for each child per year (*børnefamilieydelse*). The benefit differs according to the age-group of the child. Thus, three groups are made: the children from 0 until 3 years old, the children from 3 until 6 and those from 7 up to the age of 18. This benefit is supplemented by a lump sum per month and per child for single parents or when both parents are pensioners (old age or invalidity). This scheme is regulated in an act concerning personal income taxation and therefore no longer considered to be part of the domain of social security;
- the extra benefit for the single parent, i.e. when the beneficiary is solely responsible for the child. The extra benefit is paid per month and per household;
- the special additional benefit per month and per child when one or both parents are pensioners, or when the child is either motherless or fatherless. In case the child is orphan of both parents, the benefit amounts are to be doubled;
- the extra benefit for families of multiple births with twins or triplets etc. is granted until the children's 7th birthday; and
- the extra benefit in case of adoption of a child.

Finally, it must be mentioned that the legislation which governs family benefits also contains provisions concerning the granting of advantage payments by the state of alimony for children in cases where the liable person is not fulfilling his obligations in time. The advance payment may not exceed the amount of the special child allowance.

4.7. Need

On grounds of the act concerning social assistance the state is under a duty to provide assistance to any person who is present in Denmark and who, in view of his personal and family circumstances, needs counselling, financial or practical help and support in the recovery of his earning capacity, care, special treatment or educational support. From this provision it emerges that the scope of the assistance scheme is very wide; it contains a plethora of benefits. The Assistance Act is therefore governed by the principle that only one office, i.e. the service of the *kommune*, should deal with all questions of social assistance. Another principle is that care should be provided regardless of the cause of the need for help and the professional category to which the beneficiary belongs.
In view of the wide scope of the social assistance scheme, we shall only deal with assistance in cash; thus, the services which are provided on the basis of the Assistance Act to the handicapped, the home and child care facilities, as well as the juvenile protection measures, are not taken into consideration.

Assistance in cash may be divided into assistance for subsistence and assistance for special costs.

The assistance for subsistence is payable to those whose life circumstances have altered to such an extent that they can no longer provide for the subsistence of themselves and their families. Assistance for subsistence consists of a basic benefit, a housing supplement and a child supplement. Basic benefit for single persons consists of half the amount payable to a couple. After 9 months, the amount of basic benefit is reduced, unless it can be proved that in the near future the person in question will be able to take care of himself again. A single young person up to 25 years of age receives benefit at a reduced rate, here a distinction is made between juveniles living at home and juveniles who live on their own. The housing supplement is intended to cover the costs of rent or the costs of home ownership, after deduction of other housing subsidies. Furthermore, the housing supplement covers the costs of water, gas, electricity, heating and other costs connected with housing; all real costs are covered, unless these are considered to be excessive.

Assistance in cash is subject to an income and capital test. Furthermore, both spouses must have exhausted all possibilities of finding employment. At the latest after three months of payment of assistance in cash, the *sociale udvalg* will consider whether there is reason to move to other forms of assistance payments, for example budget advising. The total amount of assistance for subsistence may not exceed the maximum amount of daily benefit on grounds of the unemployment insurance scheme (after tax deduction).

The Danish social assistance scheme was reformed in 1997 in order to bring it more in line with a pro-active labour market policy, stressing the obligations of the individual rather than his entitlements. The effort that the social assistance authorities have to make in order to offer rehabilitation or activation to the needy person as soon as possible is very important. As a consequence unemployed persons younger than 25 years of age, will have to be activated within three months of becoming unemployed.

Special rules apply for those who do their obligatory (non-military) service in the civil sector or in a developing country, as well as for people who stay in a penal institution.

Assistance in cash for special costs is payable to people regardless of whether they receive assistance for subsistence. Assistance for coverage of justifiable isolated expenses is payable, if the payment of these expenses by the beneficiary himself would constitute a real threat to future possibilities of providing for his own livelihood. Assistance may be provided for the coverage of the costs of medical treatment, medicine, dental care, etc., as far as these are not already covered by other schemes. Furthermore, assistance may be given for expenses resulting from the exercise of parental care duties, as well as for the coverage of removal costs to a place with better housing and earning circumstances. Severely handicapped people living on their own, as well as people who care at home for a physically or mentally handicapped person, younger than 18 years of age, are entitled to compensation for the extra costs resulting from their attendance.

5. *Financing*

Social assistance and a number of social insurance benefits are wholly financed out of general taxation. The state and the *kommuner* and *amtskommuner* together bear the largest share of the total social security expenditure. The employers and the insured persons traditionally only contributed a small part of this. However, in order to cope with the State's growing social expenditures, three 'Labour Market Funds' were established. These funds are being fed by contributions paid by employers, wage-earners and self-employed. These contributions are calculated as a certain percentage of the gross wages or profits. These funds are used for financing the sickness and maternity benefits, the unemployment benefits, the early retirement benefits and employment measures. As such, they replace the earlier (tax financed) state subventions.
The daily benefits which are paid by the employer are financed fully by the employers themselves.

Social assistance in cash is 50% financed by the state and 50% by the *kommune*. Advice given on grounds of the assistance act, as well as the general administration, is financed wholly by the *kommune*; this also applies to the social assistance services for people older than 67 years of age. The assistance services which are offered to people younger than 67 years of age are mostly 50% financed by the *kommune* and 50% by the *amtskommune*.

The daily benefits in respect of sickness and maternity are 25% financed out of the budget of the *kommune*; the remaining 75% is borne by a labour market fund. The daily benefits which are paid by the employer are financed fully by the employers themselves.

Pensions to people over 60 years of age are fully financed by the state; 50% of the pensions paid to younger people is financed by the State and the remaining 50% is covered by the *kommune*.

The social and part-time pensions are fully refunded by the state to the *kommune*. However, the personal pension supplements which are granted by the *kommune* on a discretionary basis are only refunded up to 75%.

The additional labour market (*A.T.P.*) pensions are financed fully from contributions. These are borne for 1/3 by the employees and for 2/3 by the employers.

Family benefits are financed entirely by the state.

The costs of medical care are borne by the *amtskommuner* and the state.

Employers who bear contribution liability pay 12 times the amount of maximum daily (unemployment) benefit as an annual contribution toward the unemployment insurance scheme; the members of unemployment funds pay 8 times this amount. The remaining means which are necessary for the financing of unemployment benefits are financed by a labour market fund (subsidised on

the basis of the expenditure of the fund in the previous year; also here the state subsidy constitutes the major financing share). Furthermore, the members of the unemployment funds are liable to pay contributions for the costs of administration; the rates of the administration contributions are set by each fund. Employers bear no contribution liability in respect of their first employee. Further, unemployed members are liable to pay contributions; recipients of *efterløn* pay contributions at a 50% rate.
The *efterløn* scheme is mainly financed out of general taxation. The employers and employees also contribute through an increase of the contribution rate for the unemployment insurance scheme.

In respect of the insurance scheme for occupational damage, the employers pay a contribution to their private insurers corresponding to their firm's individual degree of risk. The private insurers pay back the benefits granted to the administrative body and add a sum for each case in order to cover the administrative costs. The state itself fully finances the benefits in an attempt to save human lives.

The system underlying the additional financing of the labour market pension and the income maintenance benefits on the grounds of the scheme for occupational damage bears characteristics of both the pay as you go principle and the capitalisation principle.

6. Judicial review

If a citizen wants to challenge an unfavourable decision by an administrative body, he is not dependent upon the ordinary Danish judiciary, but upon a number of judicial bodies, which constitute part of the administration, yet operate independently. These administrative judicial bodies are subject to the supervision of the ordinary courts and are controlled by the ombudsman. Each of the different acts determines which judicial body is competent to deal with particular disputes. The term for appeal is usually four weeks, counting from the moment when the litigious decision is made known to the claimant.
The adjudication system is based upon the principle that a decision of the administration can only be challenged before one judicial body, albeit that a system has been introduced which allows the administrative body to reconsider its contentious decision.
Thus, a person who wants to challenge a decision of the *sociale udvalg* or of an administrative body operating on a district level must first notify this to the administrative body. This body then subjects its decision to a reconsideration. Only if this does not result in a fresh decision which fully satisfies the claimant, will the *Social ankenaevn* take up the case.
As a rule, decisions of the *social udvalg* of the local community are open to appeal to the *Social ankenaevn*. This body is linked to the *amtskommune* of the district. The *Social ankenaevn* consists of the head of the district (the *amtsmand*) and six other members appointed by the Minister of Social Affairs upon the recommendation of the local and district councils and of the Association of organisations of the handicapped.

The *social ankenaevn* is competent to deal with complaints about decisions taken at the local or district level as well as in cases dealing with early pensions. In urgent cases the chairman may give immediate judgement; he alone is also competent to give judgement in the first instance in simple and straightforward cases. The *Social ankenaevn* is bound by the case law of the *Sociale ankestyreslse*, but not by the administrative instructions of the *kommune*, district or ministry.

The *Sociale ankestyrelse* is the highest appeal authority in matters of social affairs. Although this body is linked to the *Socialministerium*, it operates fully independently; thus it is not bound by the instructions which are issued by the ministry or by lower administrative bodies.

The appeals are dealt with by a chairman-civil servant and two further members, who are nominated by the central employer organisations and by the trade unions, the councils of København and Frederiksberg, the national association of *kommuner*, the association of district councils, the associations for the handicapped and the beneficiaries of a social pension.
As from 1983 the *Sociale ankestyrelse* only hears appeals against decisions of the *Social ankenaevn* to the extent that these involve points of principle, in particular with regard to the interpretation of the law.
Furthermore, the *sociale ankestyrelse* decides some cases in first instance, such as appeals against the decisions of the *sociale udvalg* in København and Frederiksberg (as said, these *kommuner* do not constitute a part of an *amtskommune*), appeals against the decisions which are taken on a district level, and appeals against some decisions concerning occupational damage insurance taken by the *Arbejdsskadestyrelse*.

Appeal against decisions concerning child benefits must be made to the *sociale udvalg*. Such appeals are passed through to the taxation inspection service which itself sends them to the national taxation directory, accompanied by a recommendation concerning the decision. The final decision is not subject to further appeal.

Appeals against decisions of the unemployment funds may be made to the *Direktorat for arbejdsløshedsforsikringen*; their decisions are subject to further appeal to the *Arbejdsløshedsforsikringens Ankenaevn*. The latter consists of five members, one of whom is nominated by the employers' organisations and one by the trade unions.
The *A.T.P.'s Ankenaevn* hear appeals against decisions of the *A.T.P.* concerning additional labour market pensions.
It should be mentioned that the decisions of all administrative organisations may be challenged before the ordinary courts. However, there are some restrictions with regard to the power of these courts to judge decisions which are made on a discretionary basis. In matters of social security law, appeal to the ordinary courts is very exceptional.

The ombudsman plays a much more important role in the settlement of social security disputes. The ombudsman hears complaints against decisions or against the conduct of public authorities, however not against acts and judicial decisions. His duty is to make sure that acts and other legal norms are not violated by the administration. Possibilities of administrative appeal must first be exhausted before a complaint can successfully be lodged with the ombudsman. However, if the dispute involves the treatment of a case by the administration, it is possible to address the ombudsman immediately. After investigation the ombudsman informs the plaintiff about his findings and actions; if necessary, he will also confront the administrative body with criticism or recommendations. The ombudsman can neither cancel the contentious decision or conduct, nor act as a substitute for the administrative body.

Chapter Four

FINLAND

1. Introduction: concept and sources of social security law

The Finnish concept of social security *(sosiaaliturva)* is rather broad. It covers the traditional benefit schemes as well as and health and other social services; several less traditional benefit schemes are also included, such as housing allowances.

The benefit schemes can be divided into the basic benefit schemes, which in principle cover all residents, and the employment related benefits. The employment based schemes include pensions, unemployment benefits and benefits in case of labour accident and professional disease. The basic schemes include the national pensions, sickness insurance (for medical costs), unemployment benefits, child benefits and children's home care allowances. Sickness and maternity daily allowances are schemes presenting features both of the basic and the employment related schemes. There are also social allowances (social assistance) to cover all residents and every resident of a Finnish municipality has access to the health care and social services.
It is clear that for the main risks there is a two tier approach: a basic benefit for all and an employment related benefit for the wage earners and self employed. In principle, if the employment related benefit is due, the basic benefit will not be paid out.
It should be observed that the same sickness insurance covers, as a universal scheme, the costs of health care and basic sickness and maternity allowances, and as an employment related scheme, earnings related sickness and maternity daily allowances.

The Constitution Act of Finland states that since the constitutional revision of 1995 everyone shall have the right to primary education free of charge (s.13) and that public authorities shall strive to ensure that everyone has the right to a healthy environment as well as the opportunity to influence decision-making concerning his living environment (s.14(a)). In section 15 it is stated that everyone shall have the lawful right to procure a living through the work, occupation or trade of his choice. Public authorities shall ensure the protection of labour. Public authorities shall also promote employment and shall strive to secure the right to work for everyone. Provisions on the right to vocational training shall be prescribed by an Act of Parliament. No one shall be dismissed from work without a reason prescribed by Act of Parliament.
However, section 15(a) of the Constitution Act is of the greatest importance to us, this was also introduced in 1995. It reads as follows: "Everyone who is unable to procure the security required for a dignified life shall have the right to

necessary subsistence and care. The right to security of basic livelihood at times of unemployment, illness, inability to work and old age as well as on account of childbirth and loss of provider shall be guaranteed to everyone by Act of Parliament. Public authorities shall, in the manner stipulated in greater detail by Act of Parliament, secure for everyone adequate social welfare and health services and shall promote the health of the population. Public authorities shall also support the abilities of families and others charged with the care of children to provide for their welfare and individual growth. It shall be the task of public authorities to promote the right of everyone to a dwelling and to support the efforts of persons to provide their own housing."

It remains to be seen what the practical impact of these constitutional provisions will be upon the day to day social security legislation and practice.

2. Administrative organisation

Political responsibility for social security mainly lies with the Ministry of Social Affairs and Health, except for the housing allowance which is the competence of the Ministry of the Environment. The employment offices function under the competence of the Ministry of Labour. The Ministry of Social Affairs and Health defines the social security policy; it also prepares national four year plans for the provision of social welfare and health.

The administration of the basic benefits is the responsibility of the Social Insurance Institution (*KELA*). Employment related sickness and maternity insurance is also managed by *KELA*.

KELA is an autonomous body under the authority of Parliament. A constitutional instrument, the Parliamentary Act, provides that Parliament shall appoint Governors to supervise the administration and activities of the funds for which Parliament is responsible. Parliament also appoints auditors to audit the accounts for the current financial year regarding the management of the aforesaid institutions (art. 83). Parliament shall also appoint twelve trustees to supervise the administration and activities of the Social Insurance Institution and shall issue regulations for these trustees (art. 83 a).

The employment related benefits in case of old age, survivorship and long term incapacity for work (invalidity) are managed by private pension institutions, co-ordinated and supervised by the Central Pensions Security Institute (*ETK*). Similarly the benefits in case of work accidents and professional diseases are administrated by private insurance companies, with the Federation of Accident Insurances Institution (*TVL*) acting as their central body.

The employment related unemployment benefit is managed by the unemployment fund of the insured person's sector of activity.

The Farmer's Social Insurance Institution (*MELA*) administers the farmer's pensions, employment accident insurance, short-term sickness compensation and group life insurance. *MELA* is managed by a board where representatives of the insured have a majority, the other members being the representatives of the concerned ministries. The autonomy of *MELA* is in fact less important as funding comes from the annual budget of the state.

The provision of adequate health care and other social services is the responsibility of the municipal authorities, who sometimes join in co-operation with each other to fulfil these duties. Private sector health care and service providers supplement the public services. Provinces exercise a guiding and supervisory role upon the fulfilment of this task by the municipalities

3. Personal scope of application

The national old age and invalidity pension as well as the daily sickness and maternity benefit schemes cover all residents aged 16 to 64; to qualify for the pension at least 3 years of residence after the age of 16 is required. All residents are also covered by the national survivor's pension scheme on the condition that the deceased and the survivor were resident in Finland for at least 5 years since they became 16 years of age and that they were resident at the time of the death. For Finnish citizens and nationals of other EU countries only 3 years of previous residence are required.
Maternity, paternity and parent's allowances are only paid to persons who have been resident in Finland for at least 180 days immediately preceding confinement or adoption.

The basic security in case of unemployment covers employees and self-employed persons aged 17 to 64.
The employment related security for unemployment covers the same persons on the condition that they are members of an unemployment fund. Membership of such a fund is voluntary. Members of trade unions are in practice automatically members of a fund, but they are free to refuse membership if they so wish.

The employment related old age pension scheme covers all employees and self employed persons aged between 23 and 65 years on the condition that they participated in the scheme for at least one month (wage earners) or four months (self employed); the employment related invalidity pensions covers all wage earners and self employed persons aged 14 or more. The condition of a minimum number of months of participation also applies for the employment related invalidity pensions. The employment related survivor's pension covers all wage earners aged 14 or more, whereas the self-employed are covered from the age of 18 onwards.

All wage earners and farmers, as well as some students and trainees are compulsorily insured under the labour accident and occupational disease insurances; other self employed persons can take voluntary insurance.
The farmers not only have their own employment related accident scheme, they also have their own employment-related pensions schemes and a scheme to compensate for the first days of incapacity for work that are not normally covered by the other schemes. Farmers, self-employed fishermen, and reindeer

herders over the age of 18 years, together with the family members of all the aforementioned are considered to be farmers. The farmers are compulsorily insured if the farm contains more than 5 hectares of arable land.

All residents of municipalities qualify for using the health care and other social services which are guaranteed by their municipality. The labour market support assistance benefits, under the conditions to be discussed below, are available to all unemployed residents. In this way persons who are not a member of an unemployment fund, people having exhausted their employment related benefit and persons who never worked before registering as a job seeker, may qualify. Social allowances benefit all residents, be it that social allowance will seldom be granted individually to young people under 18 years of age, as their parents are obliged to support them.

We shall not deal here with the specificalities of the social protection of the civil servants.

4. Risks and benefits

Let us observe that in Finland the pension schemes are covering within one frame both the old age, survivors and invalidity risks. We shall hereafter deal with the main features of the pension schemes under the heading 'old age', mentioning under the headings 'death' and 'incapacity for work' only the specificalities of the pension schemes in case those risks occur.

As the labour accidents and professional disease insurances cover the different risks mentioned hereafter, we shall define the ambit of these here. Under Finnish law, a labour accident is an accidental injury occurring at work in circumstances deriving from the nature of the employment or the journey to or from work. The occupational disease insurance takes a mixed approach: it defines these diseases as the diseases which are caused by exposure to a physical factor, chemical substance or biological agent at work, in such an amount that it can theoretically cause the disease in question unless it is proven that the disease has been clearly caused by exposure outside the workplace; but Finnish occupational disease insurance also works with a list of generally recognised occupational diseases.

4.1. Old age

Finland has a dual approach to the coverage of the old age risk. The national pension scheme provides pensions on the basis of residence in order to guarantee a minimum income. The employment related schemes provide earnings related benefits to former wage earners, self-employed persons and farmers. Separate employment related pension schemes for temporary wage earners, free lancers and civil servants, will not be dealt with here.

The retirement age is fixed at 65 years for all pension schemes; in case the concerned person decides to defer the pension, the amount of the pension is increased by 1% per month after reaching the age of 65.

The national pension may be accompanied by a care allowance and a pensioners housing allowance. The national pension consists of a lump sum differentiated according to marital status and according to the cost of living classification of the municipality of residence; the national pension is reduced by a sum equal to 50% of the amount of the employment related pension; it is also reduced proportionally if the pensioner has less than 40 years of residence between the ages of 16 and 65. The care allowances consist of a lump sum (one for each of the three categories which are being distinguished) to compensate for costs arising from home care or other special expenses caused by illness or injury. The pensioner's housing allowances may be paid to all pensioners residing in Finland and the amount is established in function of the income and the housing costs of the pensioner (as well as in function of a series of other factors).
The national pension is increased with fixed amounts if the beneficiary has the charge of a depending spouse without income of his own or of children under the age of 16; however no new supplements of this kind will be granted after 1.1.1996.

The employment related pension accrues with 1,5% of the 'pensionable income' per year of activity (2,5% after the age of 60). The 'pensionable income' (and thus the amount of the pension) is calculated per professional activity which the concerned person has had. To calculate that 'pensionable income' one takes the last years of the employment. The number of years to be taken into account will be gradually raised from the four previous years which are used at present to the ten last years, this reform is to be implemented gradually by the year 2005. Years with exceptionally low annual income will be disregarded.
The total amount of the employment related pension calculated in this way, may never exceed 60% of the highest pensionable salary of the concerned person. There are no maximum levels as to the amount of the pensionable salary.
The national pension and the employment related pension being integrated, their sum may never be superior to 60% of the highest pensionable salary.
The employment related pension is increased by between 1 and 20% when the beneficiary was born between 1919 and 1939 and has a dependent child.

Several possibilities to take up a pension before the age of 65 has been reached also exist.
The first consists in the early old-age pension, which can be taken up by anyone having reached the age of 60; in such a case the pension is permanently reduced by 6% per year of anticipation.
There is also the option of taking a part-time pension. In order to qualify for a part time pension the claimants must be aged between 58 and 64, their working hours must have been reduced considerably (to 16 or 28 hours a week) and their income must also have been reduced to 35 or 70 % of their earlier earnings. The part-time pension amounts to 50% of the lost income.

The unemployment pension is paid to long-term unemployed persons having received unemployment benefit for the maximum period and who are aged 60 to 64; it equals the amount of the disability pension.

Farmers also have the possibility under their own employment related scheme to take an early retirement pension between 55 and 64 years of age, they can do this when they transfer their farms to successors or to non-agricultural users.

Once on a pension, the earnings of the pensioner affect neither his entitlement to nor the amount of his pension; however, this is not valid for persons on early retirement or unemployment pension.

The national pension is annually adjusted on the basis of the cost of living index; the employment related pension is adapted annually according to the average price and wage changes ('TEL'index), two separate weights being used for pensions payable to persons under and over 65.

4.2. Death

Widows or widowers, and orphans may qualify for a survivor's pension, both in the (basic) national pension scheme and in the employment related pension schemes. They loose this entitlement if they remarry when they are under the age of 50. In such a case a grant equal to 3 years pension is awarded.

Both pensions are integrated; the maximum total amount equals 100% of the amount of the (real or fictitious) integrated pension of the deceased person.

In order to qualify for a widow/widower's national pension, the survivor must either have a common child with the deceased, or not have reached the age of 50 at the marriage, which itself lasted at least 5 years.

The national widow/widower's pension consists of a basic amount plus a possible basic amount addition. The basic amount (amount cf.old age), is paid for the first six months following the death; afterwards it is continued if the survivor supports a child under the age of 16. The basic amount addition is always paid for the first six months, its amount however depends upon the income and property of the beneficiary; afterwards the entitlement and amount depend upon the income and property of the survivor.

In order to qualify for an orphan's national pension, the beneficiary child must be under the age of 18 or between 18 and 20 and be a full-time student; the latter category of students however, only qualify for the basic amount, never for the basic amount supplement. Children under the age of 18 may also qualify for a basic amount supplement, depending upon the amount of the other survivor's pensions. Orphans of both parents qualify for two orphan pensions.

In order to open a right to an employment related survivor's pension, the deceased must have been insured at the time of his death.

In order to qualify for a widow/widower employment related pension, the widow(er) having a common child with the deceased must have married before reaching the age of 65; the widow(er) with no common child with the deceased must have reached the age of 50, have been married to the deceased for at least

5 years and have married before he/she reached 50 years of age and before the deceased turned 65.

The employment related widow/widower pension's amount is calculated as a percentage (17 to 50%) of the pension of the deceased, depending on how many children are entitled to an orphan's pension. If the deceased person was not actually benefiting from an employment related pension at the moment of his death, the survivor's pension is calculated on the basis of the invalidity pension the deceased would have been entitled to at the time of his death.

The former spouse will also qualify for the employment related pension, if he/she received alimony from the deceased.

In order to qualify for an employment related orphan's pension the beneficiary must not have reached the age of 18. The pension amounts to 33 to 83% of the real or fictitious pension of the deceased, depending on how many children are entitled to an orphan's pension.

The amounts of the employment related widow/widower and child pensions are calculated in such a way that the sum of the widow(er)'s pension and the child pension of two children, equal the amount of the deceased person's pension.

Orphans of both parents may get two separate employment related orphan's pensions; in such a case an addition of 2/12 is paid to the total of both pensions.

If the death of the insured person is caused by a labour accident or a professional disease, the labour accident or professional disease insurances will also pay out the widow(er)'s and/or orphan's pensions, the total amount of which may not exceed 70% of the earnings the victim would have earned in one year without the labour accident or the professional disease having occurred. If there are no orphans the surviving spouse gets 40%; this percentage decreases as the number of orphan beneficiaries increases. Children qualify for the orphan pension if they are under 18 years or between 18 and 24 years old and studying or handicapped. One orphan gets 25%, two 40% (together) until four or more receive 55%. The labour accident and professional disease insurance also pay out a lump sum as a funeral grant.

All payments by the labour accident and professional disease insurances are annually adjusted according to the TEL-index.

All wage earners are covered by group life insurance as a part of the collective labour agreement they work under. The benefit is a fixed sum, decreasing gradually when the deceased dies after reaching the age of 50 and increasing per child under the age of 18. The benefits are increased by 50% in case of accidental death. A similar coverage exists for farmers with *MELA*.

4.3. Incapacity for work

Short term incapacity for work as well as maternity are covered by a daily allowances scheme, covering all residents of working age, but without requiring the beneficiaries to actually participate in the labour market.

Incapacity for work needs to be certified by a doctor.

The sickness daily allowance is paid for a maximum of 300 days (excluding Sundays) over a two year period; the benefit is not paid until 9 days (excluding Sundays) after the day the illness started. The special short-term sickness compensation scheme for farmers compensates, however, for the days not covered by the general sickness daily allowance if the illness has lasted for more than three days.

The amount of the general allowance depends upon the annual earnings of the persons concerned; if they did not exceed a lower income limit, a lump sum is paid after applying a means test and in principle only if the sick leave lasts more than 60 days; according to the category of earnings the beneficiary belongs to, he will get a percentage of the annual earnings and possibly a lump sum as well. The amount of the short-term sickness compensation benefit for farmer's equals 75% of the daily income insured under the farmer's pension insurance.

We shall deal with the maternity, paternity and parents' allowances under 4.6.

In case the temporary incapacity is due to a labour accident or a professional disease, the labour accident or professional disease insurances will pay a daily allowance for up to one year. If the temporary incapacity lasts less than three days (excluding the day the accident occurred) no daily allowance will be paid. The daily allowance equals the amount of the sick pay for the first four weeks; afterwards it amounts to 1/360 of the annual earnings of the insured person.

Long term incapacity for work is covered by the national and the employment related pension schemes. We shall not repeat the general features of these here, as they are described above under section 4.1. on "Old age". We shall focus here on the specificalities of the pensions awarded for incapacity for work. Both the national and employment related pension schemes distinguish between the disability pension and the individual early retirement pensions.

The disability pensions benefit insured persons having lost 2/5 or 3/5 of their work capacity through illness and whose incapacity is estimated to last at least one year. The individual early retirement pensions cover insured persons who have reached the age of 58, who had a long working career and who are incapable of continuing in their present employment because of work related stress and fatigue or other determined factors.

The full employment related disability pension is only due when no more than 2/5 of the working capacity is left, whereas a partial disability employment related pension will be paid when no more than 3/5 of the working capacity remains.

The disability pension will start from the end of the period of payment of sickness benefit. It may be that the disability pension is only awarded on a temporary basis as a rehabilitation benefit.

Disability and individual early retirement pensions are paid for as long as the conditions are fulfilled; upon reaching the age of 65 they are automatically converted into an old age pension.

The amount of the national pension in case of incapacity for work is calculated in the same way as the national old age pension. If the beneficiary of the full national pension amount has been resident in Finland less than 80% of the time between the age of 16 and the disability, the pension will be adjusted correspondingly to the length of residence. National invalidity pensions cannot be combined with income out of work without limitations.

The employment related disability pension is equal to the full projected old age pension. The employment related partial disability pension equals to 50% of the full disability pension. The individual early retirement pension equals the disability pension.

In case the recipient of a disability pension earns at least 40 but not 60% of the 'pensionable income' from an income from work, the full disability pension is changed into a partial disability pension; if his earnings are at least 60% of the 'pensionable income', the pension is withdrawn. In case the recipient of an individual early retirement pension earns more than a determined sum, but not more than 3/5 of the 'pensionable salary, the full pension is changed into a partial pension; if his earnings exceed 3/5 of the pensionable income the payment of the pension is suspended for the working period.

Rehabilitation allowance will be paid for periods of active rehabilitation of the pensioner, arranged by the pension institution. The allowance equals the full disability pension plus a rehabilitation increment of 33%. A special disability allowance also exists, this is to be paid to persons between 16 and 64 years old, who are not in receipt of a pension but whose health is weakened through illness or injury. This benefit is intended to compensate for the related hardship and necessary services. The amount of this special disability allowance depends only on the degree of disability and this benefit is not taxed.

If the permanent incapacity for work results from a labour accident or a professional disease, the labour accident or professional disease insurances will pay a pension on the condition that the victim's working capacity has been reduced by at least 10% and the reduction in the amount of annual wages is at least 5%. The pension is calculated upon the amount the insured would probably have earned in one year without the labour accident or professional disease having occurred: in case of total incapacity 85% of this amount will be paid, except when the victim is aged more than 50 years old, in which case it will be 70%. In cases of partial incapacity, the pension is proportionally reduced. If the victim should need another person's care, a helplessness supplement of a fixed amount per day may be awarded. If the pension is no more than 20% of the full pension, the pensioner may ask the Employment Accident Board to allow for its conversion into a lump sum payment. The pension can be cumulated with other incomes out of work. An inconvenience allowance will be paid in case of permanent incapacity. The amounts are fixed in function of the degree of incapacity. Twenty degrees are distinguished; the maximum amount is paid in case of 100% incapacity for work.

4.4. Unemployment

We distinguish the insurance based basic benefit and earnings related benefit, and the labour market support assistance. All these benefits are not paid beyond the age of 65.

The insurance based benefits are only granted if the beneficiary has registered as unemployed with an employment office, is looking for full-time work and is available for the labour market.

To qualify for the basic benefit the wage earner must show at least 26 weeks of employment during the last 24 months, whereas the self-employed person must show at least 24 months of self-employed activity in the last 48 months. To qualify for the earnings related benefit the same conditions need to be met plus during the minimal periods of employment the insured must have been a member of an unemployment fund.

The insurance based benefits are not due in the first five working days of unemployment.

The insurance based benefits are paid for a maximal duration of 500 calendar days over a period of 4 consecutive calendar years; once the previously unemployed person has again fulfilled the minimally required periods of employment, a new period of 500 days will start. A person having reached the age of 55, may receive the insurance based benefits until the age of 60.

The basic daily benefit is a lump sum per working day. The earnings related benefit integrates the basic daily benefit plus 42% of the difference between the daily professional income and the basic benefit. If the monthly professional income is greater than 90 times the basic amount, the earnings related part is 42% until that limit and 20% of the excess. The professional income taken into consideration for wage earners is the average earnings of the preceding 26 weeks; for self-employed persons it is the earnings on which premiums have been paid for the last 12 months, without this sum being higher than the reported income confirmed as the basis for the pension.

In case of partial unemployment due to a shortening of the weekly working time by at least one day (or the equivalent number of hours), due to the acceptance by the unemployed of part-time work or of a job for less than one month, or due to the loss of the principal employment while preserving a secondary professional activity, the concerned person will be entitled to an adapted daily benefit. This benefit then amounts to the normal amount of the benefit minus 80% of the professional income exceeding a fixed sum.

Unemployed persons who do not fulfil the conditions for unemployment insurance (e.g. by not being member of a fund) or who have received daily allowance for the maximum period, may qualify for the labour market support assistance. Persons aged between 17 and 19 are entitled, when participating in labour market measures (work try out, apprenticeship, labour market training or rehabilitation). Persons aged 17 do not qualify if they did not complete vocational training and youngsters between 18 and 19 years old do not qualify if they have refused labour market measures or have not applied for training.

Labour market support is granted after a waiting period of 5 working days. Persons entering the labour market for the first time, have a waiting period of 5

months, except when they have completed their vocational training. The young unemployed individual living with his parents only gets 60% of the full labour market support.
The labour market support is a fixed sum, the amount of which depends upon the family composition of the unemployed.
The labour market support is only granted after a means test, except when the beneficiary participates in work tryout, apprenticeship, labour market training or rehabilitation. In the latter case the young unemployed person living with his parents also gets the full labour market support. Income above the limit of the labour market support reduces the support by 75%. The labour market support is supplemented for children at charge by a proportionally decreasing fixed amount per child.

4.5. Health care

The basic responsibility for providing health care services lies with the municipalities. They provide these services themselves or through co-operation with other municipalities. They provide the services themselves or purchase them from the private sector.
As the municipalities are competent, the scope, content and organisation of health and social services may, within the statutory framework, differ from one local authority to another.
The (universal) sickness insurance provides partial compensation for doctor's fees, examination and treatment given by private sector providers; it also refunds part of the costs of medicines and of travelling expenses in connection with both the public and private health care.

Doctors working in the public hospitals or health centres are salaried by the municipalities. The services of these doctors are free except for a personal contribution from the patient, which amounts to a maximum of 50 FIM for the first three visits in a calendar year or to double this for twelve months, depending upon the concerned municipality. Children under the age of 15 are exempt from the personal contribution. There are also fixed personal contributions for out-patient visits to hospital (specialist care) and for in-patient care per day. Patients under the age of 18 may only be charged for the first seven days of hospital treatment in a year; patients receiving care for more than three months in a hospital will be charged a fee in accordance with their means and without this charge exceeding 80% of the patient's net monthly income.
Medical checks at maternity and health care centres during and after pregnancy are free of charge.
The patient pays for dental treatment, the fee consists of a basic sum plus a fixed tariff for each visit. Within limits, the local health centres establish the amount of these fees. In the public health centres persons under the age 19 and war veterans receive dental treatment free of charge.
Persons born in 1956 or thereafter are refunded 75% of the fees for dental examinations and preventive treatment and 60% for other dental treatment. For other persons dental treatment is only refunded if the care was needed for the treatment of a disease other than a dental one.

Private doctors charge a fee, which is to be paid in full by the patient. However, the sickness insurance refunds 60% of the fee (not exceeding a maximum). The services of other health care providers, prescribed by a medical doctor, are refunded for 75% of their cost exceeding a fixed sum.

Medicine is free when prescribed at a public hospital. Other medicine has to be paid in full by the patients; they can then get a refund of 50% of the cost of the medicine exceeding the fixed sum of their personal contribution. This refund will be raised to 75% or 100% of the cost of some listed medicines exceeding half of the previously mentioned fixed sum of contribution in case of serious and chronic diseases. When the costs of pharmaceutical products which the patients have to bear themselves exceeds a certain amount during one calendar year, the excess amount is fully reimbursed.

Prosthesis, spectacles and hearing aids, may be free when provided at the local health centre.

Travel and transport costs are fully compensated from the sickness insurance after deduction of a fixed sum as a personal contribution; moreover, if the total of personal contributions over one calendar year exceeds a certain sum, the excess is fully refunded; if the travel requires staying overnight, accommodation is refunded up to a fixed sum per night.

When health care is necessitated by the occurrence of a labour accident or a professional disease, the labour accident or professional disease insurances will pay all the related costs in full; the victims have the free choice of doctor and hospital, be it that they should avoid unnecessary costs.

4.6. Family

Child benefit is paid for each child under the age of 17 residing in Finland. The amount of the benefit is linked to the number of eligible children in the family (increasing per child according to the number of children, the fifth child getting nearly double that of the first). The general child benefit will be supplemented with a fixed sum for each child of a single parent.

Maternity grant consists of either a maternity package containing necessities for the care of the child or a lump sum. The maternity grant benefits all pregnant women resident in Finland, whose pregnancy has lasted at least 154 days and who have undergone a health examination.

Maternity benefits are paid to all resident mothers for 105 consecutive days (except Sundays), 30 to 50 of which may be taken up before the expected day of birth. Paternity benefits are paid for 6 to 12 days (excluding Sundays) in direct connection with the birth and 6 days during the maternity benefit period. Parents' benefits are due immediately after the maternity benefit to either the father or the mother for 158 days; 60 days are added if more than one child is born. The amounts of the maternity, paternity and parents' benefits are calculated in the same way as the sickness daily benefits, except that the minimum benefit is not means tested.

Families caring for their children under the age of three at home or by another arrangement instead of using the municipal day care, qualify for a child home care allowance. This allowance consists of a basic amount, plus a sibling increase (both lump sums) and a means tested supplement. A partial home care allowance will be paid to the parent of a child under 3 years of age, who reduces his/her working hours to maximum 30 hours a week.

A maintenance allowance for children and a child care allowance also exists.
The maintenance allowance is paid to the single parent if the identity of the other parent has not been established or the other parent does not fulfil the obligation to pay maintenance. The child care allowance is paid for the care of severely disabled and chronically ill children under 16; three different amounts of allowance exist according to the degree of strain on the family.

Child benefits, maternity grants and maintenance allowances are not subject to taxation. Child home care allowances are, just like most other income replacement benefits, subject to taxation.

4.7. Need

Social allowance is the last resort assistance benefiting all residents who temporarily, for a shorter or longer period, remain without sufficient means to meet the necessary costs of living. A person is of course first supposed to support himself by work or by claiming other social security benefits.
As with all the other benefits under Finnish social security the right to social allowance is an individual right, be it that the situation of the whole household is taken into consideration. All the earnings of the applicant and/or the family, including family allowances, are in principle being considered.

The amount of the social allowance consists of a basic part, supplemented by the municipality with an additional allowance. The basic part equals 80% of the full national pension for a single person; other amounts have been fixed for spouses (85% of the full national pension for each), children over 17 years of age living with their parents (73%), children younger than 10 years of age (66%) and children aged between 10 and 16 (70%). Other expenses for which additional social allowance may be granted include reasonable housing costs, substantial medical expenses, child day care costs and other costs which are considered to be essential.

All low-income households, with the exception of students and pensioners who have their own schemes, are entitled to housing allowance.

The dependants of a person performing his national service are paid draftee's dependants allowance if their own income is lower than a fixed amount.

5. *Financing*

The benefits of the sickness insurance are financed out of contributions plus a state subsidy. These contributions are a percentage of the taxable income as far as the socially insured are concerned; recipients of a pension pay an additional percentage on their pension income. The contributions are expressed as a percentage of the payroll as far as the employers are concerned. There is no contribution ceiling.
National (basic) pensions in case of old age and invalidity are financed out of contributions plus a state subsidy, whereas the basic survivor's pension is fully tax financed. The contributions for the basic pensions are organised in similar way as described above for the sickness insurance.
The basic unemployment benefit and the family benefits are tax financed.

The employment related old age, survivor's and invalidity pensions are financed out of contributions; supplemented by a state subsidy as far as the farmers' and self employed persons' pensions schemes are concerned. The employment related pension contributions are expressed as a percentage of the salaries (about 4/5 employer contribution and 1/5 employee contribution); farmers and the self employed pay a percentage of their professional income which is in principle equivalent to the sum of the percentages due by employers and wage earners. If however, the farmer's income is below a fixed lower income ceiling, he only pays about half of this percentage; the percentage increases above the lower income ceiling to finally reach the percentage valid for all self-employed persons. There are no contribution ceilings. The professional income upon which the contribution percentages for the employment related specific pensions scheme for farmers are being calculated (and consequently also the farmers' contribution to the other specific insurance schemes for farmers) is determined according to the annual computed income for the farm, each insured person consequently being given a personal income assessment in function of the work done by each. The computed income for the farm is calculated in function of the strength of the amount of arable land and forest; this amount may be increased by 30% or reduced by 15% according to the estimate of the farmers. Sometimes it may be altered even more, for instance if the calculated income deviates markedly from the taxable income. The computed income of the farm established in this way has to be ratified by *MELA*.

The earnings related unemployment benefit is financed out of contributions by the insured persons, the employers and the state. The employer pays less contribution on the first 5 million FIM of the payroll.

State subsidies cover any deficit in the sickness and maternity insurance, the national pensions schemes, the self-employed persons' and farmers' employment related pensions. State subsidies cover less than half of the cost of the earnings related unemployment benefits. The state fully finances the special short-term sickness compensation for farmers and 4/5 of the special employment related pensions for farmers.

Public health care is financed by the local authorities. Municipalities receive state subsidies for arranging the health and social services. The subsidy for health care is determined in function of the number of residents of the municipality, their age structure, the area, the population density, the likelihood of the population of the municipality to get sick and its fiscal capacity.

Local authorities pay a little less than half of the pensioner's housing allowances and of the national pension basic amount addition. They pay about 3/5 of the social allowances, the remaining amounts being paid by the state. In fact, the state pays in a subsidy to the municipalities in the form of a lump sum, the amount of which is calculated according to the number of municipal residents, their age structure, the unemployment rate and the financial capacity classification of the municipality.

The labour accidents and occupational diseases insurance is fully financed by employers premiums (or premiums of the self employed participating in this scheme), the amount of which is fixed according to the risk. However, the state subsidises about one third of the costs of the accident insurance for farmers.

All schemes operate on a pay as you go basis, except for the employment old age and invalidity pensions, which are partly funded and the labour accidents and professional diseases insurances which are funded except for the index increases.

6. *Judicial review*

When dissatisfied with the decision of the social security authorities, persons first have to enter a complaint with the institution that took the decision. If the latter confirms the earlier decision, the person concerned may appeal to independent appeal boards created within the Ministry of Social Affairs and Health. We can distinguish between the Social Insurance Board, the Inspection Board, the Pension Board, the Unemployment Board and the Accident Insurance Board. Appeals against the decisions of the Social Insurance Board are heard by the Inspection Board, while higher appeal against the decisions of the other boards is the competence of the Insurance Court. Appeals against the decisions of the Insurance Court may be heard by the Supreme Court.

Chapter Five

FRANCE

1. Introduction: concept and sources of social security law

French social security has a complex structure. It distinguishes between:
a) the 'statutory social security systems' *(les régimes légaux)* of social insurance, which are basically divided into four occupationally based systems;
b) the social security schemes which are based on collective labour agreements *(les régimes conventionels)*;
c) the individual private 'social protection'; and
d) the social assistance.
Let us examine each of them separately.

Statutory social security is characterised by the simultaneous existence of separate systems for the diverse occupational groups. We distinguish:
1) the general system *(le régime général)*;
2) the agricultural system *(le régime agricole* or *mutualité sociale agricole)*;
3) the special systems of social security *(les régimes spéciaux de sécurité sociale)*;
4) the autonomous systems *(les régimes autonomes* or *régimes des professions non salariées non agricoles)*.

The general system is the most important one. To the extent that no special scheme is applicable to them, employees engaged in the private sector as well as categories of people who are considered as such, are insured for the risks of sickness, maternity, incapacity for work, industrial injuries and occupational diseases, old age and death. The scheme also covers civil servants and assimilated persons for the risks of sickness and maternity. The family benefits scheme of the general system covers all residents. Except for the family benefits scheme and the labour accident insurance, benefits of the general scheme are dependent upon the fulfilment of a minimum contribution record.
The general system is subdivided in four branches: the sickness, maternity, invalidity and death insurance; the employment injuries and occupational diseases insurance; the family benefits scheme; and the old age and survivor's, (basic) pensions.
The general system is governed by the Social Security Code, except for some means tested family benefits (e.g. for the handicapped) which are governed by the Family and Social Aid Code.

The agricultural system covers people working within the agricultural sector other than in a self-employed capacity, in a similar way as people who are covered by the general scheme. The self-employed farmers are also covered by the agricultural system, but only for the risk of old age; the self-employed farmers may join the system for sickness, maternity, injury and incapacity for work insurances on a voluntary basis. The social mutual funds (which themselves are grouped in the Agricultural Social Fund) manage the insurances of the agricultural system. They also pay out the family benefits to persons insured under the agricultural system which is a task delegated to them by the general system. The agricultural system is governed by the Social Security Code and the Rural Code.

The special systems cover the specific groups of professionally active people that escaped (totally or partially) integration in the general system, such as railway workers, miners, sailors, transport workers, gas and electricity workers, civil servants, etc. The protection varies from system to system; some special systems provide a total coverage (e.g. the system of the railway workers) whereas others only cover some risks, leaving others to be covered by the general system (e.g. civil servants covered by the general system's sickness insurance). If a certain risk is covered, the relevant benefits must be of at least the same level as the benefits within the general scheme; the differences are most important as far as the pensions are concerned. The special systems are governed by a series of different codes and statutes.

The autonomous systems can be subdivided into three:
- the system of the industrial and commercial occupations;
- the system of the craftsmen;
- the system of the free professions.

The old age insurance of the first two of these autonomous systems are in line with the general system. The system of the free professions is in fact itself composed of a range of separate professional schemes, such as those for solicitors, medical doctors etc. There is a sickness insurance common to the three autonomous systems. The affiliation of members is taken care of by 24 inter-professional regional mutual funds and the mutual organisations of the free professions. These contract with non-profit or commercial insurance institutions for the collection of contributions and the distribution of benefits.

There is a certain degree of co-ordination and harmonisation between the general scheme and the other schemes. Most importantly, for all or part of the schemes, uniform, legal rules exist with respect to, for example, administration, financing and judicial review.

The above described systems together form what is generally referred to as "the statutory social security" (*les régimes légaux*) as they were created and are regulated by statute. This is in opposition to the social security schemes which are based on collective labour agreements (*les régimes conventionels*) having been made compulsory for all concerned workers either by statute or by the collective agreement.

The unemployment insurance is such a scheme created by inter-professional national collective labour agreement and made compulsory for all workers of the private sector. The unemployment insurance is governed by the national inter-professional collective agreements and by the Labour Code.

Complementary old age insurance has also been installed by inter-professional national agreement and made compulsory for all wage earners of the (agricultural and non-agricultural) private sector. By these agreements two funds were created, one covering all workers (*Association des Régimes de Retraite Complémentaire ARCCO*), the other only covering the higher employees and management (*Association Générale des Institutions de Retraite Complémentaire AGIRC*). Whereas the *AGIRC* only uses a uniform retirement scheme, the *ARCCO* operates various complementary pensions schemes. The compulsory complementary old age insurance is governed by the inter-professional national collective labour agreements, the Labour Code and the Social Security Code.

Apart from the two compulsory schemes based on collective labour agreements, collective labour agreements may also provide additional social protection on the level of the branch of industry, the company or plant level. This additional protection improves both the quality and quantity of the social protection provided by the statutory systems and the above mentioned obligatory unemployment and complementary old age schemes. These schemes are rather numerous and very different from one another.

Since 1989, collective bargaining is not the only way of providing collective complementary social protection: it is also possible now for an employer to decide unilaterally, or after a referendum with his employees, to create such a scheme. Of course, the employee or any other person can decide for himself to buy individual private 'social protection'. In 1997 the creation of supplementary retirement savings plans was allowed and provided with an interesting tax treatment.

Social assistance consists of a minimum income scheme for persons agreeing to make an effort to reintegrate into social and professional life (the *'revenu minimum d'insertion'*) and the more classical social assistance. The Family and Social Aid Code governs social assistance.

Hereafter, we shall in principle only deal with the general scheme (*le régime général*), as it is complemented by the unemployment benefits scheme and social assistance.

The constitution of the fifth French republic (of 1958) maintained the preamble of the Constitution of 1946, in which a number of social principles are proclaimed to be "of special necessity in our time". Thus the nation must ensure the conditions which are necessary for the development of all individuals and their families (para. 10) and guarantee to everyone, especially to the child, to the mother and to elderly employees, protection of health, material means of subsistence and rest and leisure time. Furthermore, para. 11 states that each person who, due to his age, physical or mental state, or due to the economic situation, is unable to work, is entitled to suitable means of subsistence from the community.

Until now, neither these principles of social fundamental rights nor the qualification of France in article 2 of the Constitution as a social republic, would appear to have produced legal consequences for positive social security law.
In order to determine the fundamental principles of social security law, article 34 Constitution requires the intervention of a statute adopted by parliament. Where these fundamental principles are not involved, according to the French constitutional system, legislative powers lie with the government (which acts by decrees). The provisions of the different codes reflect this particular sharing of legislative power: they are preceded by the letters « L » (statutes), « R » (decrees submitted to the *Conseil d'Etat* in application of legislative competence) and « D » (ordinary decrees in application of a law). The government can also receive power in the field of competence of the Parliament by a specific authorisation of the Parliament, which then is limited in time. These acts are called ordinances (*ordonnances*); when later approved by Parliament they get the legal value of a statute; the technique of ordinances is being frequently used in the field of social protection.

Although, in principle, Alsace-Moselle falls within the scope of French social security law, there are still some derogating rules applicable in this region, e.g. in the area of contributions and benefits and in the organisation of medical care. In this book these special rules will not be dealt with.

2. *Administrative organisation*

We shall discuss consecutively the administrative organisation of the general system, the scheme for unemployment and the assistance schemes. Within the general system we have to differentiate according to the concerned branch.

Let us first observe that all the administrative bodies of the general system to be discussed hereafter are managed by boards of governors in which the representatives of the employers and the employees have, as a result of reforms in 1996, the same number of seats. They are assisted by so called "qualified persons" who are designated by the government.

On a national level, the administrations of the family benefits scheme is in the hands of the *Caisse nationale des allocations familiales (CNAF)*. This institution acts, not only for the general system, but also for all the other systems which, in consequence, do not manage family benefits. This *CNAF* is in charge of the organisation of this branch and the supervision of the lower bodies which are organised on the level of a *département (Caisses d'allocations familiales)* and pay out the family benefits. The *CNAF* has to ensure the financial balance of the system.

The *Caisse nationale d'assurance maladie des travailleurs salariés (CNAMTS)* is responsible for the administration of the branches of sickness, maternity invalidity and death and the branches of employment injuries and occupational diseases. The second branch has been managed by a special found within the *CNAMTS* since 1995. The *CNAMTS* has to ensure the financial balance of the system; its also organises medical control. It negotiates (with the other institutions of the other systems) the collective agreements with the private health care providers. It also funds the functioning of the hospitals.

On a regional level, the *Caisses régionales d'assurance maladie (CRAM)* are responsible for the prevention of industrial injuries and occupational diseases and for the relations with the recently created *Agences Régionales de l'hospitalisation*. The reform of 1996 (Plan Juppé) transferred the planning and the funding of hospitals from the state administration to these regional agencies, which are directed by a general manager.

Finally *the Caisses primaires d'assurance maladie (CPAM)* operate on a *départment* level (except for historical reasons in Alsace-Moselle where there are 8 *CPAM* for 3 *départements*). They are concerned with the granting of benefits to the insured persons.

The *Caisse nationale d'assurance vieillesse des travailleurs salariés (CNAVTS)* is responsible for the administration of the (basic) old age and survivor's branch of the general system. This body deals with the general administration of this branch, its financial balance and the granting of benefits in the Ile de France region. In the other regions, the basic pensions are served by the *CRAM*, except for Alsace-Moselle where there is a special regional institution *(Caisse régionale d'assurance vieillessse d'Alsace et de Moselle)*.

The *Union des caisses nationales de sécurité sociale (UCANSS)* is in charge of the issues of equal concern to all the above mentioned administrative bodies. It's main functions are the bargaining (with the representative trade unions) of the employment conditions of the personnel of the bodies.

The *Agence centrale des organismes de sécurité sociale (ACOSS) and the Union pour recouvrement des cotisations de sécurité sociale et d'allocation familiales (URSSAF)* on the *départemate* level are in charge of the collection and the redistribution of the contributions to the schemes and, since 1991, of the registration of the insured as well. The other *régimes légaux* and the *régimes conventionels* collect the contributions themselves.

The supervision of the general system, as well as of the other systems, is carried out on a national level by the minister responsible for social security and the minister of finance. For the other systems other ministers can be involved, such as for example the minister in charge of the public service for the social protection of the civil servants, or the minister of agriculture for the agricultural system. The state has to control every expenditure of the administrative bodies of social security, as far as these have an impact upon the financial balance of the system. These controls operate at the national level through the National Accountancy Court *(Cour des comptes)* or the General inspection of the social *security (Inspection générale des affaires sociales IGASS)* as well as on a *département* level by the state representatives *(préfets* and *direction départementale des affaires sanitaires et sociales DDASS)*. The regional agency for hospitalisation has been dealing with the hospital's budgets and policy planning since 1996.

The *Associations pour l'emploi dans l'industrie et le commerce (ASSEDIC)* are operated on a *département* level and their national organised compensation fund and control institution *Union pour l'emploi dans l'industrie et le commerce (UNEDIC)* are in charge of the administration of the unemployment scheme. The representatives of employers and employees are involved in the boards of governors of these bodies. Some benefits called 'solidarity benefits' are financed by the state, but granted by the ASSEDIC. The minister competent for labour and the minister of finance exercise a certain degree of supervision.

Since the administrative decentralisation of 1984, assistance has been organised on a departmental level. The department can make arrangements with municipalities for certain competencies to be carried out directly by the latter. A so called *Centre communal d' action sociale (C.C.A.S.)* functions on a municipal level. It collects the dossiers of claimants and recipients of assistance and sends them, accompanied by it's opinion, to the competent *Commission d' admission à l' aide sociale*, the body which, except for some specific procedures, takes the final decision.

The administration of the guaranteed minimum income scheme is organised in a different way. This is the competence of an ad hoc administration on the local level *(Commission locale d' insertion)* where members of the various administrations and local elected politicians sit in. This commission decides whether to attribute the minimum income in each individual case but the *Caisses d'allocations familiales* actually grant the benefits on behalf of the state. The accompanying measures of integration have to be financed by the *département*.

3. *Personal scope of application*

The family benefits scheme covers all persons living regularly in France. It is further required that the entitling family member is part of the household of the beneficiary. The concept of family member includes ascendants as well as descendants. The legislator is about to put every family benefit under a means-test.

The personal scope of the other three branches of the general system includes all those who carry out work for a wage under the authority of an employer of the private sector, this employer has the duty to register them and to transfer the corresponding social contributions. The insurance obligation is extended to certain categories of workers (home workers, journalists, travelling salesmen) or to some other categories of people including unemployed people during the time they receive benefits, people on guaranteed minimum income, students, war widows, etc. The coverage of these people is limited to a number of specific risks, mostly including health care and sometimes also old age pensions. The industrial injuries and occupational diseases branch also covers students in workshops, apprentices and voluntary workers.

The *assurance personelle* allows non compulsorily insured persons to join the general system's sickness and maternity insurance (benefits in kind).

The social insurances do not only provide the insured person with benefits, but also create derived rights in favour of the members of his household (including his unmarried partner).
When the status opening access to the compulsory insurance under the general system is lost (e.g. when no longer working, after exhausting unemployment benefits etc.) the entitlement to benefits under the old age and survivor's pension branch and the sickness, maternity, invalidity and death branches continues for another twelve months.

The unemployment insurance scheme extends to all those who are active on the basis of a contract of employment. The unemployment assistance scheme covers the persons who are excluded from the insurance scheme.

Social assistance and the guaranteed minimum income are payable to every person who is regularly resident in France.

4. Risks and benefits

4.1. Old age

We must distinguish between the contributory and non-contributory benefits of the general system.
The old age branch of the general system has been reformed in 1993.

The insured person who has paid contributions over 150 trimesters (in 1993; since then increased by one trimester per year in order to reach 160 trimesters in 2003) is entitled to a contributory *pension de retraite* on the attainment of 60 years of age. The pension amounts to 50% of the recipient's average salary (up to a certain maximum) over the 10 most favourable years in which work was carried out, since 1993, this has been raised by one per year in order to reach 25 years by 2008. A reduction of 1,25% of the maximum level of 50% takes place for each trimester one falls short of the required number of trimesters. Involuntary interruptions of work in cases of disease or unemployment are considered as insured periods of work. A mother is entitled to a credit of 8 trimesters for each dependent child. The maximum of 50% is automatically given if the insured person works until 65 years of age. Furthermore, a full pension when reaching the age of 60 years is payable to a number of specific categories of people, such as insured persons who get an invalidity pension or war veterans. The pension is increased by 10% if the beneficiary has had at least three dependent children or a dependent spouse of over 55 who has no means of his own above a certain level.
Entitlement to pension is subject to the condition that the beneficiary must have terminated his work with his present employer. The contributory basic pension can only be cumulated with income from work to a limited extent.

We may observe, by way of parenthesis, that the contributory (basic) *pensions de retraite* are complemented by the obligatory complementary pension scheme within the *ARRCO* for every employed persons and possibly also by a pension from the obligatory complementary pension scheme within the AGIRC for the higher employees and management.

Non-contributory benefits are payable to people over 60 years old, who are French (or assimilated) and regularly reside in France. There is the old age minimum (*minimum vieillesse*) composed of two benefits. The *allocation de base* is due to persons having a (minor) insurance record. This lump sum is supplemented by a means-tested *allocation supplémentaire du fonds de solidarité*).

The *CNAVTS,* the *CRAM*s (and the *CRAV* for Alsace-Moselle) have developed programmes to help elderly people to stay at home; by providing them help in the household (*aide à domicile*) for example. These programmes are now coordinated with the *départements* and their social assistance programmes for elderly people, especially since the introduction in 1997 of the benefit for dependent (old) people.

4.2. Death.

The a*ssurance décès* guarantees to dependants of the deceased person an amount equal to 90 times his average daily wage over the three months preceding his death. The amount is subject to an upper and a lower limit. There are minimum conditions concerning the past employment record, as well as the contribution record. The people entitled are those who, on the day of the death of the insured person, were actually, completely and permanently dependent upon the deceased. If no priorities can be determined on the basis of this starting point, the entitled person is the spouse who was neither divorced nor separated; if there is no such spouse, the descendants or, failing them, the ascendants are entitled.

The spouse of a person who was insured for old age, or who was entitled to an *allocation aux adultes handicapés*, or to benefits in kind from the sickness insurance scheme for three months preceding his death, is entitled to *allocation de veuvage*. There are conditions in respect of age (younger than 55), dependent children (the claimant must be raising at least one child or have raised a child during at least 9 years preceding the child's 16th birthday), the place of residence (in France) and personal means. The benefit is temporary (maximum three years); however, beneficiaries who have reached 50 years of age on the death of their spouse, remain entitled until they reach 55 years of age. The benefit is flat-rate and decreases yearly. Entitlement ends upon remarriage or cohabitation.

The spouse of the deceased person who, in due course, was, or would have been, entitled to a *pension de retraite*, is entitled to the *pension de réversion*. There are conditions with regard to the means of the spouse, the age of the spouse (minimum of 55 years) and the duration of the marriage (minimum of two years, unless there are children from the marriage). The divorced spouse of the deceased person, who has never remarried, is equally entitled to the pension. In some cases there is a pro rata division of the pension between the surviving spouse and the divorced ex-spouse(s) who has/have not remarried, depending upon the duration of the respective marriages. The scope of the pension amounts to 54% of the *pension de retraite* to which the deceased was or would have been entitled upon his death, if he was insured for a minimum of 15 years. In cases of a shorter period of insurance there is a pro rata reduction. If the beneficiary has been responsible for the raising of at least three children, the pension will be increased.

The spouse of an insured person who (in due course) was (or would have been) entitled to a *pension de retraite* or a *pension d' invalidité*, is entitled to a *pension de veuf ou veuve*, provided he is younger than 55 and is himself incapable of work to such a degree that, if he had been insured, he would have been entitled to an invalidity pension. The pension amounts to 54% of the pension to which the deceased person was or would have been entitled. The benefit is subject to a lower limit and will be increased in cases where the claimant has been responsible for the raising of at least three children. Entitlement terminates upon the remarriage of the beneficiary. Upon reaching 55 years of age the pension is automatically changed into a *pension de réversion*.

If death was due to an injury or an occupational disease, the dependent spouse and children up to a certain age are entitled to a *rente viagère*. With regard to the spouse there is a condition that the marriage must have taken place prior to the injury or two years preceding the death, unless there are one or more children from the marriage. The divorced spouse is only entitled to a pension if he enjoyed an alimony from his ex-partner. In case of remarriage, entitlement to a pension is suspended, but a lump sum is paid. Entitlement can be revived in case of divorce or renewed widow(er)hood. To the extent that the deceased person had neither a spouse nor children, the ascendants of the deceased person are entitled to a pension if they can demonstrate that they would have been entitled to maintenance from the deceased person; if the deceased person had a spouse and/or children, the ascendants are entitled to pension, if they were dependent upon the deceased person.
The pension for the spouse amounts to 30% of the wage of the deceased person or to 50%, if the spouse is older than 55 years of age, or is 50% or more incapable of work. A divorced spouse is entitled to 20% of the wage. The pension for the first two semi-orphans amounts to 15% of the wage and 10% for each subsequent semi-orphan. Dependent parents and grandparents receive a benefit of 10%, each with a maximum of 30% for all the ascendants in total. The total pensions may not exceed 85% of the wage of the deceased person.
In addition to the pension there is entitlement to a reimbursement of the funeral costs, which is borne by the administrative authority.

In case of death during the receipt of an unemployment benefit under the insurance regime, an amount is paid to the spouse equal to 120 times the daily benefit of the deceased person, increased by 45 times the daily benefit in respect of each dependent child.

4.3. Incapacity for work

If the insured person is diagnosed by a doctor as being incapable of work, the sickness insurance scheme (*assurance maladie*) provides daily benefits (*indemnités journalières*). This is subject to minimum conditions concerning the employment and contribution record of the insured person.

For certain long term disorders, benefit is payable, and this for a maximum period of three years, from the fourth day of incapacity. Otherwise, a person is entitled to benefit over a maximum of 360 days during a term of three years. The level of benefit amounts to half the average daily wage during the three months preceding the incapacity. There is both an upper and a lower limit. After 31 days, benefit is increased to 2/3 of the daily wage, provided that the beneficiary has at least three dependent children.

The conditions with respect to entitlement to cash benefits (*indemnités journalières de répos*) within the *assurance maternité* are the same as those which apply in the *assurance maladie*. However, in addition, a woman has to be shown to have been insured for at least 10 months before the expected day of confinement. The benefit is granted for a minimum period of 16 weeks (6 weeks before and 10 weeks after the birth). Providing the birth increases the total number of children to three, the duration of the benefit is 26 weeks (8 weeks before and 18 weeks after the birth). In case a twin is born, the benefits last for 34 weeks, of which 12 have to be situated before confinement. Regarding a multiple birth, the duration amounts up to 42 weeks (of which 24 weeks before confinement). The level of the benefit amounts to 84% of the average daily wage during the last three months of work. Here also there is an upper and a lower limit.
The man or woman who adopts a child may also qualify for the benefit, as well as the father on the mother's death due to the birth.

Occupational schemes generally provide additions on top of sickness benefit, up to the level of the wage.

Beneficiaries of the *aide médicale* (benefits from which are subject to a means test), who have received this benefit for at least three months, who are 15 years of age or older and, due to their sickness, are not capable of carrying out any occupational activity, are entitled to a monthly cash benefit, the *allocation d'aide médicale*. Neither the *aide médicale* nor the *allocation* are of much importance in practice.

Under the invalidity insurance scheme (*assurance invalidité*) the insured person, younger than 60 years of age, whose work or earning capacity is reduced by at least 2/3, is entitled to *pension d'invalidité*. The beneficiary must be incapable of earning a wage from any occupation that amounts to more than 1/3 of the normal wage for employees within the same region and active in the same occupational category as the claimant himself. In assessing the incapacity for work, not only the remaining capacity is taken into account, but also the general state of the claimant, his age, his physical and mental capacity, as well as his education and past employment record.

Entitlement to the benefit depends upon the claimant having registered himself as an insured person for at least twelve months, as well as upon his past employment record.

In determining the level of benefit, those incapable of work are sub-divided into three categories:
- people who are capable of carrying out a certain activity;
- people who are incapable of doing this;
- people who are incapable of doing this and who, furthermore, need the help of a third person regarding the daily necessities of life.

With respect to the first category, the benefit amounts to 30% of the average salary during the ten most favourable working years, with respect to the second category the rate is 50% and for the third 90%. There are upper and lower limits. Possibly, in combination with the means tested *allocation supplémentaire F.N.S.* a *minimum invalidité* is attained, equal to the *minimum vieillesse*.

The beneficiary may undergo rehabilitation training; during the training the pension is fully or partially maintained.

With respect to temporary or permanent incapacity due to an industrial injury or an occupational disease there may be entitlement to benefit under the industrial injuries and occupational diseases branch .

In case of temporary incapacity a person is entitled to an *indemnité journalière* (daily benefit). Entitlement exists from the second day of the incapacity for work (the first day is payable by the employer) until full recovery, the consolidation of the injury or the death of the claimant. Consequently, the duration of benefit is unlimited. Initially the level of the benefit amounts to 60%, and from the 29th day 80% of the average daily wage during the last period of payment. The benefit is subject to an upper and a lower limit, both of which are more favourable than those applied in the other social security schemes.

In case of permanent incapacity, that is to say the consolidation of the physical state, the claimant is entitled to a pension. This is calculated on the basis of the wage during the twelve months preceding the incapacity (there is also a relatively favourable lower and upper limit here), and the degree of incapacity for work. The latter is determined by comparing the nature of the injury, the general state of the claimant, his age, his physical and mental capacity, as well as his education and work experience, taking into account a list drawn up for this purpose.

In determining the level of the benefit an incapacity of less than 50% is only taken into account for half of its amount; it is taken into account in full if the incapacity for work is above 50%. If the claimant requires the permanent help of a third person, the pension is increased by 40%.

Entitlement to the pension only exists if the incapacity for work is estimated to be at least 10%. If not, a person is entitled to a lump sum payment (*indemnité en capital*) which is flat-rate and dependent upon the percentage of incapacity for work.

A special compensation is granted to the employee who, due to a certain occupational disease, has to change his job in order to prevent the worsening of his condition, yet who does not satisfy the conditions for a pension. This compen-

sation, the *indemnité de changement d'emploi*, is equal to 60 days wages for each year in which a person has been exposed to the risk, with a maximum of 300 days wages.
Special rules apply if the industrial injury is due to the deliberate or serious misconduct of the victim or of the employer (or his representative). The application of these rules can lead to the loss (deliberate action of the victim), reduction (serious misconduct of the victim) or increase (serious misconduct of the employer) of the benefits to the victim or to the survivors. Benefits exist for physically or mentally handicapped persons who are not entitled to a benefit in respect of incapacity for work, within the framework of the invalidity insurance scheme.

The person with a dependent, handicapped child younger than 20 years of age, is entitled to the *allocation d'éducation spéciale*, provided the degree of incapacity of the child is at least 80%. The benefit amounts to 32% of the basis applied for the family benefits. There is entitlement to an increase of benefit if there are extremely high costs associated with the handicap or if the help of a third person is required. The increase varies in accordance with the costs and the need of help (between 24% and 72% of the basis).
The benefits can also be granted in respect of a child with a degree of incapacity of between 50 and 80%, if the child attends a special school or the condition of the child makes educational help necessary at home.

The *allocation aux adultes handicapés* is payable to handicapped persons of French (or assimilated) nationality, who are between 16 years and 60 years old, are not entitled to the *allocations familiales* and whose degree of incapacity amounts to at least 80%, or who, due to their handicap, are not in a suitable condition to procure a field of activity for themselves. A further condition is that the claimant may not be entitled to an invalidity or old age pension on the same level as the *allocation*. The benefit is equal to the *minimum d'invalidité* and is subject to a means test.

The same conditions with respect to age and incapacity apply for the *aide sociale aux personnes handicapées* as for the *allocation aux adultes handicapés* described above. Entitlement to a cash benefit, the *allocation compensatrice*, also exists. Furthermore, there are specific possibilities of placement, for example in sheltered workshops. The benefits are subject to a means test.

4.4. Unemployment

In order to be entitled to a benefit within the framework of the unemployment insurance scheme (*assurance chômage*) the unemployed person must have lost his job involuntarily; furthermore, he must be capable of work, actively looking for employment and younger than 60 years of age. Finally, he must have been insured for a certain duration during the reference period.
Since a national collective agreement from 1993 there is only one benefit remaining: *the allocation unique dégressive*. This benefit is characterised by the fact that its amount gradually decreases the longer the unemployment lasts.

There is a first period in which the benefit is the highest. The duration of this first period depends upon the former work record. During this first period, the unemployed person receives a benefit of 40,4% his average gross wage earned during the reference period plus a lump sum, or simply of 57,4 % of the same average gross wage instead. The unemployed person receives the highest of the two amounts.
In the next period, this amount is reduced by 8% or 15% or 17%, according to the age of the unemployed person and his work record. Elderly unemployed individuals who have acquired more than 160 trimesters of insurance, will not be subjected to the decreases and will maintain the full benefit until they reach the age of 60 years.
The unemployed person remains insured under the sickness, maternity, invalidity and death branches as well as under the old age branch (both the general system and the compulsory complementary schemes), for the period during which they receive unemployment insurance benefits.

The unemployed insurance system, financed by contributions, is supplemented by two unemployed assistance schemes (*régime de solidarité*). The first of these schemes provides the *allocation de solidarité spécifique,* a benefit granted to long term unemployed people after the exhaustion of their entitlement to contributory benefits. This benefit is allocated for periods of six months, which can be prolonged. There are special rules for unemployed persons over 50 years of age. The second assistance scheme provides the *allocation d'insertion,* which is payable up to one year to a limited number of categories of people such as ex-convicts, refugees, expatriated workers who are not entitled to social insurance benefits or employed persons who had an industrial injury or disease and are waiting for a rehabilitation measure.
Both schemes make benefit dependent upon passing a means test; the benefits are flat rated.

The employee who is engaged in full time work (a minimum of 39 hours a week or less according to what is the conventional working time in the plant or branch of industry he works in) and of which the working time is temporarily reduced as a result of a decision of the employer or of economic difficulties, will be compensated for the loss of wage due to the reduction of his working time. To this end an *allocation de chômage partiel* is paid to his employer. The latter then compensates the employee.

4.5. Health care

Among others, the sickness insurance scheme covers the costs of medical, dentist and pharmacist care as well as hospital costs. Not only the costs of the insured person himself, but also those of other people are covered. These other co-insured people are the spouse of the insured person, a cohabitant who is actually, completely and permanently dependent upon the insured person, dependent children until the age of 20 and relatives to the third degree who live with the insured person in the same household.

As health care is covered under a professional social insurance, entitlement to compensation for health care costs depends upon specific employment and contribution conditions; however they can easily be met. As a result of this, and of the co-insurance, most residents of France are covered for the risk of health care.

In the first instance, the insured person must pay the costs himself. He is then compensated for these costs. There is never a full compensation. For each activity regulations determine a personal cost sharing amount by the insured person (*ticket modérateur*). However, in practice the system of the personal cost sharing does not apply; often, such personal contributions are no longer applicable. For example, this is the case for very expensive operations; if the personal cost sharing amounts which have previously been paid by the insured people are in excess of a certain amount; or for certain categories of people such as those in receipt of an invalidity pension. Furthermore, it must be pointed out that when the personal cost sharing amount is still due, it will often be reimbursed by a *mutualité*, an insurance fund to which most insured persons are affiliated voluntarily or by collective agreement.

The doctor's fees, medicine and entry into hospital, regarding pregnancy or birth, and other related costs are covered by the maternity insurance scheme. Entitlement exists for women who are insured under their own title as well as dependent spouses, cohabitees and daughters of insured people. The conditions with respect to the employment and contribution record are the same as those which apply in the sickness insurance scheme. The costs of medicine are only compensated for up to a flat-rate amount and the remaining benefits are free of charge.

With respect to temporary or permanent incapacity due to an industrial injury or an occupational disease there, may be entitlement to benefit under the industrial injuries and occupational diseases branch .
The benefits in kind encompass, *inter alia,* compensation for the costs of medical treatment, medicine, artificial aids and the costs of rehabilitation. The costs are paid directly to the concerned care providers; the victim pays nothing.

Assistance (*aide médicale*) provides benefits in kind, comparable to those of the sickness and maternity insurance schemes. Also the sickness costs which remain payable by the claimant may be reimbursed. Entitlement to benefit exists when the costs payable by the claimant bear no relation to his means. In view of the extensions of the personal scope of application of the sickness costs insurance scheme, the *aide médicale* is of minor significance.

4.6. Family

We must distinguish between social insurance family benefits and assistance to families.

There are a large number of family benefits within the general statutory scheme, to be divided into three groups:
- *prestations générales d'entretien*;
- *prestations liées à la naissance*;
- *prestations à affection spéciale*.

Subject to certain exceptions concerning specific family benefits, there are general rules with regard to the scope of the children giving rise to entitlement and the basis of calculation of the benefits.
Every child living in France (exceptions are possible) gives rise to entitlement until the age when compulsory education ceases (18) on the condition that he does not earn an income of more than 55% of the minimum wage. Beyond this age, entitlement to benefit also exists for children until they reach the age of 20 years, if they are engaged in education or apprenticeship, or if they are handicapped.

The level of the family benefits depends upon the so called monthly calculation base (*base mensuelle de calcul*). This basis is fixed twice a year by decree.

Various *prestations générales d'entretien* also exist; these are payable on a monthly basis and, since 1997, they are all means tested. Let us briefly discuss most of them.
The family benefits in the strict sense (*allocations familiales*) are payable as from the second dependent child. The benefit amounts to 32% of the calculation base for the first two children and 41% for the third and subsequent children. The benefit is to be increased for children of 10 years of age and older (9% as from the 10th year of age and 16% as from the age of 15); the increase is also applicable in respect of the first child, provided that the total number of dependent children is at least three.
The family complement (*complément familial*) is payable to a household or to the person whose means do not exceed a certain limit and who has at least three dependent children older than three years of age residing in France. The level amounts to 41.56% of the monthly calculation basis.
The family support benefit (*allocation de soutien familial*) is payable in respect of the full or semi-orphan, as well as the child whose descent from one or both parents is unknown and the child whose parents, or one of them, are not willing or capable of maintaining him. Benefit is payable to the father, the mother or a third person who actually and permanently takes on the maintenance of the child. The father or mother who remarries or who cohabitees loses, entitlement to benefit. The level of benefit amounts to 30% of the monthly calculation basis for full orphans and comparable children and 22,5% in other cases.
The single parent benefit (*allocation de parent isolé*) is payable to the single parent who is exclusively responsible for the maintenance of at least one child. The surviving, divorced, separated, abandoned and unmarried parent, as well as

the single pregnant woman, are all considered to be single parents, provided that they do not cohabit. The allocation amounts to 150% of the basis for the single parent increased by 50% for each child, and is subject to a means test. Benefit is payable for a period of twelve months and possibly for a longer period until the moment that the youngest child has reached the age of three years.
We can distinguish three *prestations liées à la naissance*.

The young child benefit (*allocation au jeune enfant*) is payable from the fourth month of the pregnancy until the end of the month in which the child has reached three months. One can also be entitled to benefit after this time, albeit subject to a means test and maximally until the moment that the child reaches three years of age. The benefit amounts to 45.95% of the basis.

If a birth or an adoption brings the total number of children to three or in case of a second birth after 1 July 1994 and the person on whom the child is dependent no longer carries out any paid employment, there is a right to a parental education benefit (*allocation parentale d'éducation*), until the moment that the youngest child reaches the age of three years. The claimant must have been employed for at least 2 years during the 10 years preceding the birth or adoption. The benefit amounts to 142.57% of the basis (the *allocation au jeune enfant* is included within this amount). Those who, during the child's third year, resume at the most either half time paid employment or paid training, remain entitled to benefit, albeit at a 50% level. There are important anti-cumulation provisions which are intended to prevent the *allocation* (which in view of its level threatens to take on an income maintenance character) from coinciding with, for example, a wage or an income maintenance benefit in the case of maternity.

The *allocation de garde d'enfant à domicile* is payable to the family which, or the person who, has appointed one or more people to care for the children at home, due to the fact that the parents or the single parent carry out an occupational activity of a certain scope. The level of the allocation is equal to the social security contributions which are payable by third person(s), subject to an upper limit.

Of the *allocations à affections spéciales* we will only deal with the back to school benefit (*allocation de rentrée scolaire*) (see section 4.3 for the *allocation d'éducation spéciale* which also belongs to this category). The back to school benefit is payable to families who are also entitled to another family benefit for children attending school between the ages of 6 and 18. The benefit amounts to 20% of the calculation basis for each child and is paid at the beginning of the school year. It is subject to a means test.

The head of a family with at least two dependent children and without sufficient means to raise the children is entitled to the *aide sociale aux familles*. This benefit is subject to an extensive means test. However, due to the extension of the scope of application of the family benefits from the general scheme, this assistance scheme is of little practical significance.

Although the family allowance scheme (of the general system) covers all residents, some systems provide additional family benefits; this is the case for the civil servants scheme or the agricultural system for example.

4.7. Need

French social security uses a whole series of specific assistance benefits, which are designed for special categories of persons or for the coverage of specific needs. Recently a more general assistance scheme has been established, the *revenu minimum d'insertion*.

Entitlement to guaranteed minimum income benefit (*revenu minimum d'insertion*) depends upon a person residing in France. Nationality requirements are not imposed, although for non-EEC nationals there are requirements regarding the duration of residence; for this category entitlement to benefit only exists after a minimum period of residence in France of three years.
The claimant must be older than 25 years of age; if he is younger, he must have one or more dependent children. Students and apprentices are excluded from entitlement.

There are various benefit rates depending upon the composition of the households. The basic amount for the single parent is increased by 50% for the lone spouse or the partner; for each child, in respect of which there is entitlement to family benefits, there is another 30% increase; the latter also applies for each person younger than 25 years old who belongs to the household and is dependent upon the claimant. For each further person after the third person (without taking into account the partner) the basic amount is raised by 40%. The level of benefit is determined by deducting all the means within the household from the applicable rate. The means include all income with the exception of a limited number of specific benefits; the tested income also includes rights to alimony payments. The means of all the persons belonging to the household are taken into account.

The claimant must agree to participate in activities aimed at integration. The *revenu minimum d'insertion* is at first granted for a period of three months. During this period a "contract" is proposed by the authorities, which includes a plan for integration. The integration should not necessarily be aimed at paid employment; training or an apprenticeship are equally valid objectives; the act even allows for the drawing up of a more social integration programme, for example aimed at fighting illiteracy or the combat against alcoholism. After the conclusion of the contract, benefit is granted for a period of 3 to 12 months; when this period has expired, benefit may be renewed, for an equal period each time. If the claimant does not fulfil his obligations under the contract, the benefit will be terminated.

In 1997, a new assistance benefit was created, the specific dependency benefit (*prestation spécifique dépendance*). The benefit is means tested and replaces the former advantages granted to handicapped people in need of special care which were given to the elderly. The benefit consists of help in the household and co-ordinated care. The latter co-ordination is in the hands of the *département*.

5. *Financing*

The general system is, in principle, financed by contributions from the insured persons and the employers. The state is only involved in the financing on an incidental basis, especially in making contribution payments for certain categories of persons. The state will also supplement possible shortages, especially in the sickness insurance funds.
Contributions are levied on the wages or the occupational income of the insured people, subject to an upper earnings limit. Furthermore, some social security benefits are also subject to contribution liability.
Generally, contributions have a proportional character. The rates differ from scheme to scheme. For certain categories of people, such as domestic personnel, hotel personnel and taxi drivers the contributions are flat-rate.
Contributions are generally jointly paid by the employers and the employees, according to a certain ratio of distribution. However, the contributions for the industrial injuries and occupational diseases branch are completely borne by the employers. They pay a standard contribution (in small companies) or a risk related contribution (in larger enterprises).
The employer deposits all the contributions, including those of the employee, with the fund of the *U.R.S.S.A.F./A.C.O.S.S.* These divide the contributions between the various branches of the general system (except the family benefits scheme).
The financing of the general scheme is based upon the pay as you go principle.

A contribution on all income, the *contribution sociale généralisée (C.S.G.)* has been introduced in 1991. The proceeds of this 2,4% contribution on personal income are used to finance the family benefit scheme (common to all residents) as well as some non-contributory benefits paid by the National Solidarity Fund Elderly (*Fonds National de Solidarité Vieillesse*) under the old age branch of the general system.

The unemployment benefits scheme is financed out of employee and employer contributions as well as out of state subventions. The latter cover the 'solidarity benefits'.

The proactive social policy of government also included the reduction of the employer contributions under specific circumstances. In principle, the concerned schemes are compensated by the state for the loss of income.

A source of financing of a supplementary nature consists in taxing alcohol, tobacco, pharmaceutical advertising and the possession of a car; the proceeds of these additional taxes being earmarked for the financing of social security.

Since the so called "reform Juppé" in 1996, the Parliament has to adopt a statute on the overall financing of the social security each year, it must indicate the maximum growth of the expenditures of the social security systems.

Except for a limited number of benefits which are financed by the government, the expenses of the *aide sociale* are borne by the departments. However, part of the financial obligations are transferred to the municipalities. The new *prestation spécifique dépendance* fully financed by the *départements*.
The expenditure of the *revenu minimum d' insertion* is entirely borne by the central government.

6. Judicial review

Judicial review in the area of social security is subject to a special procedure for the settlement of disputes. The procedures are simple, fast and inexpensive. In special cases, the regular courts are competent, e.g. in disputes concerning the recovery of benefits from third parties, in disputes concerning the election of governing boards of the administrative bodies, in disputes concerning the application of penal sanctions and in respect of disputes concerning the occupational pension scheme and the unemployment scheme.

The special procedure for the settlement of disputes is subdivided into the *contentieux général* and a number of *contentieux spéciaux*.

The *contentieux général de la sécurité sociale* governs all disputes in the field of statutory social security, which, due to their nature, do not fall under another procedure for judicial review. It mainly covers all disputes concerning insurance obligation, contribution liability and the granting of benefits.
Competent in first instance is the *tribunal des affaires de sécurité sociale* which is chaired by a judge and assisted by a representative of the employees and the employers. Before the claimant can turn to this tribunal, he must address a *commission de recours amiable* within two months after the litigious decision. This commission, which constitutes a part of the administrative body in question, takes a fresh reasoned decision. If after one month the claimant has not received a decision, or if he wishes to challenge the decision, appeal to the *tribunal* within a period of two months is open. The parties can appear personally before the *tribunal*, but they may also be represented or accompanied by certain people (a spouse, direct ascendants and descendants, a lawyer, a colleague or a representative of a union). The *tribunal* may order a further inquiry to be carried out, summon advisory experts and, in short, collect all the necessary information. If the case concerns a dispute of a medical nature, the *tribunal* is obliged to apply a special procedure (see below).
If the case which is subject to the judge's decision, does not amount to a certain level, determined by legislation, then the decision of the *tribunal* constitutes a final judgement which is not subject to further appeal. Otherwise, appeal is possible within one month to the *Cour d'appel, chambre sociale*. The decision taken by this court can be disputed within two months in the *Cour de cassation, chambre sociale*.

With respect to disputes of a medical nature, there is the separate procedure of the *expertise médicale*. This procedure must be started within one month after the litigious decision. A physician or a board of physicians, appointed by the attendant doctor and the doctor from the administrative body, give their opinion. Subject to further conditions, that opinion is binding upon the claimant, the administrative body and the judge.

Apart from the *contentieux général* there are two special procedures for judicial review.

The *contentieux du contrôle technique* is a procedure which must be followed in cases of error, misuse, fraud and facts concerning the performance of the medical profession, in the framework of medical care provided to insured persons.
The *contentieux technique de la sécurité sociale* is the judicial procedure applicable with respect to disputes concerning the degree of invalidity within the meaning of the social insurance schemes, the incapacity for work in the old age insurance scheme and the state of permanent incapacity in the scheme regarding industrial injuries and occupational diseases. In first instance the disputes are dealt with by the *Commissions régionales*, consisting, among others, of physicians. Appeal is possible to the *Commission nationale technique* and in the last instance to the *Cour de cassation*.

Objections against decisions taken by the *Commissions d'admission d'aide sociale* can be made with the so called *Commission départementale*, a commission which, in composition, is similar to the *Commission d'admission*. The claimant is heard at his request. The *Commission centrale d'aide sociale* hears appeals; it is chaired by a member of the *Conseil d' Etat* and further composed of members of the *Conseil d' Etat*, judges and members appointed by the competent minister on grounds of their specific expertise in the assistance field. If required, the commission is supplemented by advisory physicians. In view of the administrative character of this judicial procedure, further appeal can be made with the *Conseil d'Etat*.

Chapter Six

GERMANY

1. Introduction: concept and sources of social security law

After the unification of East and West Germany took place in 1990, the social security system of East Germany has been replaced by the social security system of West Germany. The process of transformation started on July 1st, 1990, when the currency union between the former two German states had been shaped. The transitional period will end in the next decade after a full adaptation of the economic efficiency of the economy of the eastern part of Germany. The social security system of Germany is based on the laws, enacted by the former West Germany.

In Germany we can distinguish three branches of social security, namely social insurance, social compensation and assistance.

Traditionally the system has been based upon the principle of social insurance (*Sozialversicherung*); in addition to a health insurance scheme, an industrial injuries insurance scheme and an invalidity and old age insurance scheme, (together referred to as classic social insurance schemes), there is also an unemployment insurance scheme. Since 1995 a specific scheme for long term care also exists (*Pflegeversicherung*).

As a consequence of the first world war a new branch of social security was created for war veterans, called the *Kriegsopferversorgung*, which constituted the first element of the *soziale Entschädigung*. The State took the responsibility upon itself to compensate for damage to health suffered by persons as a result of services offered to the state. By this way of thinking, the *Bundesversorgungsgezetz* aimed to compensate war victims. Later, this branch of social security was extended to cover, inter alia, victims of compulsory vaccination or crime.

The third and, at the same time, the oldest branch of social security is assistance (*Sozialhilfe*).

In addition to these traditional branches of social security, a number of more recent branches may be distinguished, these do belong to the social security scheme, but are difficult to place within the three given sections. Here we may mention the system of study grants (*Ausbildungsförderung*), family benefits (*Kindergeld, Erziehungsgeld, Unterhaltsvorschuß*) and housing benefits (*Wohngeld*). This branch of law is referred to as *soziale Förderung* (social promotion).

The German Constitution includes hardly any provisions which are of direct importance for social security law. Social security is only expressly mentioned as 'Sozialversicherung' in respect to the rule concerning legislative competence (Art. 74, n° 12 Constitution); which appoints the Federation as the competent body. Of indirect, but great importance, is the *Sozialstaatsprinzip*, derived from case law and legal doctrine from articles 20 and 28 of the Constitution. It authorises and justifies legislative activities in the various fields of social policy. A comparison with social rights, yet to be discussed, is called for here; many people characterise social rights as a realisation of the *Sozialstaatsprinzip*. Finally, albeit very indirectly, some fundamental rights, are of importance for social security, for example the principle of equality (art. 3), the right of free personal development (art. 2), the special protection provided for marriage and the family (art. 6) and the protection of property (art. 14). In addition to the Federal Constitution, attention should also be paid to the Constitutions of the single states. Within these we often encounter fundamental social rights which are described in detail but from which no subjective rights can be derived.

In 1970 it was officially resolved to codify social security law within one Code, called *Sozialgesetzbuch*. The aim of this codification was to simplify, to unify and to clarify social security law, which was haphazardly regulated by numerous separate acts. It was hoped that all the social security laws could be shaped into one comprehensive system of law in order to promote the citizens' understanding of the law and thereby their trust in the constitutional welfare state, as well as to simplify the application of the law and to guarantee legal certainty.

In the meantime, a general part has been realised, which includes introductory material as well as formal legal provisions which, with some exceptions, cover the entire ambit of the *Sozialgesetzbuch*. The general part includes a chapter concerning common provisions for social insurance and a chapter regulating the benefit payment procedure, data protection, and the co-operation between the administrative bodies and their relationships with third parties.
From 1984 onwards further sections of the *Sozialgesetzbuch* have been enacted about the main provisions on administrative procedures, the health insurance, the social assistance for children and young adults (*Jugendhilfe*), the old age, invalidity and survivors pensions, the industrial injuries insurance and the unemployment insurance. On the grounds of article 1 of the transitional and final provisions, a whole series of acts are considered to be special parts of *Sozialgesetzbuch*, until they are actually adopted within it. The exhaustive enumeration of the specific acts also provides us with a possible delimitation of the concept of social security; which is often understood to include all the laws that are regulated in the *Sozialgesetzbuch*.

Within articles 3-10 of the general part of the *Sozialgesetzbuch* there are a number of so called "social rights" (*soziale Rechte*) with reference to the branches of social security mentioned above. No entitlement to benefits can be derived on the ground of these provisions. For this the articles refer to the relevant provisions of the special acts. The law requires that social rights must be taken into consideration in interpreting the remaining provisions of the statute book and in applying any discretion. In this, care must be taken that the social rights are extensively realised.

From the above it can be deduced that the act is the most prominent source of social security law. Legislative norms are regularly supplemented by changing the Code itself or by subordinate legislation. Jurisprudence also forms an important source of law, both for the interpretation of legislative concepts and for the review of decisions taken by social security institutions. For the purposes of this chapter, two schemes will not be considered, although they do fall under the formal social security concept. The schemes in question are the system of study grants and the system of housing benefits.

2. *Administrative organisation*

At the federal level, the Ministry of Labour and Social Affairs is competent for social security, except for the health care insurance and social assistance, that are of the competence of the Ministry of Health.

In respect of the administration of the social security schemes, a fundamental distinction must be made between the social insurance schemes on the one hand and the remaining schemes on the other.

The administration of the three classic insurance schemes is charged to corporations under public law. The common provisions for social insurance schemes within the *Sozialgesetzbuch* contain elaborate rules explaining the existence and the structure of these corporations. The principle of *Selbstverwaltung*, self-government, is applied to the social insurance schemes. This is apparent from the composition of the various bodies of those corporations. Firstly we may distinguish the general assembly which is composed, on equal shares, of representatives of the insured people and by the employers for a period of six years, on the ground of lists of preference, submitted respectively by organisations of employers and employees (*Sozialwahlen*). Usually the relevant organisations are able to agree on the composition of the preference lists, and a vote is not necessary. The general assembly subsequently chooses the members of the governing board. With regard to the mutual divisions of tasks, the general assembly takes decisions of a general nature, for example the determination of internal regulations, the fixing of the contributions and the issuing of administrative directives; the managerial activities are divided between the other two bodies. The general secretary, for instance, is responsible for current affairs, for which he represents the legal person to the outside world.

In the light of detailed legislation, one wonders whether one should speak of indirect state government rather than self-government. In this respect the state supervision of administrative bodies is of importance. This too is regulated by the general provisions for the social insurance schemes within the *Sozialgesetzbuch*. According to these provisions, supervision is aimed at examining the lawfulness of the acts of administration; in addition, the management and book keeping of the administrative body is also controlled. On a federal level, supervision is carried out by the *Bundesversicherungsamt* and on a state level by the *Arbeits- und Sozialminister* of the different Länder.

The three separate insurance schemes have the following administrative bodies. The *Krankenkassen* are responsible for the administration of the health insurance scheme. They are also responsible for the administration of the long-term care insurance. The *Krankenkassen* are divided into the *Orts-, Betriebs-* and *Innungskrankenkassen*, as well as the so called *Ersatzkassen*. Since 1996 all persons covered by the German health insurance have the right to opt for one of these bodies. The general assembly of such a fund is entirely composed of representatives of the insured persons. It enacts the level of contributions autonomously, but the expenditure is limited by a fixed budget.

The injury insurance scheme is administered by the so called *Berufsgenossenschaften* on the one hand, and on the other by the so called *Eigenunfallversicherungstrager*. The *Berufsgenossenschaften* are divided into industrial bodies, agricultural bodies and bodies for mariners. For special categories of insured persons, either the federation, the states, the municipalities, or the *Bundesanstallt für Arbeit* (see below) may act as the *Eigenunfallversicherungstrager*. In these cases administration is carried out by civil servants of one of those bodies. Administration of the invalidity and old age insurance scheme for workers is the responsibility of the *Landesversicherungsanstalten*; administration of the insurance scheme for *Angestellte* is the responsibility of the *Bundesversicherungsanstalt für Angestellte*. The *Bundesknappschaft* administers the invalidity, worker's injuries and old age insurance scheme for mine workers and the *landwirtschaftliche Alterskassen* administers the old age and invalidity insurance scheme for farmers.

To strengthen their position, nearly all categories of administrative bodies have federations on a national level: these constitute corporations under public law. Another example is the *Verband Deutscher Rentenversicherungsträger*, a corporation under private law. The administration of the unemployment insurance scheme is organised, in a slightly different way, under the specific provisions of the *Arbeitsförderungsgesetz*. This administration is in the hands of the *Bundesanstalt für Arbeit*, a corporation under public law; it is subdivided into a headquarters (the *Bundesanstalt*), the *Landesarbeitsämtern*, and the *Arbeitsämtern*. The *Bundesanstalt für Arbeit* has a *Verwaltungsrat* and a *Vorstand*, the *Landesarbeitsämter* and *Arbeitsämter* have administrative commissions. These bodies are composed of representatives of the employees, employers and public bodies (federal, state and municipal). However, the representatives are not elected but appointed, albeit on the recommendation of the organisations of employers and employees.

All social security schemes, with the exception of social insurance schemes, are directly administered by the State on a decentralised level. Thus the states are responsible for the administration of the *Bundesversorgungsgesetz*, a task which is carried out via the *Versorgungsämter* and the *Landesversorgungsämter*. Firstly the *kreisfreie Städte* and the *Landkreise*, and in addition the *Länder* are responsible for the administration of the *Bundessozialhilfegesetz* and *Jugendhilfe*.

The *Bundesanstalt* für Arbeit takes a somewhat special place as administrator of the *Bundeskindergeldgesetz*. In this capacity the *Bundesanstalt für Arbeit* carries the title of *Familienkasse*. It is further subject to the administrative directives of the minister. Decisions in individual cases are taken by the competent *Arbeitsamt*. The states may appoint the *Bundesanstalt für Arbeit* as the administrative body for the *Bundeserziehungsgeldgesetz*. Since 1997 the family benefits are administered for income tax payers by the tax offices.

Recently, non-profit and even commercial employment agencies have been allowed to carry out (specified) labour exchange activities.

3. *Personal scope of application*

The four social insurance schemes do not have the same scope of personal coverage; there are differences which vary according to the aim of the scheme. Nevertheless, in view of the existence many similarities between these schemes, the following overview is focused upon categories of people and not upon separate insurance schemes

An important distinction exists between compulsorily insured people and voluntarily insured people. People in gainful employment are obligatorily insured. The legislation uses the term *"beschäftigt sein"* and takes the *Beschäftigungsverhältnis* as a point of departure for the insurance obligation. Those employed in gainful employment must be distinguished from self-employed workers. According to jurisprudence, the main characteristic of the *Beschäftigungsverhältnis* is the personal dependence of the employee on the employer. This dependence is notably assumed when there is a duty to follow various instructions in respect of work or behaviour during work.

Arbeiter and *Angestellte* are insured according to the criteria mentioned above. *"Arbeiter"* means an employee who executes predominantly manual work; *"Angestellte"* means an employee who executes predominantly intellectual work. In a post-industrial society this distinction becomes old fashioned; however it still exists. This distinction is important for determining the competent administrative body in old age invalidity and survivor's insurance: For *"Arbeiter"* the *Landesversicherungsanstalten* is the competent administrative body, whilst for *"Angestellte"* this is the *Bundesversicherungsanstalt für Angestellte*.

The compulsory insurance exists only in respect of activities which are carried out for a wage. All income from work is included within this concept, regardless of the name or form under which it is paid, whether there exists a right to it or whether it is gained in cash, goods or services. These rules are further elaborated in regulations, in respect of which one has aimed at the greatest possible harmony with the concept of wage used in taxation law.

All those who are participating in vocational training are also compulsorily insured. However, the wage requirement is not applicable in respect of these people.

Furthermore, some smaller groups of self-employed people, whose economic position is comparable with that of people in a position of a dependent labour relationship and who are consequently considered to be in need of protection, are also subject to obligatory insurance. Home workers, midwives, artisans, manual workers, artists and writers can all be mentioned here. Those who execute so called "liberal professions" (e.g. physicians, dentists, lawyers, architects, notaries, etc.) as self-employed are compelled to integrate into a pension scheme, framed for the various professions and regulated by various state laws. The insurance obligation of these self-employed people does not extend to the health, long term care, work injuries and unemployment insurance schemes. Sometimes special rules are applicable for them, for example in respect of farmers.

In addition to the self-employed people mentioned, there are other people included within the obligatory insurance scheme who are considered in need of protection by the legislator. To be mentioned here are co-operating family members in the agricultural sector, students, apprentices and handicapped people who are active in a work place for the handicapped. Generally, the compulsory insurance only covers the sickness (costs), long term care, invalidity and old age insurance schemes.

A final category of compulsorily insured people consists of those who interrupt a dependent labour relationship or terminate it without losing the need for protection, for example those executing military service and those in receipt of an unemployment benefit or pension.

All civil servants are excluded from the compulsory insurance; while they are protected under a special scheme. All those who carry out minor activities are also excluded.

Apart from these statutory exclusions, in some cases the opportunity of applying for exemption from the insurance obligation exists. In respect of these cases the legislator has attempted to gain some control with regard to the existence of other adequate forms of protection.

All the insurance schemes, except for the unemployment insurance scheme, offer the opportunity of voluntary insurance. The old age and invalidity insurance scheme offers this opportunity to all Germans and EC-citizens and to everyone who lives or whose usual place of residence is within the Federal Republic; those who make use of this possibility are, for example, people who carry out domestic activities.

To the extent that they presuppose the existence of a labour relationship or a self-employed activity, the provisions with regard to compulsory and voluntary insurance only apply when the activity is carried out within the Federal Republic. The place of residence of the employee or self-employed person is not the deciding factor, but the place in which the activity is performed (*Beschäftigungsort*). There are two exceptions to this rule. Persons insured in Germany who are temporarily sent abroad in the course of their activities remain insured (*Ausstrahlung*). In contrast to that, people insured under a foreign system who are only temporarily active in the Federal Republic do not fall under compulsory insurance (*Einstrahlung*). The so called principle of territoriality (*Territorialitätsprinzip*) is applicable to the remaining social security schemes. This principle, as laid down within the general part of the *Sozialgesetzbuch*, declares the law of the *Sozialgesetzbuch* to be applicable to all people whose ordinary or habitual place of residence is within Germany, irrespective of his nationality. The term ordinary residence (*Wohnsitz*) refers to the place where a person has a house under circumstances which indicate that the house is kept up and used on a long term basis. The term habitual residence (*gewöhnlicher Aufenthalt*) refers to the place where a person stays with a certain regularity and for a certain time.

The principle of territoriality or residence, must yield to derogating rules within the specific parts of the *Sozialgesetzbuch*. It has already been shown that the social insurance schemes depart from the principle of residence by focusing upon the place where the activity is carried out. We also encounter modifications in the other social insurance schemes. Thus in the field of the *soziale Entschädigung*, the principle of residence has been extensively modified by the principle of nationality (*Personalitätsprinzip*). Therefore benefits are awarded only to Germans, even if they live abroad, although this award is subject to certain conditions. The principle of residence has also been moderated within the *Bundessozialhilfegesetz* by the principle of nationality, albeit to a lesser extent.

4. Risks and benefits

4.1. Old age

When the insured person reaches a certain age he is no longer expected to provide for his own livelihood. The usual limit, as laid down by the legislator, is 65 years of age. When this age is attained, one is entitled to old age pension (*Altersrente*) even though the activity carried out until this time may not actually have been abandoned. Furthermore, the old age insurance scheme operates with a flexible pensionable age and an early (*vorgezogenen*) pensionable age, two concepts that must be distinguished from each other.
The flexible pensionable age enables the insured person to apply for the benefits usually given to someone who is partially incapable of work on the condition that he is 60 years old and carries out no, or very minor, activities.
Several specific categories of people qualify for an early pension under conditions established by law. Severely handicapped persons, people who have been unemployed for more than 18 months and all women, are allowed to retire at an age no younger than 60 on the condition they fulfil certain requirements as to the number of years they have been insured. Here too, no or only a very minor activity may be carried out in order to qualify for the full early pension.

However, in order to make the transition to the full pension easier, a partial retirement pension has been introduced, allowing its recipients to partially continue substantial professional activities.

The system of the early pensionable age will be given up in the next few years. The political intention behind this change is to make it more attractive to the insured person to apply for benefits at a later age. For this purpose deductions of increasing percentages are made in case of earlier retirement and supplementary benefits are paid to those applying for a pension after reaching pensionable age. The political aim is to re-establish 65 as the regular pensionable age.

With respect to entitlement to old age pension, the actual or fictitious completion of a waiting period of sixty months is required; when making use of the flexible or early pensionable age, the contribution period is equal to 180 months and an insurance period of 35 years. Periods of payment of contributions are recognised as periods of completion of the waiting periods (*Beitragszeiten*). Furthermore, subject to certain conditions, periods are taken into account during which no contributions were paid, due to specific reasons, e.g. military service or raising children (*Ersatzzeiten*).

The amount of the pension is dependent upon four factors, these are the general basis of calculation, the special basis of calculation, the number of insurance years and a multiplication factor (for this scheme 1%). The general basis of calculation is an amount determined by regulation, derived from the average annual income of all insured people. It is adjusted annually to increases in net wages and salaries (*Dynamisierung*). The special basis of calculation reflects the relationship between the individual income of the insured person during his insured career and the average income of all insured persons. Finally, the number of insurance years to be taken into account constitute, on the one hand, the sum of periods to be counted for the completion of the waiting period (see above) and, on the other, the so called *Anrechnungszeiten* and *Zurechnungszeiten* which are periods in which the insured person was prevented from carrying out obligatorily insured work, due to circumstances beyond his control, for example periods of incapacity for work or education. *Zurechnungszeiten* play a role in situations of early invalidity (see section 4.3.). *Anrechnungszeiten* as well as *Zurechnungszeiten* are only taken into account when a certain number of contributions have been paid.

Benefits from the statutory old age insurance scheme are often supplemented by occupational schemes set up on a collective agreement between employer and employees or an individual basis.

4.2. Death

Death of an insured person gives the right to benefits for the survivors. The widow or widower is entitled to *Witwen-* or *Witwerrente* if the deceased was entitled to a pension, or had satisfied, actually or fictitiously, a waiting period of 60 months. The widow/widower is the person who was married to the insured person at the time of his/her death. The survivor's pension is derived from the pension rights of the deceased person and amounts to respectively 60% of the pension on account of *Berufsunfähigkeit* (small survival pension). The latter is only granted to survivors who are 45 years of age or older or who are incapable of work, or who are raising at least one child. For the first three months the survivor's pension amounts to 100% of the insured person's pension. The survivor's pension is income-tested: apart from a disregard determined by legislation, all earnings of the beneficiary are deducted from the pension. These benefits are income-tested.

In case of divorce, widow's or widower's pension is paid if the insured person had to maintain his/her former spouse before death and the divorce was enacted before July 1st 1977. For divorces after this date, a credit splitting is provided, designed to split credits earned by the married couple during the period of marriage equally. The split and the transfer of credits is carried out immediately at the moment of the divorce.

Children are entitled to orphan's pension (*Waisenrente*) until the age of 18 or until the age of 27 if they are following vocational training. The amount of the orphan's pension is also related to the pension of the insured person. If the death of the insured person was due to an industrial injury or an occupational disease, the widow(er) or the orphan are entitled to *Hinterbliebenenrente* on the basis of the injuries insurance scheme. Following the same criteria as above, a distinction is made between a small and a large pension. The amount is respectively three tenths and two fifths of the basis of calculation for the *Verletzenrente*, and two thirds of this for the first quarter following the death of the insured person. The survivor's pension is subject to an in-come test. On the grounds of the injuries insurance scheme benefits are also payable to ex-spouses and orphans.

Within the framework of the *soziale Entschädigung* the survivors are entitled to benefit on the death of the victim. If death was due to a cause covered by the *soziale Entschädigung* (see section 4.3.), there is a right to *Hinterbliebenenrente*, otherwise there is a right to *Beihilfen*. The pension for the surviving spouse is made up of different components. Firstly there is the flat-rate *Grundrente*. The supplementary *Ausgleichsrente* is also flat-rate, but is only granted to the spouse who, due to certain circumstances, is expected to be unable to earn any income; it is means-tested. If the spouse earns an income amounting to less than half the amount which would have been earned by the deceased person, there is a right to *Berufsschadensausgleich*. Within certain limits the compensation amounts to four tenths of the difference between both incomes.

Subject to further conditions, the above benefits are also granted to the ex-spouse of the deceased person.

Orphans receive a flat-rate *Grundrente* and possibly a means-tested *Ausgleichsrente*.

Subject to further conditions, the parents or grand parents of the deceased are entitled to a means-tested *Aszendentenrente*.

Beihilfen are granted with a view to the fact that the deceased person, due to damage suffered to his health, has not been able to build up sufficient rights for his spouse and children during his lifetime. As a rule they are smaller than the *Hinterblienenrente* and, within a certain limit, are subject to a means-test.
All cash benefits are annually adjusted by law as in the old age insurance scheme.

4.3. Incapacity for work

The health insurance scheme is a social insurance scheme which offers coverage against the risks of sickness-related loss of income, maternity and medical care (see section 4.5.). By sickness (*Krankheit*) the *Bundessozialgericht* means an upset of the physical or mental condition which requires medical treatment by physicians and/or results in incapacity for work. The cause of the upset is not important nor is the duration of it. The system operates on the principle of 'all or nothing': one is either fully incapable or fully capable of work.

The risk of maternity (*Schwangerschaft/Mutterschaft*) is understood as being limited to the condition of pregnancy, the birth and the period 8 weeks after confinement.

The most prominent benefit in cash of the health insurance scheme is sick leave payment (*Krankengeld*). In order to be eligible for sick pay, a person must be incapable of work due to sickness. Sick leave payment constitutes an income maintenance benefit: thus it is not granted to (insured) students and apprentices. The benefit amounts to 70% of the so called *Regellohn*, i.e. the wage or income which also formed the basis for the calculation of contributions. In respect of one and the same disease, sick leave payment is to be paid for a maximum period of 78 weeks within a three year period.

In respect of maternity, the woman is entitled to *Mutterschaftsgeld*, the amount of which is equal to her net wages, subject to a rather low flat-rate maximum. If the real wages are higher than this limit, the employer is obliged to give a supplement on the grounds of the *Mutterschutzgesetz*. Benefit is granted for six weeks preceding the birth and for eight to twelve weeks thereafter.

Two types of incapacity for work are distinguished under the invalidity insurance scheme, the *Berufsunfähigkeit* and the *Erwerbsunfähigkeit*. According to the legislative definition, a person is considered to be *berufsunfähig* when his capacity for work, as a result of sickness or disablement, is considered to be less than half that of a healthy person with a comparable education and with equivalent knowledge and ability. The determination of the remaining capacity of a person depends upon an assessment of the extent to which he is still able to carry out an occupation that reflects his strength and ability and with which, taking into account his previous occupation, he can reasonably be charged. Then there is an assessment of the extent to which the remaining capacity to work can be realised on the labour market (*konkrete Betrachtungsweise*). The risk of *Erwerbsunfähigkeit* is also further defined within the legislation. According to the definition a person is considered to be *erwerbsunfähig* when, as a result of sickness or disablement, he cannot, for an unforeseeable time, regularly carry out an occupation, or earn more than only a minor income in such an occupation.

The insured can be compared with any occupation that is compatible with his strength and ability; his education or previous activities are not taken into consideration, which constitutes a major difference with the concept of *Berufsunfähigkeit*.

Similarly to the determination of the *Berufsunfähigkeit*, it should further be assessed to what extent the remaining capacity for work can be realised on the labour market.

The existence of *Berufs-* or *Erwerbsunfähigkeit* is not in itself sufficient to give rise to entitlement to benefit. There are two more conditions. The first condition is that in the five years preceding the moment of incapacity, work should have been carried out on the grounds of which contributions must have been paid over at least 36 months. Furthermore, a waiting period of sixty months must have been completed, similar to the one which applies in respect of entitlement to old age pension. Here too, account is taken of contributory periods (*Beitragszeiten*) and non-contributory periods (*Anrechnungs-* und *Ersatzzeiten*). If the risk is realised as a result of a circumstance for which society must take responsibility, the waiting period is always considered to be completed. This is the case for instance with industrial injuries. The completion of the waiting period is also fictitious if the risk occurs before the waiting period could possibly have been completed. This covers the situation whereby a person has only worked for a short period because he had previously followed vocational training. In principle, the waiting period must be completed prior to the moment that the risk materialised. However, there is a special rule concerning the early handicapped. They may claim invalidity pension if they have been insured for 240 months, irrespective of the fact that the incapacity for work existed at the onset of the insurance. A reform of this system of invalidity pensions is under discussion.

In certain cases the invalidity insurance scheme provides rehabilitation benefits. There is no right to such benefits; the granting of them is at the discretion of the administrative body. The law distinguishes between medical benefits, supplementary benefits, and benefits which are designed to improve the chances of carrying out an occupation.

The most important cash benefit is invalidity pension. This benefit is calculated in the same way as the old age pension (see section 4.1.). A multiplying factor of 1% is applicable to the *Berufsunfähigkeitsrente* and 1,5% to the *Erwerbsunfähigkeitsrente*. The difference arises from the presumption that the person who is *berufsunfähig* is still supposed to realise his remaining earning capacity. The *Zurechtnungszeiten* play a special role here. These are the periods between the occurrence of *Erwerbs-* or *Berufsunfähigkeit* and the attainment of 56 years of age. They are intended to ensure that persons who become invalid at an early stage of their career receive an adequate pension.

In principle, invalidity pensions are payable till the beneficiary reaches pensionable age, then the pension is transferred into an old age pension. If there are well founded expectations that the incapacity will terminate within the foreseeable future, the pension is granted only after 26 weeks, and at the most for three years. A period of three years is considered as foreseeable.

There are special rules within the injuries insurance scheme regarding cases of incapacity for work as the result of an industrial injury or an occupational disease.

Firstly, the injuries insurance scheme provides benefits in kind. These include medical and surgical help, home care or care within an institution and help within the occupational sphere aimed at future rehabilitation into working life. Secondly, benefits in cash consist of *Verletztengeld* and *Verletztenrente*. The former is payable to a person who is incapable within the meaning of the injury insurance scheme. It amounts to 80% of the gross annual income. If, after thirteen weeks, there is still a reduced incapacity as a result of the injury and if this is at least 20%, a person is entitled to *Verletztenrente*. There is a distinction between a permanent (*Verletztenrente*) and a provisional pension (*Verletztengeld*). If the condition is not yet stable enough to fix the pension on a permanent basis, the latter is granted for a maximum period of two years after the injury. In cases of full incapacity, the pension amounts to two thirds of the gross earnings of the previous year, and in cases of partial incapacity to a percentage of these earnings.

Entitlement to benefit in the field of the *soziale Entschädigung*, as regulated in the *Bundesversorgungsgesetz*, exists for those who have sustained a service injury as the result of military service during the time of national socialism, or who have suffered health damage as the result of actions which were characteristic of this service (*Wehrdienstbeschädigung*). A number of other possible causes of damage to health are treated as those under military service activities, for example the direct effects of war (in respect of civilian victims) and war imprisonment. Other acts within the field of the *soziale Entschädigung* are set up along the lines of the *Bundesversorgungsgesetz*. They apply when the damage to health occurred as a result of particular causes. For example, within the *Soldatenversorgungsgesetz*, this is the service activities of soldiers in the present *Bundeswehr*. In the *Opferentschädigungsgesetz* it is the premeditated, unlawful assault on a person. In the *Bundesseuchengesetz* it is forced or recommended vaccination.

There is entitlement to benefits in kind, as well as to cash benefits. The package of benefits in kind largely coincides with medical and surgical help from the sickness insurance scheme. If the damage results in the incapacity for work of the claimant, then he may be entitled to *Übergangsgeld*, which is calculated in the same way as the *Krankengeld*.

If the incapacity is permanent, a person has the right to a pension. This pension (*Rente*) consists of a number of components. Firstly, there is a non meanstested *Grundrente*, payable to those who are at least 30% incapable of work.

Depending upon the degree of incapacity for work, the *Grundrente* is determined as a fixed amount. Subject to further conditions, those who are 50% incapable, or more, may also be entitled to an *Ausgleichsrente*. This also consists of fixed amounts corresponding to the degree of incapacity for work, although, except for certain disregards, it is means-tested. Finally, every beneficiary of a *Rente* is entitled to the so called *Berufsschadensausgleich*. This benefit covers the loss of income due to the reduced incapacity; within certain limits, it is payable at a rate of four tenths of the loss of income.

Legislative fixed supplements are payable in respect of the spouse and/or the children of the victim.

4.4. Unemployment

The unemployment insurance scheme is designed to avoid and combat unemployment as well as to replace lost income (*Arbeitslosigkeit*). Employees who are available for work, but who are temporarily without employment and whose previous employment was not a minor activity, are considered to be unemployed. An employee is any person who at the time of the claim and during the consecutive period is considered to belong to the category of persons who normally carry out a dependent activity, other than of a minor character. The employee must be available for the labour market. This is the case if the person is both capable and willing, to carry out suitable employment, or to comply with suitable measures within the framework of education or rehabilitation. The definition of suitable work has been changed recently in order to make in principle all activities suitable ones.

Another risk covered by the unemployment insurance scheme is the temporary reduction of working hours (*Kurzarbeit*). The cause must lie in economic circumstances (e.g. decline in trade) or in unavoidable events (natural disasters), it must not be caused by something within the power of the employer. The reduction of working hours must be unavoidable and must have a certain dimension. It must also result in a reduction of wages for the employee. Apart from that, there is a separate benefit for workers in the construction industry in case of reduction of working hours due to bad weather.

Finally, the unemployment insurance scheme also covers the risk of the employer's insolvency in respect of overdue wage claims of the employees, albeit limited to the last three months prior to the bankruptcy of the employer (*Insolvenzversicherung*).

An important benefit in kind for the unemployed person is the labour exchange. Other important benefits in kind are vocational training and retraining. The most important cash benefit is *Arbeitslosengeld*. Entitlement depends upon the registration of the unemployment with the *Arbeitsamt* and the completion of the so-called *Anwartschaftszeit*. The latter is comparable to the waiting period within the old age insurance scheme. It is considered to be completed if, in the three years preceding the unemployment, the unemployed person has carried out 360 days compulsory insured work for which he received wages. Again, certain periods of non-contributory activities may be credited, e.g. periods of executing military service.

The level of unemployment benefit for unemployed persons with at least one child amounts to 67% and for all others to 60% of the average net income from work enjoyed during the period of reference, i.e. the average weekly wage for the last six months. The duration of the benefit is limited and varies, depending on the employment record, from 156 to 832 days. If the *Arbeitslosengeld* is exhausted, the unemployed may be entitled to *Arbeitslosenhilfe*. This benefit is means-tested. Nevertheless, the level of the benefit is related to net income from work; for the unemployed persons with at least one child, it amounts to 57% and for all others to 53% of this income. In principle, the duration of entitlement to *Arbeitslosenhilfe* is unlimited.

Benefits on the same differentiated level as the unemployment benefit are payable in cases of reduction in working hours, but for a maximum of six months (*Kurzarbeitergeld*). The same applies with respect to the loss of work due to bad weather.

In cases of insolvency of the employer, employees receive a benefit equal to their net labour wage, as already stated, for the income loss of a maximum period of three months (*Insolvenzgeld*). In addition to the payments made for income losses, social security contributions are paid to the social security institutions.

4.5. Health and long-term care

The medical care branch of the health insurance scheme provides for a whole series of diverse benefits. There are benefits of a preventive character, for example the annual check-ups for specific categories of insured individuals for certain diseases (cancer) and the granting of artificial aids and help in respect of a threatening handicap. Benefits with a curative function are to be found within the package for medical and surgical help, to be distinguished between help to out-patients and clinical help (*Kranken- und Krankenhauspflege*). The out-patient's help encompasses treatment by a doctor or a dentist, the granting of medicine and wound dressings, as well as occupational therapy. The granting of these curative benefits is subject to further legislative conditions and limitations, e.g. the help must be truly sufficient and appropriate, yet may not exceed what is necessary. Entry into, and nursing in a hospital is indicated when this is necessary for diagnosis, treatment or cure of the disease. Instead of this, or to prevent it, nursing at home is also possible. Furthermore, the administrative body is authorised to grant treatment in a health resort (*Kurort*).

Medical and surgical help is granted through a system of benefits in kind (*Sachleistungen*) and, only by way of exception, through reimbursement of costs ensued by the insured person. The administrative body does not provide the benefits itself, but this is done by third parties, such as dentists, doctors, hospitals and pharmacists. The relationship between the *Krankenkassen* as the administrators of the insurance scheme and respectively the dentists, doctors and hospitals is regulated by legislation. It gives competence to regulate the system by contracts (collective agreements). The concerned parties are united in organisations on a federal state, and on a *Land,* level and on these levels they negotiate. Such negotiations should result in agreements governed by public law; if not, a court of arbitration determines similar agreements. Individual dentists, doctors and hospitals may only become involved in treatment with the permission of the administrative authorities of the sickness (costs) insurance scheme. If permission is refused by the competent authorities, appeal is possible to the *Sozialgerichte*. The insured person has the freedom of choice of doctor, dentist and hospital.

Insured persons are not only entitled to benefits for themselves, but also to benefits for their spouses and their dependent children, albeit with the exception of sick leave payment. There is a condition that the family members of the insured person can not have any income in excess of a certain level. *Familienhilfe* has no effect upon the contributions to be paid by the insured person.

The long-term care insurance provides benefits in kind or in cash for long-term care at the house of the person entitled or in specific institutions. Three categories of persons are distinguished, depending upon their degree of need for long-term care. In the first place, there are the people who need help at least once a day for at least two activities in the fields of personal hygiene, alimentation or mobility and the people who require help with household tasks several times a week (considerable need). Second, there are the persons in need of help at least three times a day at different hours and in respect of household affairs (severe need). Last, there are those people who need help around the clock (day and night) and also require help in the household.
Furthermore a distinction is to be made whether the benefits concern home care or institutional care. Concerning home care, a benefit in kind is provided for in the first place. It means that the person in need can use a home care service at the expense of the insurance, although this is limited by a statutorily provided maximum amount. Costs exceeding this amount are to be borne by the persons in need themselves. Next, benefits in cash are provided when a third person takes care of the person in need. The allowance is paid to the person in need himself and is not liable to taxation. It is to the beneficiary's discretion whether the sum or part of it will be forwarded to the carer as a reward or remuneration. In case the usual third person is not available, the long-term insurance pays the expenses for another care person for four weeks a year. The combination of both benefits is only possible to a certain extent. All home care benefits differ according to the category the beneficiary belongs to. In addition, the long-term care insurance bears the costs for nursing aids and supplements and the care related construction works at the beneficiary's home up to a certain sum per measure. Training courses for honorary care persons and family members are moreover offered free of charge.
In case of institutional care, the costs for board and lodging are to be borne by the persons in need themselves. Other benefits in kind however, are provided for up to a certain amount per month, regardless the category the beneficiary

belongs to. Concerning this limit, an exception can be made for persons of the third category in order to avoid social hardship.

4.6. Family

German social security law contains a number of diverse benefits in respect of the economic burden of the family.

Thus, *Kindergeld* is payable to everyone who maintains a child, irrespective of marital status, for one's own or adopted children, provided that the children belong to your household or get alimony in cash. When more than one person is entitled to benefit, the actual maintenance of the child is decisive. Benefit is only payable until the moment that the child becomes 16 years old. Subject to further conditions (especially concerning study or occupational training) the limit is extended to 27 years of age, or even more. *Kindergeld* forms a legislatively fixed supplement to the family's income. Its amount varies according to the number of children and the income of the family. *Erziehungsgeld* is payable to parents with a child less than one year old, living within the household. The parents must be alone in the upbringing of the child and, as a consequence, carry out no or little work (i.e., less than 19 hours per week). *Erziehungsgeld* is especially aimed at encouraging the working parent to devote time to the raising of the child. For parents in similar circumstances, under labour law one may be entitled to *Erziehungsurlaub*, which is complementary to *Erziehungsgeld*. However, *Erziehungsgeld* is equally granted to the parent with no labour record. The benefit is flat-rate and only available for the first six months, it is non means-tested but income-tested. Since 1993 it is paid for a maximum of two years.

Finally, a single parent benefit (*Unterhaltsvorschuß* or *Unterhaltsausfallleistung*) will be paid to children under the age of 12 living in a single parent household and being resident in Germany, if maintenance is not paid by the other parent (due to unwillingness, death, ...) The benefit will not be paid for more than six years. The income and capital of the parent with whom the child lives has no influence upon the (scope of) entitlement to benefit. The maintenance liability in respect of the child is subrogated to the administrative authorities.

4.7. Need

The *Bundessozialhilfegesetz* offers coverage for the risk of an existing emergency situation in the form of requirements which cannot be met by the individual himself, and thus is coupled with need. In certain circumstances the danger of the (re)occurrence of an emergency situation may also give rise to entitlement to benefit. Benefits are in principle not payable in respect of the past. The cause of the need is of no importance. A distinction is made between need in respect of living costs (general need) and special needs; the special needs are defined with reference to specific situations, such as sickness, blindness, need of long-term care, handicap, old age or pregnancy (*Hilfe in beson-*

deren Lebenslagen). With regard to benefits for general needs there is a right to benefit. Benefits for special needs are granted, subject to the discretion of the competent administrative bodies.

The benefits in respect of special needs are nearly all benefits in kind. On the contrary, general needs give rise to entitlement to cash benefits, the *Hilfe zum Lebensunterhalt*. The level of this benefit is determined according to a mechanism set up by legislation on a federal state level; according to the *Bundessozialhilfegesetz* the amount of benefit payable must be below the wage level of the lowest paid wage groups. The characteristic of this scheme is its subsidiary nature. This implies that the granting of a benefit is subject to an unlimited income and asset test of the claimant and of the people within his household.

5. *Financing*

Two thirds of social security expenditures are financed out of contributions. The level of contributions is dependent upon two factors, the basis of calculation of the contributions and the contribution rate. The basis of contribution is respectively made up of the wage or the income from employment. In delegated legislation these concepts are to a large extent harmonised with the relevant concepts under taxation law. There is a statutorily fixed wage ceiling for contribution liability (*Beitragsbemessungsgrenze*). In the health insurance scheme this limit is 75% below that of the remaining insurance schemes and at the same time it forms the *Versicherungspflichtgrenze*. This means, employees earning more than this wage ceiling are dispensed from coverage in health insurance. Within the health insurance scheme the contribution rate is determined by the *Krankenkassen*; for the other insurance schemes it is determined by statute. The contribution level must be sufficient. This means that the income from contributions together with other income (for example from capital), is sufficient to cover the expenditure of a given year. Thus, apart from a compulsory reserve, the system operates upon the 'pay as you go principle'.

In respect of those who carry out wage labour, the employer and employee each pay half the contributions for the insurance schemes, except for the injuries insurance schemes. However, only the former must actually pay contributions; the employer may deduct the contributions payable by the employees from their wages. For people with a small income, i.e. less than 10% of the *Beitragsbemessungsgrenze*, the employer must make all contribution payments at his own expense. Equally, the employers are responsible for all the contributions regarding the injuries insurance scheme, the *Insolvenzversicherung* and the *Winterbauförderung*. This arises from the special character of these insurance schemes (covering employers risks). For all these schemes there is a special basis of calculation of the premiums. Sometimes it is the insured person himself who is liable to pay all the contributions. This is the case for self-employed persons and for voluntarily insured persons. Finally, in some cases contributions are paid by a third party, not being the employer. For example, the administrative bodies which are responsible for the payment of income maintenance benefits may operate as such.

The contributions for all the insurance schemes are collected by the *Krankenkassen* as so called *Gesamtversicherungsbeitrag*. These *Krankenkassen* decide in cases concerning contribution liability. Besides income from contributions, State subsidies (*Zuschüsse*) also play an important role within the old age and invalidity insurance and the unemployment insurance.

The State also finances all the social security benefits outside the sphere of the insurance schemes; the source of this financing is general taxation. The Federation is responsible for all the costs arising from the *Bundesversorgungsgesetz*, *Arbeitslosenhilfe*, *Kindergeld* and *Erziehungsgeld*. The Federation and the states each bear half the costs of the *Unterhaltsvorschüsse*; the costs of the *Opferentschädigung* are met in a ratio of 40:60 respectively. The states are wholly responsible for the expenditure arising from the *Bundesseuchengesetz*. Finally, the expenditure of the *Sozialhilfe* is met respectively by the *kreisfreie Städte*, the *Kreise* and, to a small extent, by the states.

Employers dismissing older workers who worked for many years with them, may have to take financial responsibility for the unemployment benefits to be paid to these older unemployed persons.

6. Judicial review

In 1953 the *Sozialgerichtsgesetz* introduced a special branch in the judicial system for the settlement of social security disputes, which is separate from the general administrative system for the settlement of disputes. However, judicial review via the *Sozialgerichtsgesetz* does not extend to all social security law. It is limited to disputes within the framework of the social insurance scheme, the remaining tasks of the *Bundesanstalt für Arbeit*, the *soziale Entschädigung* and the relations between physician and health insurance (*Vertragsartzrecht*). Other social security disputes are subject to the jurisdiction of the administrative courts (*Verwaltungsgerichtsbarkeit*).

The *Sozialgerichtsgesetz* firstly regulates the existence and the composition of three different judicial authorities, i.e. the *Sozialgericht*, the *Landessozialgericht* and the *Bundessozialgericht*. The *Sozialgericht* consists of a professional judge and two lay judges. The other tribunals are composed of three professional judges and two lay judges. The lay judges are appointed by the state on the recommendation of the organisations for employers, employees, doctors, handicapped people and victims of war.

The procedure is set in process by the lodging of a complaint with the competent *Sozialgericht*. In some cases the lodging of a complaint entails a preliminary procedure. This *Vorverfahren* does not belong to the actual judicial procedure and gives the administrative body the opportunity to reconsider the legality and the suitability of its decision.

The procedure according to the *Sozialgerichtsgesetz* is characterised by a number of procedural principles. Thus there is the so called principle of easy access

to court (*Klägerfreundlichkeit*). This results for example, in a large degree of freedom of form, the absence of obligatory representation in the first two instances and in the fact that the procedure is costless. Another important principle is that of *Amtsermittelungsgrundsatz,* which obliges the judge to search independently for the truth; he does not play a passive role. The final procedural principle is the right to be heard; according to this principle an oral hearing forms the heart of the process. The tribunals make their decisions on the basis of the oral hearing.
In principle, the decision of a judge is expressed in a judgement. However, if a judge regards the appeal as inadmissible, or without grounds, he can settle it by reasoned decision. Nevertheless, parties still have the opportunity of enforcing an oral hearing of their case.

In principle, decisions of the *Sozialgerichte* are subject to further appeal with the *Landessozialgerichte*. The *Sozialgerichtsgesetz* contains an exhaustive list of cases, in respect of which further appeal is excluded. Among others, such cases concern disputes relating to lump sum benefits or benefits with a duration of less than three months. In principle there is no appeal against a decision of the *Landessozialgericht*. However, in certain cases the *Landessozialgericht* or the *Bundessozialgericht* may give leave to a plaintiff for a revision of the decision by the *Bundessozialgericht*. The disputes must then either involve points of law of fundamental significance, a judgement which deviates from a decision of the *Bundessozialgericht*, or certain procedural irregularities. The revision serves, in the first place, legal certainty and also the development of the law. For this purpose a separate chamber has been established within the *Bundessozialgericht*, the so called *Großer Senat*. This chamber decides on cases in which a chamber of the *Bundessozialgericht* intends to deviate from a decision of another chamber, as well as in cases of fundamental significance.

To the extent that the competence for judicial review does not lie with the *Sozialgerichte*, the administrative courts (*Verwaltungsgerichte*) are competent. The procedure regulated in the *Verwaltungsgerichtsordnung* mostly corresponds to that of the *Sozialgerichtsgesetz* and is characterised by equivalent principles. Here too, judicial review is carried out by three judicial bodies, i.e. the *Verwaltungsgerichte*, the *Oberverwaltungsgerichte* and the *Bundesverwaltungsgericht*. A preliminary procedure before the actual process begins (*Widerspruchsverfahren*) also exists.

Chapter Seven

GREAT BRITAIN

1. Introduction: concept and sources of social security law

The institutional concept of social security law covers benefit schemes which provide cash benefits under the competence of the Department of Social Security.
The social security benefits may be divided into three categories:
1) *contributory benefits.* These are insurance benefits which exist for the risks of unemployment, pregnancy, incapacity for work, old age and death.
2) *non-contributory benefits.* These are benefits financed out of general taxation for the risks of disability and old age, they are intended for specific categories of people who are not covered by the insurance system. This category also includes child benefits.
3) *means tested benefits.* These benefits are also financed out of general taxation, albeit that they are subject to a means test. Means tested benefits include *income support* and *family credit.*

Medical care, as provided by the *National Health Service,* is traditionally excluded from the ambit of social security. However, in line with the framework chosen for this work, we shall nevertheless pay some attention to this service. The same applies to *statutory benefits*, which are payable by the employers.

The most important source of social security law is the statute. Nonetheless, the statutes merely offer a general framework of legislation. The main body of material law is contained in a range of *statutory instruments* (commonly referred to as 'regulations'). The regulations are enacted by the Secretary of State in pursuance of specific delegation powers laid down in the statutes. A third source of social security law is case law, this plays a role in clarifying vague legal concepts and in assessing the validity of 'delegated' legislation.

Most social security legislative provisions refer to "Great Britain" as a geographical unit. Thus, the general legislation applies to England, Wales and Scotland. Other parts of the British Isles, such as the Channel Islands, the Isle of Man and Northern Ireland fall outside the territorial scope of British social security law. However, legislation applicable to Northern Ireland is often similar to legislation in Great Britain.

2. Administrative organisation

The administration of social security in Great Britain lies almost exclusively in the hands of the *Department of Social Security (DSS)* under the authority of a *Secretary of State*. The DSS is the competent department concerning the administration of all social security schemes which provide cash benefits. The scheme for unemployed people (*the jobseeker's allowance*) is jointly administered by the *Benefits Agency* and the *Employment Service* of the *Department for Education and Employment*. Housing benefit and council tax benefit are paid through local government departments.

Since April 1991 most operational tasks within the Department have been undertaken by separate executive bodies, known as *'Next Steps Agencies'*, in which the great majority of the Department's staff work. By far the largest of these units is the *Benefits Agency* which is responsible for the delivery of benefits through some 500 local offices in some 125 districts in 2 territories. These offices usually deal with routine administration of the social security schemes. The Benefit Directorate in Newcastle deals, among others, with the administration of contribution records, while another in North Fylde concerns itself with claims for war pensions, *constant attendance allowance* and *income support*). A *Child Support Agency* and a *War Pension Agency* were also created and have been given some social security related tasks. In order to improve the efficiency and quality of administration *'one stop services'* have been introduced, enabling customers to obtain information on all benefits and to lodge claims for any benefit through one single point of contact. Within the *Benefits Agency* a special branch was created to co-ordinate anti-fraud activities.

The departmental headquarters remain responsible for policy development and central research allocation. Decisions concerning individual cases are taken by *adjudication officers*. These are active in the local offices of the Benefits Agency and in the *job centres*. The *adjudication officers* act independently of the department, but are subject to the directives and guidance of the *chief adjudication officer*. The latter is required to report annually to the Secretary of State on the standards of adjudication.

The *Department of Health* is responsible for the administration of the *National Health Service (N.H.S.)*.

At the operational level three divisions are distinguished: the personal practitioner services (doctors, dentists, etc.), which conclude agreements with the competent authorities, *N.H.S.* managed hospitals (each district has a general district hospital and one or more specialised hospitals) and the *community health services*, e.g. home help and family planning.

The *District Health Authorities* are responsible for the hospitals and the *community health services*. These bodies consist of up to eleven members, the chairman of which is appointed by the Secretary of State. Most of the other members are representatives of the medical profession or officers of the District Health Authorities. The *District Health Authorities* are advised by *District Management Teams*, of which most of its members are medical specialists.

On a higher organisational level there are the *Regional Health Authorities* which are appointed by the minister to carry out supervisory and administrative tasks. The minister himself, as head of the Department of Health, is responsible for the overall strategic control of the *N.H.S.*

It appears from the administrative structure of the British social security system that the authority of the State in the running of the social security schemes is virtually omnipotent. The recent trend towards privatisation, which puts greater emphasis on the role of new 'statutory' benefits administered by the employers, does little to change this. In fact only the routine application and administration of these benefits is dealt with by the employers; the detailed provisions of the statutes leave the employers little room for discretion.

The administrative structure does not make provision for the insured population to be directly involved in the administration. They can only voice their opinions via advisory bodies such as the *Social Security Advisory Committee*. Within the sphere of the *N.H.S.*, the *Community Health Councils* watch over the interests of the patients.

3. *Personal scope of application*

Both employees and self-employed people belong to the group of compulsorily insured people for *contributory benefits*, although the insurance scheme for the latter does not continue during unemployment and incapacity. Thus it is important to distinguish between these two categories.

An employee is a person who is gainfully employed on the basis of an apprenticeship or a contract of employment.
This rule is further elaborated in case law, which recognises a number of relevant factors, the relative importance of which vary from case to case. Important factors to be considered are, among others, the question of who bears the financial risk of the professional activity, whether there is supervision of the work, whether the person can send a substitute to do his job or whether there is discretion as regards the hours of work, etc. In regulations issued by the Secretary of State, certain activities are specifically classified as employed activities, e.g. cleaning and agency work. Special rules to this effect apply to the insurance scheme for industrial injuries and occupational diseases; here for example probationers and firemen are considered as employees. Self-employed people are not covered by the insurance scheme for industrial injuries or occupational diseases at all.

Apart from compulsorily insured people there are also voluntarily insured people. Voluntary insurance is available to all employees and self-employed people who satisfy the relevant contribution conditions, to self-employed people who are not covered by the compulsory insurance scheme, for example because of low income, and to certain categories of non-active people.

The types of contributions payable are divided into five classes (see section 5). Employees and their employers pay class 1 contributions, the self-employed class 2 and 4 contributions and the voluntarily insured class 3 contributions. Employers only pay class 1A contributions in respect of their employee's private use of company cars. The scope of coverage and the contribution rates are different for each class. Employees paying class 1 contributions are insured against all risks. The self-employed paying class 2 contributions are excluded from entitlement to benefit during unemployment and incapacity. Class 3 contributions are only made for the purpose of insurance against death and old age. Class 1A and 4 contributions are pure taxes, giving rise to no benefit entitlement.

Both compulsory and voluntary insurance are subject to age limits, i.e. from 16 years up to pensionable age.

The personal scope of application of the *non-contributory benefits*, *means tested benefits* and *child benefit* is delimited on the basis of territorial criteria. In respect of some benefits the 'residence test' is fairly simple and straightforward. Thus, for example, in respect of *income support* it is merely required that a person is present in Great Britain on the day of the claim. Other benefits, however, impose much more stringent residence conditions. Thus, with regard to *severe disablement allowance, constant attendance allowance, invalid care allowance* and *disability living allowance* the basic conditions are that the claimant must have been:

1) present in Great Britain on the day that the allowance is claimed;
2) ordinarily resident in Great Britain at the time of the claim;
3) present in Great Britain for at least 26 weeks in the past year.

For certain categories of people (e.g. the terminally ill) there are less stringent conditions.

Apart from residence conditions, each scheme imposes certain other qualifying conditions which result in a further delimitation of the personal scope of application. For example, war pensions are only payable to former members of the armed forces.

The essential feature of the *National Health Service* is that it covers all people who are in need of medical care in Great Britain. Nonetheless, the applicable legislation allows the Secretary of State to enact regulations providing for the recovery of charges from people who are not ordinarily resident in Great Britain.

4. Risks and benefits

Before embarking upon a discussion of the various risks and benefits, attention must be paid to two general points which are relevant for all the insurance schemes, i.e. the contribution conditions and the benefit structure.

Entitlement to all contributory benefits depends upon the fulfilment of contribution conditions. These conditions are not the same for all benefits.

For the right to *contribution-based jobseeker's allowance* and *incapacity benefit* the insured person must:
- have paid contributions in one of the last two years preceding the tax year in which the benefit is claimed (*contribution-based jobseeker's allowance*) or in any year before the benefit is claimed (*incapacity benefit*), on an income corresponding to at least 25 times the lower weekly contributions limit in that year;
- have paid or been credited contributions in each of the last two tax years preceding the claim, over an income corresponding to at least 50 times the lower weekly contributions limit in that year.

In order to be entitled to *maternity allowance* only one contribution condition is imposed: within the 52 weeks preceding the 14th week before the expected date of birth, the insured person must have paid at least 26 weekly contributions.

Also for the *widow's payment* there is only one condition: that the late husband of the widow has paid contributions during any one year on an income corresponding to at least 25 times the lower contributions limit.

The right to *widowed mother's allowance, widow's pension* and *retirement pension* is again dependent upon the fulfilment of a double contribution condition. The insured person must:
- have paid contributions during any one year on an income that corresponds to at least 52 times the lower contributions limit in that year;
- have paid or been credited contributions for not less than 90% of his working life on an income again corresponding to 52 times the lower contributions limit.

If a person only satisfies part of the latter condition, benefit is paid at a reduced rate (subject to a minimum contribution condition).

Certain categories of people who are clearly established within the contributory scheme (this must be apparent through the people having paid a certain number of contributions), but who have failed to make the requisite number of contributions for making up entitlement to benefit, are credited with contributions. Credit facilities are open to, among others, unemployed people and people incapable of work, those caring full time for invalids and new entrants to the contributory scheme.

If the entitlement conditions of the contributory benefits are satisfied, the claimant has the right to a basic benefit. Furthermore, subject to the satisfaction of further conditions, there may be a right to additions for an adult dependant, usually the spouse of the claimant, and/or for any children.

In principle, the right to additions for children exists only in respect of long-term benefits; in respect of short term benefits only those above pensionable

age are entitled to such additions. Entitlement to an addition exists when the following conditions are satisfied:
- the claimant concerned must be entitled to *child benefit* in respect of the child;
- the child must live with the claimant or be maintained by him/her;
- when a person is married or cohabiting, the partner's income may not exceed a certain level.

The right to an adult dependant addition exists first of all for the spouse of the person entitled to the basic benefit. The latter must live together with his/her spouse or maintain him/her. Furthermore, the income of the spouse may not exceed a certain level.

The right to an adult dependant addition also exists for an adult who is caring for the children of the entitled person (a child carer). Here, too, the right to the addition is subject to the conditions that the entitled person lives with the dependant or maintains him and that the income of the dependant does not exceed a certain level.

Basic contributory benefits, as well as the dependency additions, are flat-rate. Furthermore, in the area of widow's and retirement pensions, there may be a right to certain earnings related supplements under the *State Earnings-Related Pension Scheme (S.E.R.P.S.)*. These supplements are calculated on the basis of payment of contributions on the income that is 52 times the lower earnings limit. Over a maximum period of 20 years a person will build up pension rights up to a maximum of 25% of the upper minimum income level.

The contribution liability constitutes a certain percentage of the weekly earnings above the lower earnings limit. In the period of 20 years a person will build up pension rights up to a maximum of 25% of his extra-minimal earnings. For each year that a person contributes less than 20 years, the pension rate will be reduced by 1%. As the system was first introduced in 1978, no full supplements will be payable until the end of this century. However changes in the social security law mean that, for people retiring after 1998, the maximum amount of *S.E.R.P.S.* payable will be only 20% of a person's extra earnings over their whole working career. However, this change will not become fully effective until the year 2010.

The Secretary of State is legally bound to review annually most of the social security benefits. The increase in benefits has usually been based on the impact of inflation in a twelve month period before the uprating.

4.1. Old age

The right to *contributory retirement pension* exists for all people who have attained pensionable age (60 for women, 65 for men) and who satisfy the contribution conditions. Over the period from 2011 to 2020 the age for women will be raised to 65.

A claimant's earnings do not affect the pension, although an addition may not be payable for an adult dependant if the latter receives any income from work.

A person may defer drawing his pension and carry on working for a maximum period of five years, i.e. up to the age of 65 (women) or 70 (men). The deferred pension is increased by 7.5% for every year (up to five years) that the retirement is postponed.

Approximately half the working population enjoys some additional protection from occupational pension schemes, which are established on a collective or individual basis. If their occupational pensions are considered to offer sufficient protection, these people are offered the opportunity to opt out of *S.E.R.P.S.*

Non-contributory retirement pensions exist for two special categories of people. Here contribution conditions are replaced by residence conditions. The level of these benefits is markedly lower than that of the contributory retirement pensions.
All pensioners over 80 years receive a very small weekly *age-addition* on top of their pension.

4.2. Death

Subject to the fulfilment of contribution conditions, a widow is entitled to a number of benefits. When the death of the spouse is due to an industrial injury or an occupational disease, no contribution conditions are applicable. On the death of her spouse, a widow is, in the first place, entitled to a *widow's payment,* which is a flat rate benefit payable in a lump sum.
Furthermore, there are two periodic benefits, i.e. the *widowed mother's allowance* and the *widow's pension.* The former benefit is intended for the widow who is expecting a child of her deceased spouse or who already has a child in respect of whom she receives child benefit.

A widow, who at the time of death of her spouse or at the time of the termination of the *widowed mother's allowance* has attained the age of 45, has the right to a *widow's pension.* If the widow has attained the age of 55 or older at these times, she receives the maximum pension. For every year that she is younger than 55 there is a reduction of 7% in the pension. For the further duration of the benefit this reduction is not reversed.
The right to benefits terminates if the widow remarries. A *war widow's pension* however is reinstated on termination of the subsequent marriage.
If the widow cohabits with a man, the right to benefit is suspended for the duration of the cohabitation.

Those who have an orphan living with them or who maintain an orphan who gives rise to entitlement to *child benefit*, are entitled to a *guardian's allowance.* Entitlement to this allowance depends upon the fulfilment of residence conditions.

4.3. Incapacity for work

A person who is physically or mentally incapable of work, and who satisfies the relevant contribution conditions, is entitled to contributory *incapacity benefit*. The first three days of incapacity count as waiting days; the maximum duration of the benefit is 28 weeks. Whereas this scheme was previously restricted to short term incapacity, it now also covers long term incapacity for work. After 28 weeks of incapacity or from the start of the incapacity, if the claimant had no regular job, an 'all works test' is being applied in order to determine the degree of incapacity. The claimant, his personal medical doctor and an official medical doctor are involved in the assessment of the medical condition of the claimant. This medical assessment concerns his ability to carry out a range of work-related activities. In principle, the same test is applied throughout all social security, whenever incapacity for work needs to be assessed. Three rates of *incapacity benefit* are being distinguished: the highest is payable after 52 weeks, except for a small number of severely ill or disabled persons, which are already eligible after 28 weeks.

In practice for most employees the importance of *incapacity benefit* is very minor. For the first 28 weeks of their incapacity they are entitled to *statutory sick pay*, payable by the employer. The entitlement conditions for this benefit are very similar to those for *incapacity benefit*, but the flat-rate amount is higher, although there are no additions for dependants Through individual or collective labour agreements many employees are guaranteed extra protection.
If incapacity for work continues after the maximum duration of the statutory sick pay or there is no entitlement to it, there is a right to *incapacity benefit*. This incapacity must not only exclude the person from his own work but also from other suitable employment.

A person may be disqualified from receiving *incapacity benefit* or *statutory sick pay* during a period of up to six weeks, if he became incapable of work through his own misconduct or if he fails without good cause to attend for or submit himself to medical or other treatment.

Various benefits exist for long term incapacity caused by industrial injuries and occupational diseases, or as a result of military service; there are also *non-contributory benefits* in respect of special groups of handicapped people.

When, as a result of an industrial injury or an occupational disease, there is a loss of physical or mental capacity, a right to *disablement benefit* exists. There does not have to be a loss of earning capacity, but the self-employed are excluded. No contribution conditions are applied. *Disablement benefit* is payable from the fifteenth week after the accident, and may continue until the death of the beneficiary. The amount of the benefit depends upon the extent of the disability. This is judged by comparing the disabled claimant with a person of the same age and the same sex whose physical and mental state is normal.
Special supplements are payable on top of the disablement benefit to those with 100% disablement and therefore requiring constant attendance: *constant attendance allowance* and *exceptionally severe disablement allowance*.

The scheme for *war disablement pensions* largely resembles that for industrial accidents and occupational diseases. The pension is payable in respect of disablement which is attributable to service in the British forces. Here too the amount of the pensions depends upon the extent of the disablement, and extra supplements and allowances are payable on top of the basic pension.

The following *non-contributory* benefits are payable in respect of invalidity:
1. *disability living allowance*, payable to severely disabled people under the age of 66 who need help with personal care and/or getting about;
2. *attendance allowance*, payable to severely disabled people over the age of 65 who require continuous attention or supervision by another person;
3. *invalid care allowance*, payable to a person between the ages of 16 and 65, who is providing regular and substantial care for someone in receipt of specific disability benefits, and who, as a result, is not available for employment, or for full-time education;
4. *disability working allowance*, payable after a means test to people in full-time employment whose earning capacity is affected by illness or disability;
5. *severe disablement allowance*, payable to long term severely handicapped people who normally do not qualify for benefits under the war pensions or contributory benefit schemes.

A woman who satisfies the relevant contribution conditions is entitled to *contributory maternity allowance*, for 18 weeks starting from between 11 to 6 weeks preceding the expected date of birth. A woman may be disqualified from receiving benefit if she fails to attend a medical examination or if she is engaged in any employment. In view of the existence of a *statutory maternity pay* scheme (payable by the employers), the *contributory maternity allowance* has little practical importance; the statutory scheme is available to all female employees who have worked for the same employer for at least 26 weeks and in addition have average earnings in excess of the lower earnings limit. Benefit covers the same period as the *contributory maternity allowance*. During the first 6 weeks the benefit amounts to 90% of the normal weekly income, providing that the claimant has worked for the same employer for 16 hours per week for two consecutive years (or 8 hours per week for five consecutive years). If the claimant does not satisfy all the necessary conditions, as for the period after the expiry of the first 6 weeks, she is only entitled to a flat rate benefit.

4.4. Unemployment

Jobseeker's allowance has replaced both contributory unemployment benefit and means-tested income support for unemployed people with a single benefit which has two elements - contribution-based and income-based. The first is dependent on the meeting of contribution conditions with an allowance at income support rate paid only for the person out of work for a maximum of 26 weeks according to age (under 18; 18 - 24 and 25 and over). The receipt of any occupational or personal pension above a low amount will result in a reduction of the allowance.

The contribution-based jobseeker's allowance is payable for a maximum of 26 weeks: after that it cannot be paid until the contribution conditions have been met in a new benefit year.

If the maximum period has been exhausted or there is no entitlement to the contribution-based element, income-based jobseeker's allowance may be paid if income and savings are low enough. This is closely comparable to income support (see 4.7 below) and is dependent upon a test of means. The basic allowance is the same, but there are additional allowances for adult and child dependants, and premiums for family and disability.

A person is not eligible for the allowance during the first three days of unemployment. Periods of unemployment are added together if they are interrupted by periods of not claiming shorter than 13 weeks.

The unemployed person must be available for and capable of work; be actively seeking work; and have a personal jobseeker's agreement in force which specifies the type of work sought and the actual steps to be taken to look for work and to improve the chances of finding work.
If a person has lost his employment through his own misconduct, or has voluntarily left his employment without just cause, he will be disqualified from receiving benefit for a maximum period of 26 weeks. The same is possible if the unemployed person refuses to accept or fails to apply for employment without good cause. People are also disqualified from benefit if they are unemployed by reason of a stoppage of work, due to a trade dispute at their place of work. However, this disqualification rule does not apply for those who are not directly interested in the trade dispute, or who otherwise do not withdraw their labour in pursuance of it.
The unemployed person is obliged to sign on at the job centre office, this is usually done every two weeks, and to be actively seeking employment.

There are special rules with regard to the position of certain groups of unemployed people, such as fishermen and seasonal workers. The same applies for part-time workers and those whose contract of employment is suspended until more work is available.

4.5. Health care

The *National Health Service (N.H.S.)* is open to all British residents. Among other things, it provides care by general practitioners; the general practitioners have a contract with the local *N.H.S.* branch. Equally covered is the entry into and care in an *N.H.S.* hospital. The beneficiary is not required to pay any personal contributions for either of these two services. This is not the case for optical or dental care; for the latter the beneficiary is liable for 80% of the costs, albeit up to a certain maximum level. Certain people are excluded from the payment of dental charges such as, for example, pregnant women and women who have recently given birth, juveniles up to 16, 18 or 19 years of age, depending upon their circumstances, and people on means-tested benefits or with low income. People may qualify for free sight tests and vouchers for glasses or contact lenses depending on their age, any income from means-tested benefit they may receive and their health, including the degree of poor sight. The vouchers may not cover the full cost. There is also a flat-rate, personal contribution for all prescribed medicine but, here too, different categories of people are excluded from payment such as, for example, people under 16 years of age (or under 19 if still in full-time education) and those who are 60 or over, as well as and persons on means-tested benefits or with low income.

4.6. Family

Above we have seen that there are dependency additions payable on top of social security benefits in respect of the children of the beneficiary. Besides this, the *child benefit* scheme aims at helping to meet the costs of bringing up children. Entitlement to *child benefit* exists for every child up to the age of 16 or up to the age of 19 if the child is still in full-time non-advanced education. It may also be paid for a short 'extension' period if seeking employment and receiving no other income immediately after leaving school. The child must live with the beneficiary or be maintained by him. Residence conditions apply in respect of both the child and the beneficiary.
Child benefit is, at present, paid at three rates. The higher rate for the elder eligible child is increased even further if he is living with a single parent (but this is due to be abolished in April 1998).

The *family credit* scheme is intended for low paid workers with children. Those who claim benefit (or whose partner claims benefit) must be carrying out paid work for a minimum time of 16 hours per week, be it as an employee or as a self-employed person. Besides this, there must be at least one child of 16 years of age or younger, or between the ages of 16 and 19 years of age, who follows full-time education. Again residence conditions apply.
The right to maximum *family credit* exists when the income or capital of the family falls below a legally fixed threshold. If the family income lies above this threshold, the maximum credit is reduced by a percentage of the amount by which the income exceeds the threshold.
The maximum *credit* consists of an adult credit and child credits for each child. The former is the same for a beneficiary with a partner and for one without a partner, but is increased if an adult works more than 30 hours a week. There are three different *credits* for children depending upon their age, and *credits* for additional partner in a polygamous marriage.
A characteristic feature of this benefit is that it is payable for a period of 26 weeks, during which no account is taken of a change in circumstances.

The *Child Support Agency* has the responsibility for the means-tested support of people for whom child maintenance is an issue and assists in the collection of any maintenance due from absent parents.

4.7. Need

The *income support* scheme (including income-based *job-seeker's* allowance) acts as a safety net under the social security system. In order to be entitled to benefit, the means of the claimant (income and capital excluding the value of the home) must lie below a legally applicable level. Besides this, there are a number of supplementary conditions. Thus, in principle, one must be 18 years of age or older (or between 16 and 18 and belonging to a specific category of persons), be present in Britain, not be in full-time employment (normally, 16 or more hours per week) and be available for work. This last condition does not apply to everybody; those above a certain age, those caring for children or ill family members and those who are incapable for work are excluded.

The '*applicable amount*' constitutes the starting point for the calculation of *income support*. This amount is made-up of three separate parts, i.e. the *personal allowance*, any *premiums* and the *housing costs*. The personal *allowance* constitutes the basis of *income support*. Standard amounts exist for married couples, single parents, single persons and children. Within these categories various amounts apply which are dependent upon the age of the claimant.
Fixed *premiums* are paid on top of the basic amounts in respect of family responsibility, age and disability. The increases are also standardised. There is no possibility of obtaining income support payments for exceptional costs.
Housing costs constitute the final part of *income support*. These consist of payments mainly covering the expenses of owner occupiers. People in rented accommodation are covered by the *housing benefit* scheme.
Special rules apply for different categories of people, such as, for example, those who have been admitted into residential accommodation or a hospital.
After the applicable amount for the claimant has been determined, the next step is to determine his means which include those of any partner and a contribution from adult non-dependants. A limited amount of income and capital may be disregarded. The difference between these two amounts constitutes the amount of *income support* payable.
Income support for families is not granted individually but on a household basis, i.e. in respect of the claimant, the claimant's partner and any children. Married people and cohabitants are treated the same.

Apart from the *income support* scheme, some attention should be given to the *social fund*. This fund provides benefits for special needs. Some benefits are granted on a discretionary basis, others according to regulation.

The regulated *social fund* provides three types of payment to people already receiving certain specified means-tested benefits. The *maternity expenses payment* is a flat-rate benefit which is intended to defray some of the costs of giving birth. The *funeral expenses payment* compensates for certain costs arising from a funeral. Both benefits are means tested. The '*cold weather payment*' is a small fixed amount automatically allocated to many categories of *income support* recipients with pensioner or disability premiums or with a young child, for each period of seven days of exceptionally cold weather.

Three more benefits are payable out of the *social fund* on a discretionary basis, *budgeting loans, crisis loans* and *community care grants*. Each of these benefits is means tested. The first two benefits are payable as a loan, subject to a maximum limit. The *budgeting loans* are meant to cover sudden expenses for which a person has no reserves. Certain costs are excluded from indemnification, others are given priority. *Crisis loans* are intended for emergencies, in which there are not enough personal means to meet certain unavoidable costs. Some people are excluded from receiving *crisis loans*; furthermore, certain expenses are excluded from *crisis loan* coverage. Guidelines determine in which situations *crisis and budgeting loans* should be granted.

The *community care grants* help people in their return to, or maintenance in the community. Here too, certain expenses are not covered by the grant. Guidelines determine in which situations a grant should be awarded.

In the awarding of discretionary payments account should be taken of the fact that there is only a limited budget available which is set annually for each local office. There is no right of appeal against decisions concerning the granting of benefits, but merely an internal review procedure.

Home-owners on income support may claim payment to cover their housing costs (e.g. interest on a housing loan or mortgage subject to a ceiling on the size of the loan). Except for those aged 60 or over, no payment is made for the first 39 weeks of receiving income support if the loan was taken out after 1 October 1995, but there is full payment afterwards subject to the ceiling. For mortgages raised earlier, nothing is paid for the first 8 weeks on income support, then 50% for the next 18 weeks and the full rate after that subject to the ceiling.

People who have a low income and who pay rent, whether or not the person is in employment or receiving any other benefit, may apply for housing benefit paid on a means-tested basis. Similarly, those who have to pay council tax on property which they normally occupy as their home, whether they own or rent it, may receive council tax benefit on a means-tested basis. The two schemes are administered by local government, although they are national schemes and the rules are mainly determined by DSS regulations.

5. *Financing*

The costs of the *contributory benefits* are covered by the contributions paid by the insured people and the employers. The contributions are deposited in the *National Insurance Fund*. This Fund can be supplemented with funds from general taxation. In order to help meet existing spending commitments and to maintain a balance in the Fund, a treasury grant can be drawn up to a maximum amount which is defined in accordance with the estimated expenditures for that year.

Five contribution classes are distinguished. Employees and employers pay class 1 contributions. Contributions from employees are paid on all earnings up to an upper earnings limit being over seven times the amount of the lower earnings limit. For employers earnings are divided into four bands; for each band there is a specific contribution rate which increases when one reaches a higher band. The upper earnings limit does not apply for the employer; four further income bands and corresponding contribution rates are distinguished in respect of the employer.

Class 1A for private use of company cars, paid only by employers.

Class 2 contributions payable by self-employed people are flat-rate and are to be paid when earnings exceed a certain level. Self-employed people are simultaneously liable to pay class 4 contributions. These are income-related and consist of a percentage of the income of a person between certain lower and upper limits.
Finally, voluntary class 3 contributions are flat-rate.

Expenses within the framework of the *non-contributory benefits, means tested benefits* and the *child benefit* scheme are fully financed from general taxation.

The *National Health Service* is also almost entirely financed by the government. Furthermore, a small amount is born by the *National Insurance Fund*.

6. Judicial review

A more or less uniform machinery for the adjudication of benefits does exist, this operates independently of the ordinary British courts and the *DSS*.
As we have seen above, the *adjudication officers* decide in the first instance upon almost all questions concerning social security.

Appeal against the decision of the *adjudication officer* may be made within three months to the *Social Security Appeal Tribunal,* which is part of the *Independent Tribunal Service* and not of the *Department of Social Security*. Each *Tribunal* consists of three members: a legally-qualified chairman and two lay members. The *Tribunals* can, if they do not confirm the decision in issue, substitute the decision of the *adjudication officer* with a fresh one. The decision may be taken with a majority vote.

The claimant as well as the *adjudication officer* can appeal against the decisions of the *Tribunal* to a *Social Security Commissioner*. Appeals must be made with the leave of either the chairman of a *Tribunal* or a *Commissioner*. Appeal may only be made on points of law and not on points of fact. The *Commissioner* usually decides a case himself, although he can refer it back to a *Tribunal*. Apart from the *Chief Social Security Commissioner*, there are thirteen *Commissioners*.
In principle the decision of the *Commissioner* is final, albeit that further appeals on points of law may be made to the *Court of Appeal* (in England and

Wales) or the Court of Sessions (in Scotland), and even to the *House of Lords*. For this, leave is required from either the *Commissioner* or the *Court of Appeal*.

The procedure applied in *Social Security Appeal Tribunals* and before *Social Security Commissioners* is partly determined by legislative rules. These relate to matters such as the right to representation, the right to call and to cross-examine witnesses and the presence of medical assessors. The fairness of the procedure is guaranteed through the application of the *rules of natural justice*.

In addition to the usual machinery for adjudication, there are a number of special provisions.
Thus only the Secretary of State is competent to take decisions in questions concerning insurance obligations or contribution conditions. He also takes decisions relating to the granting of a number of special benefits, such as, for example, *constant attendance allowance*. Only some decisions of the Secretary of State are subject to appeal to the *High Court*.

Certain medical questions, which are relevant for entitlement to *disablement benefit*, are determined by special medical adjudicating authorities: the *Adjudication Medical Practitioners* or a *Medical* Board; appeals go to the *Medical Appeal Tribunals*. The latter is composed of three members, one of whom is a legally qualified chairman, two of whom are medical practitioners. On points of law decisions of the *Tribunals* are open to appeal to the *Social Security Commissioners*.
There is also a special adjudication procedure with regard to the entitlement to *attendance allowance* (the *Attendance Allowance Board*) and for the entitlement to war pension (*Pension Appeal Tribunals*). The *Disability Appeal Tribunals* hear appeals about disability questions within *disability living allowances* and *disability working allowances*.

Individuals who feel unjustly treated by an administrative body can complain to the *Parliamentary Commissioner for Administration*. Although the ombudsman is in fact not a part of the system for the settlement of disputes, due to his practical importance, he must still be mentioned. The ombudsman cannot alter or rescind decisions, but he can make a report on his investigations which may have some influence.

Chapter Eight

GREECE

1. Introduction: concept and sources of social security law

The Greek social security system can be divided into social insurance, social assistance and the national health scheme. The term social security is not commonly used in Greece. Instead one speaks of social insurance systems (*systima koinonikis asphalisseos*). Indeed a characteristic aspect of Greek social security is the relatively minor importance of social assistance, together with the existence of five major and a total number of over 300 social insurance schemes, the scope of protection of which may vary considerably.

The pluriformity of the social insurance schemes makes it impossible to link the concept of social insurance systematically to clearly defined social risks. This is all the more true, since the schemes also cover atypical risks, for example, the loss of income as a result of a call-up for military training (referred to below as reservists benefit) which features in the social insurance of most employees, another atypical benefit covers the destruction of agricultural production within the insurance for farmers.

Social assistance is not very developed due to the absence of a general social assistance scheme, covering all persons in need. The only existing rudimentary minimum income schemes are categorical: they cover the elderly, the handicapped, single parent families and children in need. Moreover, until recently assistance focused upon the coverage of emergency situations for example by providing relief for hundreds of thousands of refugees, victims of the civil war or victims of earthquakes. Presently, the introduction of a general assistance scheme is on the political agenda.

The main gaps of the fragmented social assistance system are often covered through so-called "mixed social security benefits". The term "mixed benefits" refers to benefits with an assistance character which are granted by the administrative bodies of social insurance schemes (for example a pension for each Greek citizen who is older than 65 years of age, living in Greece, who is not entitled to any social insurance benefit and whose income is below a certain income level).

The large number of social insurance schemes and the absence of a guaranteed general minimum income are responsible for the fact that social security law has been laid down in hundreds of legislative texts. A degree of harmonisation is urgently required and indeed efforts to this effect are currently being undertaken. Already, at this stage, the legislative framework of the social insurance schemes of the *I.K.A.* (to be discussed below) serves as a model for the other social insurance schemes. All employees who are not affiliated to another social insurance scheme are affiliated to *I.K.A.*, and the minimum benefit level under the *I.K.A.* scheme is also applicable for other social security schemes. Hence, it is obvious that we will pay attention mainly to the employee insurance schemes as administered by the *I.K.A.*

Today the Greek health care system can be characterised as a mixed system: the health care schemes of the various social insurances co-exist with the national health system (*ethniko systima ygeias*). The national health system was established by law in 1983 and designed to guarantee free health care for all residents of Greece. Although from a legal point of view the national health system constitutes the cornerstone of health care protection, this harmonising concept suffered serious drawbacks due to the parallel functioning of the health care schemes of the various social insurances. Policy makers are discussing the possibility to integrate the health care schemes of the various social insurances into the general framework of the national health care system. So, as far as health care is concerned, Greece finds itself in a transitory stage, which makes any description of it even more difficult. In view of the fact that the transition will still take quite a number of years, we have opted to discuss both the scheme of medical care for employees, as governed by the *I.K.A.* scheme, and the main features of the national health system.

The common basis of all social security schemes is embodied in the Constitution. Although the Constitution itself does not mention the concept "social security", two provisions of the Constitution are particularly relevant for the recognition of the right to social security:
Section 21
(1) "The family, as the basis for the preservation and progress of the nation, as well as marriage, mother and childhood are under the protection of the State.
(2) Large families, war invalids and invalids of peace time, victims of war, war widows and orphans, as well as the incurable physically and mentally sick, are entitled to special State care.
(3) The State will care for the health of its citizens and will adopt special measures for the protection of young people, the elderly, invalids, as well as for assistance to the needy.
(4) For those without any or with insufficient accommodation, housing is subject to special State care".
Section 22
(1) "Employment is a right and is placed under the protection of the State which watches over the creation of conditions for full-time employment for all citizens, as well as over the moral and material progress of the active, agricultural and urban population.
All people in employment are entitled to equal remuneration for equivalent work, without distinction on grounds of sex or any other grounds."
(4) "The State will care for the social insurance of the working people, as specified by law".

Social assistance and the national health system find their legal basis in Section 21(3) Constitution; the social insurance schemes, in Section 22(4).

It is difficult to determine the legal effect of these social fundamental rights in a general manner because there is a strong tendency to deny them enforceability and to require the interposition of the legislator. Both in legal doctrine and in case law the legislator is given a wide discretion with regard to the concrete implementation of social rights. It should also be pointed out that in Greek law no legal remedy by which the legislator can be forced to act exists.

There can be no doubt that the statute constitutes the main source of social security law. Special statutes regulate the social insurance and social assistance schemes, sometimes in their entirety, sometimes in respect of certain parts thereof. Furthermore, the setting up of social security institutions, as well as their main principles and procedures, are regulated by statute.

In the Greek context, the term "statute" must be understood as referring to acts which stem from a plenary session of the Parliament or the departments thereof, as well as the legislative texts issued by the government or, under certain conditions, by the President of the Republic.

The legislator has delegated certain legislative powers to the executive, which may be charged to give further rules concerning specific parts of social security law. Such delegated legislation may take the shape of a decision of the President, a ministerial decision or a decision of the social insurance administration. In the case of delegation to an administrative body, the previous approval of the competent Minister or of a supervisor body is often required. Delegation is often used as a technique. The pluriformity of the social security schemes obliges the legislator to delegate extended powers to administrative bodies for the direct regulation of detailed subjects.

The Greek legal system recognises general principles of law, considered as unwritten fundamental rules, justified by rational thinking and deduced from the meaning or the scope of the existing written law. In the field of social security law, principles such as the principle of social solidarity and the principle of the favour to the insured, are regarded as autonomous sources. As such principles we can also regard the general principles of, among others, proper administration, equal treatment, legal security and trust.

Jurisprudence does not constitute a source of social security law. Nevertheless, case law may play an important role in practice. For instance, if the highest judiciary overrules a precedent in a concrete case, the relevant social insurance institution will have to re-examine every case that has a strong connection with the change of the jurisprudence.

In 1955, the Greek legislator prohibited the establishment of social insurance rules through collective labour agreements, in order to guarantee the public character of social insurance. Nonetheless, the social partners introduced social insurance provisions through collective labour agreements; mostly this was favourable to the socially insured persons. Since 1990, the legislation was changed and social insurance issues can be dealt with in collective labour agreements, albeit under two conditions:

a) the provisions should not be related to pensions (neither compulsory nor voluntary pensions);

b) the provisions should not violate the constitutional order nor the policies of the public social insurance institutions.

This prevailing, restricted approach is the object of serious legal controversy. New legislation to clarify the debate is expected.

2. *Administrative organisation*

Social insurance benefits are provided for by several independent institutions of public and private law, aiming to protect the individuals of a certain category against certain risks. These institutions, according to the structure of the insurance branches, are divided into institutions of main insurance, auxiliary insurance and sickness insurance. There are also institutions which provide lump sum benefits and institutions which provide complementary protection.

In 1996 there were as many as 236 social insurance institutions, each of them being more or less different from the others. The majority (215) are supervised by the Ministry of Labour and Social Insurance; they correspond to 26 institutions of main insurance, 51 institutions of auxiliary insurance, 19 sickness insurance institutions, 66 institutions which provide lump sum benefits, 50 mutual aid societies and 3 labour oriented institutions (the Manpower Employment Organisation, the Organisation for Housing Benefits and the Workers Foundation). Other institutions fall under the competence of the Ministry of National Defence (10), the Ministry of Finance (1), the Ministry of Mariners (6) and the Ministry of Agriculture (1). There is no autonomous fund for the social protection of civil servants; these are directly covered through the national budget, which also receives the relevant contributions directly.

According to the professional status of the insured, these institutions can be divided into the following categories:
a) institutions of employees and workers under private law,
b) of employees in the banking sector,
c) of public servants
d) of self-employed people,
e) of people employed in the press,
f) of farmers,
g) of the clergy,
h) and institutions for auxiliary insurance of public servants.

Almost the totality of the Greek population is covered by one of these insurance institutions. This is also now the case for part-time and home-based workers.

As a rule, the social insurance institutions have their own legal personality and exercise public authority in the form of legal bodies under public law. In principle, each institution has its own administrative structure with its own administrative bodies. However, there are certain institutions which have been created by private initiative or have been qualified by the legislator as belonging to the private sphere of law. The common legislator has, however, tried to limit the operation of private social insurance. Since 1970, it seems to be impossible to establish new private mutual aid societies. Now, employers only have the possibility to open special accounts or to provide bonus payments to their employees. Private group insurance has slowly started to play a significant role.

Where the social insurance schemes are administered by many different legal persons, it could be expected that these institutions enjoy a certain degree of self government. Yet autonomy is very restricted.
The powers of the administrative bodies concern, in principle:
- the determination of the budget of the social insurance institution;
- the proposal of internal administrative rules;
- the decision with regard to affiliation, contribution liability and benefit entitlement;
- taking all sorts of other decisions.

However, autonomy is in reality very limited, as a result of a number of powers which have been attributed to the State. Thus the State (the competent minister) has substantive supervisory powers which, for example, result in the power to withhold approval of the budgets of the social insurance institutions and to check their accounts and book-keeping. Furthermore, for each important administrative decision, the social security institutions require the approval of the competent minister. Thus, the administrative bodies must first receive ministerial approval before they can introduce qualitative or quantitative improvements of social insurance benefits. Moreover, the administrative bodies are not free in the way they spend their reserve assets; these are blocked by the Greek National Bank at a relatively low interest rate. However, institutions which have the form of legal bodies under public law can establish mutual funds for the financial management of their property or invest in existing mutual funds or on the stock-exchange.

As early as 1946 it was determined that the boards of management of the administrative institutions must be composed of representatives of the State, the insured population, pensioners, and employers. The members of the boards of managers, as nominated by the representative organisations, are appointed by the competent minister. In the past the Council of State has provided that the nominations by representative organisations are not binding upon the competent minister but merely have an advisory character. However, since 1985 this situation seems to have been changed; an act of that year provides that the majority of members of the board of managers must consist of representatives of the insured population and of pensioners. As a result of the application of this new act, the competent minister is obliged to appoint the representatives, who have been chosen by the trade unions which represent both the insured population and pensioners.

The most important social insurance system is that of the majority of the employees. It's schemes are administered by the Institute for Social Insurance (*I.K.A.*). This public law institution insures the whole range of traditional social risks for the employees. The *I.K.A.* is operationally divided into three main branches:
a) a compulsory pension branch (old-age, invalidity and survivors' pensions);

b) an auxiliary pension branch (*T.E.A.M.-I.K.A.*) to which all *I.K.A.* insured persons are compulsorily affiliated; and
c) a sickness insurance branch providing benefits in kind and in cash as well as maternity allowances.

Family and unemployment benefits for *I.K.A.* insured people are, however, administered by *O.A.E.D.* (the Manpower Employment Organisation). This public law institution is also in charge of the provision of reservists benefits.

The *I.K.A.* is charged with the levying of contributions in respect of all the benefits mentioned above.

There is a certain tendency of the *I.K.A.* to incorporate smaller social insurance schemes, resulting in a gradual extension of the scope of the system administered by the *I.K.A.*

On a local level there are a number of *I.K.A.* offices. In larger towns there are *O.A.E.D* offices as well, but in other places this institution makes use of the offices of the *I.K.A.* The *I.K.A.* is supervised by the Minister of Labour and Social Insurance.

For the sake of completeness some attention must be paid to other important administrative bodies of the larger insurance schemes. The *T.A.E.*, the fund for trade insurance, is charged with insuring the risks of sickness and maternity, invalidity, old age and death in respect of the self-employed. The same risks in respect of farmers are insured by the *O.G.A.*, the Organisation for Agricultural Insurance. The *O.G.A.* also administers the assistance scheme for people older that 65 years of age. Mostly, the state itself administers the schemes for civil servants, where the Minister of Finance acts as the competent minister.

The social assistance schemes are administered on a local level under the supervision of the Minister of Labour and Social Insurance. In each prefecture there is a social welfare department which bears the responsibility for the assistance schemes in its region; furthermore, some powers in the area of social assistance have been delegated to the local communities. In some cases the administration of social assistance schemes is charged to separate legal persons under public law, which were specially created for this purpose. Since the introduction of the so-called 'prefectural self-government' in 1993, these public law bodies were made responsible for certain activities in the social welfare area. For example, they became competent for the establishment of social services for the elderly, the handicapped and other welfare target groups. Charities and voluntary organisations may also provide social services.

3. *Personal scope of application*

There is no general social insurance system covering all active persons in the case of the occurrence of any of the traditional social risks. Of the large number of social insurance schemes each has its own affiliation conditions. A common general characteristic is that, in order to be affiliated to a scheme, a person must be engaged in employment. It depends upon the character of the specific employment (sometimes also upon the region) to which social insurance institution a person belongs. Not only those who are actually in employment are insured, but sometimes their spouse, children, brothers or sisters, or even grandchildren as well. The actual scope of the group of insured people varies from scheme to scheme.

This leads to inequalities as social protection against all the traditional social risks is only provided to white collar workers of the private sector and blue collar workers, insured under *I.K.A.* Other categories will often lack family or unemployment benefit schemes. Farmers and self-employed persons also lack supplementary insurance schemes..

With regard to the main categorical schemes, the personal scope of application of the various social insurance schemes may roughly be described as follows.

Most employees are affiliated to the *I.K.A.* The affiliation conditions for the *I.K.A.* apply for the whole nation; if a person satisfies the affiliation conditions, he is insured with the *I.K.A.* wherever he works in Greece (or sometimes even outside the country). A worker is affiliated to the *I.K.A.* scheme unless he is covered by another insurance scheme for employees. Such special social insurance schemes exist, for example, for employees in the banking sector and for employees of state companies. The main condition for affiliation to the *I.K.A.* is that one carries out professional employment in a subordinate relationship. Thus, it is essential that employment is carried out professionally, that it constitutes the main profession of the person concerned and that wages are being paid. Apart from employees stricto sensu, there are also a number of categories of people who are treated as such, i.e.:
- people who do not carry out employment as recognised under labour law, for example state accountants;
- people whose employment is not really subordinate, such as those without a regular employer or persons without a fixed place of employment; such as newspaper sellers and writers.
- unpaid workers, for example apprentices.
- people whose employment is not their main profession (e.g. members of administrative boards).
- managers.

Some limited categories of individuals are not covered under the *I.K.A.* despite fulfilling the conditions, such as extraordinary civil servants, prefects, and persons with a foreign nationality who carry out only temporary employment Since 1990, part-time and home-based workers are compulsorily affiliated to the *I.K.A.*; members of the family of an *I.K.A.* insured person, are also insured under *I.K.A.* under the condition that they work for an employer who is also head of their family and that they are not affiliated with any social insurance institution. Housewives enjoy social protection only in their capacity as family members of an insured person.

With regard to the medical care branch of the *I.K.A.* health insurance covers not only the active insured population but also retired pensioners, insured unemployed persons, and their dependants. Benefits in kind in respect of maternity are also payable to the non-dependent spouse.

Farmers are affiliated to the *O.G.A.* (Organisation of Farmers Social Insurance); due to the high number of active and retired people it insures, the *O.G.A.* constitutes one of the most important social insurance institutions in Greece.

The term "farmer" is understood to refer to each person who personally carries out an agricultural activity as his main profession. Agricultural activity means an activity in farming, cattle raising or forestry. The scheme also extended to some additional groups of persons, i.e.:
- self-employed people and craftsmen working in villages of less than 2.000 inhabitants;
- employees of all categories living in areas or communities with a population of up to 5,000 persons, on the condition that they are not affiliated to any other social insurance institution;
- fishermen;
- Greek priests and nuns working in the agricultural sector.

In respect of the free professions, there is a large number of social insurance schemes. Here the term "free profession" refers to intellectual professions, traders and craftsmen.

For each intellectual profession there is a separate administrative body and social insurance scheme. Thus, there are separate insurance schemes for practising lawyers, doctors and engineers. The effective legal exercise of the profession constitutes the main affiliation condition.

Also traders and craftsmen have their own insurance scheme. The statute determines which trade activities must be carried out in order to qualify as a trader. Engaging in trade is not sufficient for affiliation to the categorical social insurance scheme; it is also required that a person is more than 18 years of age and is registered with the Chamber of Commerce, the Chamber of Industry or the Chamber of Crafts. Finally we mention that the absence of a statutory definition of 'craftsman' causes many difficulties with regard to the delimitation of the scope of application of the social insurance scheme concerned.

The national health system (*E.S.Y.*), covers the entire Greek population, without any special entitlement condition, regardless of professional category or region.

The categorical social assistance schemes normally require Greek nationality and permanent residence in Greece in order to qualify for the benefits.

Finally, we must mention the different types of social insurance periods as they are distinguished in Greece. The most usual form of a permanent legal relation, referring to social insurance, is the compulsory social insurance period. Only the state or legal persons under public law can be institutions of compulsory insurance. Other forms of social insurance are the formal insurance and the voluntary insurance. The former refers to the period in which a person contributes to a social insurance scheme, for a reasonable time and in good faith, without actually fulfilling all the legal conditions to affiliate to the concerned institution. Although the legal conditions were not met, the social insurance institution which accepted the contributions under those circumstances must accept the contributor as a member. Within the voluntary insurance three forms must be distinguished. In the strict sense of the word, voluntary insurance is mainly created for Greek nationals living abroad. A second form is the voluntary continuation of an interrupted compulsory insurance, the third form is the additional voluntary insurance for which a special branch has been established within the *I.K.A.* In order to qualify for the second form of voluntary insurance, the person who was insured with the *I.K.A.* should request, on termination of his employment, to continue the insurance relation in the pension, sickness and auxiliary insurances; the voluntary insurance period can, however, not be taken into account for the completion of the 10.500 working days required for entitlement to a full old-age pension.

4. Risks and benefits

As the conditions for entitlement for social insurance benefits under the *I.K.A.* were changed in 1992 for the future, it will be important to make the distinction between persons who first joined the *I.K.A.* after 31.12.1992 and those already insured before 1.1.1993.

4.1. Old age

For those persons already enrolled with the *I.K.A.* before 1993, entitlement to a full-rate pension depends upon the establishment of a contribution record of 4.050 working days. For each year after 1991 the required record of working days is increased by 150 days per year (so this will be 4,200 in 1992). The termination of employment is not required but if the monthly income exceeds 35 times the statutory minimum daily wage for unskilled workers, payment of the pension is suspended.

There are several opportunities for early retirement but these are subject to various conditions, which are:

a) People who have carried out heavy and unhealthy work can retire at the age of 60 (men) or 55 (women) if they have established a contribution record that corresponds with four fifths of at least 4.050 working days (plus the 150 which will be added each next year after 1991). From these working days at least 1.000 must be included within the 10 former years before the claim for pension.

b) People who have a contribution record of 10.500 working days (approximately 35 years) can retire at the age of 58 (both for men and women). For those who enrolled after 1.1.1983 the retirement age has been increased to 60 years.

c) People who have a contribution record of at least 10.000 working days can retire at the age of 62 (men) and 57 (women). We must note that there is no reduction in the amount of pension as far as the three aforementioned possibilities for early retirement are concerned.

d) There is also the opportunity to retire at the age of 60 (men) or 55 (women) when a person has a contribution record of 4.050 working days (plus 150 x n) of which at least 100 days must have been worked in each of the five calendar years preceding early retirement. However, the amount of benefit

is reduced by 1/200 of the basic amount for each month till 65 or 60 year of age.
e) The person who has established a contribution record of 10.000 working days, of which at least 100 days must have been worked in each of the five calendar years preceding early retirement, can retire at the age of 60 (men) or 55 (women).
f) Finally, if a person has established a contribution record of 10.500 working days, it is possible to retire at the age of 56. The reduction is then also 1/200 for each month till 65 or 60 year of age.

Married women and widows with unmarried children under 18 years of age, are entitled to a complete old age pension from the age of 55 onwards, on the condition that they have contributed during at least 5.500 days and have no entitlement to another pension. They can enjoy early retirement at the age of 50; in that case the pension benefit will be reduced by 1/200 for each month of early retirement, however, the level of benefit may not fall below the minimum amount of pension. For the blind, the above mentioned contribution conditions are halved.

The pension amount consists of a basic amount (the so called "basic pension") plus different supplements. The calculation of the basic amount depends on the insurance record of the pensioner and his estimated daily income, which is linked to the real previous earnings of the employee. There are now 28 classes of real earnings, each of which corresponds to a set amount of estimated daily income. The basic amount of old age pension is calculated as a percentage (usually between 70% and 30%) of the estimated daily income within the particular earnings class. The pension rates decrease as the pensioners move from a low earnings class to a higher one: thus, the rate is 70% for the 1st class and 30% for 26th, 27th and 28th classes.

The basic amount of old age pension may be augmented by a supplement. The amount of the supplement is connected with the specific number of working days. For each 300 working days on top of 2.999, the basic amount of old age pension is augmented by 1% up to 2,5% of the estimated daily income within the earnings class. If a person has established a contribution record between 2.999 and 7.799 working days, the increase of the basic amount is 1% for each of the earnings classes. On a contribution record of 7.800 working days and more, the increase is 2,1% for the 5th class, 2,2% for the 6th class, 2,3% for the 7th to the 11th classes and finally 2,5% for the 12th to the 28th classes.

It is important also to notice that the basic amount of the pension is augmented by a flat-rate supplement (its percentage corresponds with one and a half times the minimum daily wage of an unskilled worker) if the spouse of the pensioner does not work and she does not receive a pension from any Greek social insurance. In practice it is also accepted that this supplement can be provided for a needy and handicapped wife or husband.

Another supplement (20% of the basic pension) is payable in respect of the first unmarried dependent child younger than 18 years of age or 24 years of age if the child is still in full-time education and does not work. If the child is not able to work due to a serious disease or sickness, the supplement is payable without an age limit. This supplement is 15% in respect of the second child and 10% for the third, but is not provided if any of the children receives a lump-sum benefit due to their incapacity for work. The supplements are calculated on the

basis of the basic pension corresponding to the estimated daily income of the 10th class.
The total pension amount may not exceed 80% of the estimated earnings.

For persons first affiliated with the *I.K.A.* after 1992, the pensionable age is 65, both for men and women. Under certain conditions, specific groups are entitled to early retirement:
a) workers in unhealthy and hazardous occupations (60 years of age);
b) actors and musicians (60 years of age);
c) mothers of minors or children unable to work, when they have fulfilled a contribution record of 6.000 working days (55 years of age);
d) mothers of at least three children, when they have fulfilled a contribution record of 6.000 working days (in this case the pensionable age of 65 is reduced by three years for each child up to the fifth).

The minimum period required to receive the full rate pension is 4.500 working days (15 years) for which contributions have been paid. Exceptions include tetraplegics and paraplegics (then 4.050 days) as well as the above mentioned category c) of mothers.

The pension amount also consists of a basic amount (the 'basic pension') plus different supplements. The calculation of the basic amount takes into account income from employment during the last five years before retirement. The full rate equals 60% of the pensionable income and corresponds to an insurance period of 35 years, each year being counted as 1,714% of pensionable income. No supplement for the spouse is provided anymore. The supplements for dependent children (unmarried children below the age of 18 years or below the age of 24 years if they are still in full-time education and out of work) are now calculated as proportions of a complicated index; this index equals 50% of the 1991 Gross National Product per capita, adjusted annually according to the increases in the pensions of the civil servants. The supplements correspond to 8% of this index for the first child, 10% for the second and 12% for each following child. Termination of employment is not required; however, in such case, the pension amount will be reduced by one third, without the reduced pension becoming less than half of the minimum pension.

Both persons insured before 1993 and those insured since cannot get a pension greater than four times the 1991 Gross National Product per capita, indexed in the same way as the pensions of civil servants. There is also a minimum pension amount; it equals the amount of a pension paid after the establishment of a 15 year contribution record. All old age pensions are adjusted according to the civil servants' pensions and not the consumer price index.

The *O.G.A.* provides non-contributory flat rate pensions to men and women, who have reached the age of 65, have worked as farmers for at least 25 years and do not receive a pension from any other social insurance. Due to serious problems in funding the scheme, a compulsory contributory pension scheme for farmers with seven insurance classes was introduced by a statute of 1997 and implemented as from 1998. The entitlement to the contributory pension depends upon a minimum contributions record of five years. After 2004 this minimum will be increased by one year per calendar year until a minimum record of 15 years will be reached.

For civil servants appointed before 1993 there is a complex set of rules that provides for different pensionable ages (for men and women) according to the length of insurance. The maximum retirement age is 65 years for men and 60 years for women, whereas many possibilities for early retirement on favourable conditions are offered, particularly to unmarried women or mothers of many children. For civil servants appointed after 1992 the legal retirement age is 65 years for both men and women, with exceptions for totally blind, paraplegic and tetraplegic civil servants and civil servants who are mothers of minors or of at least three children.

Apart from the strict contributory pensions that are provided under the various categorical social insurance schemes, a new type of benefit for pensioners was introduced in 1996: the 'social solidarity allowance for pensioners'. All persons receiving an old age, survivor's or invalidity pension under a social insurance scheme falling under the competence of the Ministry of Labour and Social Insurance (except *O.G.A.*-pensioners) qualify for this benefit, as long as they satisfy the following conditions:
a) they are at least aged 65 years of age. However, no age limit is set for recipients of an invalidity pension;
b) their annual income out of pensions and employment does not exceed a fixed amount (in 1996 this was 1,4 million Drachmas);
c) the annual personal taxable income of the applicant does not exceed about 130% of this fixed amount;
d) the annual family taxable income of the applicant does not exceed 200% of this fixed amount;
e) the monthly amount of the pension received should not exceed about 1/13 of this fixed amount.

The amount of the social solidarity allowance for pensioners depends upon the amount of the supplemented pension; there is a minimum and a maximum amount. The benefit is adjusted to the consumer price index.

4.2. Death

Normally, the death of an insured person gives rise to a benefit for the survivors. To illustrate this we shall discuss the *I.K.A.* pension scheme for survivors, again distinguishing between persons insured before 1993 and those first affiliated after 1992.

In order to be entitled to widow's pension the deceased, affiliated to *I.K.A.* before 1993, must either
- have a contribution record of 1,500 working days, 300 of which were acquired during the last five years preceding their death;
- have a contribution record corresponding to the number of days required for entitlement to an invalidity pension; or

- have been entitled to an old age pension.

The former two conditions do not apply if their death resulted from an industrial injury or an occupational disease. In case of death as a result of a normal injury the conditions are halved.

An additional entitlement condition is that the marriage must have lasted at least six months, unless the death resulted from an injury, there is a dependent child, or the child has been conceived before the moment of death.

Widow's pension is not payable if, on the day of marriage, the employee enjoyed an invalidity pension or old age pension and the marriage had not yet lasted two full years, again unless the death resulted from an injury, there is a dependent child, or the child has been conceived before the moment of death.

The widower is entitled to the same survivor's pension as the widow, however only on the condition that he is incapable of work and was formerly dependent upon the deceased wife or insured person.

The pension constitutes 70% of the old age pension to which the deceased would have been entitled. There is a minimum monthly level of 18 times the statutory minimum daily wage for the unskilled worker. Entitlement to widow's pension comes to an end in case of remarriage.

Mutatis mutandis, the entitlement conditions and modalities in respect of orphan's pension are the same as those for widow's pension. Orphan's pension is payable to each unmarried child older than 18 years of age (or 24 if the child is in full-time education; there is no age limit in respect of incapacitated children). The pension amount is 20% of the old age pension which the deceased enjoyed or would have enjoyed. If both parents have died the child receives 60%.

Widow's pension and orphan's pension together may not exceed the amount of old age pension to which the deceased has been (or would have been) entitled. If a widow's pension is not payable, the total amount of orphan's pension may not exceed the amount of old age pension which the deceased enjoyed (or would have enjoyed). The minimum amount of orphan's pension is equal to the minimum widow's pension.

For persons insured with the *I.K.A.* after 1992 the same contribution conditions on behalf of the deceased prevail. However, entitlement to the survivor's pension is then dependent upon the fulfilment of the following conditions:
- as far as the widow or widower are concerned:
  a) the surviving spouse has to be unable to work (invalidity rate of at least 67%);
  b) the monthly income of the survivor does not exceed a specified amount (40 times the minimum wage of an unskilled worker, adjusted by 20% per dependent child);
  c) the survivor does not remarry.
- as far as the orphan is concerned, he should not be over 18 years of age or, if attending university, be no older than 24 years of age. No age limit is applied in case of permanent incapacity to work.

The amount of the survivor's pension for the widow(er) is equal to 50% of the pension the deceased spouse received or would have received. It is 25% of this pension for each orphan; in case of an orphan of both father and mother this is increased to 50%. The total of the survivor's pensions must not exceed 100% of the pension the deceased person received or would have received; the minimum rate of survivor's pension corresponds to 80% of the old-age pension paid on the basis of a contribution record of 15 years.

The health care insurance scheme of the *I.K.A.* also provides a death allowance of at least eight times the estimated income of the lowest earnings class.

4.3. Incapacity for work

In respect of social insurance schemes, we normally make a distinction between sickness insurance and invalidity insurance. The sickness insurance schemes cover medical care and the loss of income as a result of sickness and maternity. Invalidity insurance schemes cover permanent incapacity for work; the benefits which are payable under these schemes often bear strong similarities to the old age pensions. Again we shall discuss the *I.K.A.* scheme to illustrate this.

The insured person who is not able to exercise his job due to illness, is entitled to sickness benefit.
In order to be entitled to a sickness allowance a person must satisfy the following conditions: he must be incapable for work and abstain from work; he must have established a contribution record of at least 100 working days in the year before the sickness or in the first 12 of the previous 15 months; he must not be a pensioner. In respect of incapacity for work due to industrial accident or occupational disease there are no contribution conditions.
In principle, sickness benefit provides 70% of the estimated income of the insurance class to which the claimant belonged during the last 30 days of the previous year. A sickness benefit is payable from the fourth day of incapacity (3 waiting days) over a period of a maximum of 6 months. However, if the claimant has established a contribution record of 300, respectively 1500 working days in the two, respectively five last years preceding the sickness, the maximum duration is 1 year, respectively 2 years. It must also be noted that during the first month of sickness the employer is obliged to make additional payments, as a supplement on top of the sickness benefit; so the last wage level remains intact.
Sickness benefit is also payable in respect of maternity; in order to qualify for such cash benefit, a woman must have worked 200 days in the two years preceding the expected day of birth. The period of entitlement is 102 days; half before the expected day of birth and half after this event. The woman must also not work during this period.
There are also additional benefits payable by the *O.A.E.D.* The main supplement is calculated over the same period (105 days) and covers the difference between the *I.K.A.* maternity allowance and the previous monthly earnings of the beneficiary.
The *I.K.A.* provides lump-sum benefits in case of maternity, in order to replace hospital and medical care. Those payments consist of 30 times the minimum wage for an unskilled worker.

All the women who are not entitled to any of these allowances and are not affiliated to another social insurance institution, can claim for a social assistance benefit. This means-tested benefit consists of a lump-sum paid by the Minister of Health and Social Insurance for a period of 105 days.

Invalidity benefit is payable after the right to sickness benefit has expired. The insured person is regarded to be invalid when a medical committee assesses a serious illness or physical or mental disability resulting in a radical reduction of the earning capacity. The person concerned should therefore not be able to earn more than 1/5 of the normal average earnings of a worker in his own profession for at least one year. The amount of the pension is related to the degree of invalidity:
a) an invalidity rate of 80% or more opens a right to a full pension;
b) an invalidity of between 66,6% and 80% gives entitlement to 3/4 of the full pension rate, unless the insured person has established a contribution record of at least 6.000 days or 20 years; in the latter case he receives a full-rate pension;
c) an invalidity rate of at least 50% but no more 66,6% entitles the recipient to half of the full rate pension, unless the insured person shows a contribution record of at least 6.000 days or 20 years; in the latter case he receives 3/4 of the full-rate pension.

The basic amount of the pension is increased by specific supplements for a dependent spouse and/or dependent children. The spouse supplement is, however, only awarded to persons insured with the *I.K.A.* before 1993; this monthly benefit amounts to one and a half times the daily wage of an unskilled worker. Paraplegics and tetraplegics who have established a contribution record of at least 1.000 days are entitled to a special monthly allowance equal to 20 times the minimum daily wage of an unskilled worker. Persons with an invalidity degree of 100% who are in need of constant care by a third person are entitled to a monthly allowance equal to 1/4 of the 1991 Gross National Product per capita, adjusted to the index of the civil servant's pensions.

The minimum levels of invalidity pension are the same as those for old age pension; also the method of calculation is the same as for old age pension (mutatis mutandis).

There are no contribution requirements with regard to industrial injuries and occupational diseases. The normal invalidity pension is payable, albeit that for persons insured with the *I.K.A.* before 1993, the minimum benefit level is 60% of the estimated income in the relevant earnings class. The minimum rate for persons insured since 1993 is equal to the amount of an old age pension paid after the establishment of a contribution record of 15 years. In cases of temporary incapacity for work due to an industrial injury or an occupational disease, sickness benefit is payable during a period of six months.

4.4. Unemployment

In order to become entitled to unemployment benefit under the *O.A.E.D.* (the Manpower Employment Organisation) an *I.K.A.* insured person must be capable of work, involuntarily unemployed and registered with the labour exchange. Furthermore it is required that a person has established a contribution record of 125 working days during a period of 14 months preceding the two months prior to the commencement of unemployment. In cases of first claims, proof must be given of at least 80 working days in each of the three years prior to the commencement of unemployment. Those who are older than 65 years of age are not entitled to unemployment benefit.

Benefit is paid after a waiting period of six days. The period during which the unemployment benefit is being paid depends upon the contribution record the applicant established during the 14 months before becoming unemployed:
- the benefit is paid for 5 months when the beneficiary shows a contribution record of 125 days;
- the benefit is paid for 6 months when the beneficiary shows a contribution record of 150 days;
- the benefit is paid for 8 months when the beneficiary shows a contribution record of 180 days;
- the benefit is paid for 10 months when the beneficiary shows a contribution record of 220 days;
- the benefit is paid for 12 months when the beneficiary shows a contribution record of 250 days.

The unemployment benefit is paid at a reduced rate for three additional months if the unemployed person has established an over all contribution record of 4.050 working days. For unemployed persons aged 49 or more the unemployment benefit is paid for 12 months if they show a contribution record of 210 working days over the last 14 months.

Young people between the ages of 20 and 29 years, who have recently entered the labour market and have been unemployed for more than one year, are entitled to a flat-rate unemployment benefit during a period of maximally five months.

Both for manual workers and white collar workers the rate of unemployment benefit is 50% of the estimated income within the relevant earnings class. Furthermore, there are dependency additions of 10% in respect of each dependent (subject to a maximum of 70% of the basis of calculation). The minimum level of unemployment benefit is equal to two thirds of the statutory minimum daily wage for unskilled workers. The level of reduced benefit payable after expiration of the initial benefit period is 50% of the benefit previously enjoyed.

Those who are not eligible for unemployment may, in certain extraordinary circumstances, nevertheless, receive benefit for a period of a maximum of 45 days. Examples of such circumstances are catastrophes, violent stoppages of work and long-term unemployment within certain professions. The decision to award benefit is taken by the Minister of Labour and Social Insurance. Equally, during Christmas or Easter special forms of assistance may be granted to the unemployed who are not entitled to unemployment benefit.

Two typical Greek schemes which are related to the coverage of the unemployment risk (yet to be discussed separately) are the reservists benefit scheme for employees and the insurance scheme for the loss of agricultural produce for farmers.
Reservists benefit is payable by the *O.A.E.D.* to employees who remain in military service for a longer period than their regular service term, or to employees who are called up for military training for the second or subsequent time. On a loss of income as a result of military service a person may receive benefit at a rate of between 50% and 100% of their lost income.
If the agricultural production of an *O.G.A.* insured person is destroyed by hail, frost, flooding, drought or a storm, benefit may be payable on the grounds of the insurance scheme for the loss of agricultural production.

4.5. Health care

As a result of the introduction of the National Health System (N.H.S.) in 1983, the present situation with regard to the coverage of the costs for medical care (practitioner, hospital and medicine) has become rather complicated. On the one hand there is the national health system (not linked to any social insurance scheme) which is currently being gradually phased in, on the other hand there are a number of categorical social insurance schemes which still provide medical care (for example the medical care branch of sickness insurance under the *I.K.A.*). The statute of 1983 provided that the branches of medical care of the national insurance schemes shall be incorporated within the national health system; also their capital should be transferred to this system. However, this transference has not yet been realised. Consequently, both systems still lead a parallel existence, the whole system is therefore in a transitory period. Below, we will first look into the national health system and then into the insurance scheme for the costs of medical care, as set up by the *I.K.A.*

The N.H.S. is intended to cover the costs of medical care for the entire Greek population on the basis of equality. In order to become eligible for medical care under the national health system a resident should only satisfy one condition: he should be in need of medical care. Since the system is entirely financed by the State, there are no contribution requirements.

Under the N.H.S. primary health care services are provided through rural health centres and provincial surgeries in rural areas, the outpatient departments of regional and district hospitals, the polyclinics of the social insurance institutions and specialists in urban areas. Secondary care is provided by public hospitals, private profit-making hospitals and clinics or hospitals owned by the *I.K.A.* Specific categorical social insurance schemes arrange contracts with private commercial clinics in order to provide services to their members.

Under the social insurance scheme, as managed by the *I.K.A.*, there is a right to medical care for those who have worked 50 days in the preceding year; also the dependants of such persons are entitled to care. Days of sickness benefit, unemployment benefit or pension are treated as working days. The working day requirements are waived in case of an occupational disease or industrial injury. In cases of injury not related to a person's work, the requirements are halved. Medical care is permanently covered by the *I.K.A.* from the first day of the disease.

The *I.K.A.* employs salaried doctors who provide primary medical care and dental services; it also contracts out private doctors for primary care services reimbursed on a fee for service basis. *I.K.A.* members receive free treatment in public hospitals or contracted private clinics. The insured people are entitled to free consultations from a local *I.K.A.* practitioner (both general practitioners and specialists). Furthermore, the costs of medicine on prescription of an *I.K.A.* doctor, are covered by the *I.K.A.*, subject to a personal charge of 25% of the costs of the product. A personal charge is not demanded if the patient is being treated in a recognised hospital, in cases of pregnancy, when the patient is suffering a chronicle disease or in cases when medicine is prescribed in respect of an occupational disease or industrial injury. Tuberculosis patients only pay a personal contribution of 10% of the costs. For prosthesis a personal contribution of 25% is required.

In order to become entitled to treatment in a sanatorium, tuberculosis patients need to have worked at least 350 days in the preceding four years.

Employees in higher earnings classes and their dependants may have a right to treatment in hospital accommodation of a higher grade than the one to which persons from lower earnings classes may be entitled. However, such a right is subject to extra working days requirements. The higher category of hospital accommodation does not apply for the medical treatment but only for the "hotel function" of the hospital (rooms for four, two or only one person). Better hospital accommodation can only be enjoyed for a period of a maximum of six months and the employee has to pay 10% of the extra costs during the first month of hospitalisation. However, the 10% charge is not required from victims of industrial injuries and occupational diseases. Under certain conditions, the *I.K.A.* also covers the travelling expenses of the sick who live in remote parts of the country.

4.6. Family

In Greece there is no uniform family benefits scheme. There are no family benefits in respect of the children of persons who carry out an intellectual profession, of traders, craftsmen or farmers. Sometimes family benefit is granted by different social insurance institutions in respect of the same child, which results in an overlap. Here we only discuss the family benefits as payable by the *O.A.E.D.* to the majority of employees.

Each employee with children under the age of 18 years (22 years in cases of full-time education and without an age limit in respect of incapacitated children) is entitled to family benefits. The contribution requirement is that a record of at least 50 working days must have been established during the previous calendar year.

Family benefit consists of a flat-rate amount corresponding to four recognised earnings classes. Within each earnings class this amount differs depending on whether there are one, two, three, four or more children. If one of the parents is handicapped or has died and the widow is not entitled to invalidity or widow's pension or when the spouse is doing his military service, the amount of family benefit is doubled, if there are one or two children and increased by 50% if there are more children.

The family benefits are paid annually in a lump sum between April and June; large families receive the benefit first.

Furthermore, the *O.A.E.D.* pays a lump sum benefit at the end of the period of pregnancy and maternity leave. The amount of this benefit is equal to the difference between the *I.K.A.* benefit and the real lost wages during the 105 days of pregnancy and maternity leave. Lastly, certain lump sum birth premiums are payable by the *I.K.A.* Entitlement to this birth grant depends upon the establishment of a contribution record of 200 days during the last two years; the amount of the benefit equals 30 times the minimum wage of an unskilled worker.

Apart from the family benefits paid by the *O.A.E.D.* to wage earners, special programmes providing benefits to large families and to mothers of many children also exist. These benefits should be regarded as 'mixed social security benefits' as they combine elements of social insurance and social assistance.

4.7. Need

Instead of setting up a general social assistance scheme, Greece preferred to build assistance elements within the social insurance schemes (such as the minimum pensions or the social solidarity allowance for pensioners). There were legislative attempts to introduce a general assistance scheme and to improve existing categorical programs, the introduction of a general decentralised social assistance scheme still being under consideration.

Greek social assistance consists today of a number of specific programmes for certain groups of the needy, e.g. families with children, handicapped people, victims of catastrophes and the elderly. The assistance schemes are comprised of both preventive benefits in kind (e.g. medical care, family care) and curative benefits, both in kind and in cash. The benefits in cash are regulated in detail in statutory provisions, thus leaving the administrative bodies with little room for discretion. As a rule, only people who are not eligible for any social insurance benefit are entitled to assistance. The levels of assistance benefits vary considerably from scheme to scheme, but are generally very low. Usually the benefits are subject to a means test.

Assistance may also be provided in kind. Benefits in kind may consist of help from social counsellors, rehabilitation services for the handicapped, child care facilities, etc. With regard to benefits in kind the administrative bodies have much wider discretionary powers. Usually there are more claimants than means, so that a selection must take place. Not all benefits are means tested; some benefits in kind are not available upon the free market (e.g. rehabilitation centres for the handicapped), and so those who are better off may be dependent upon them.

Finally, it should be recalled that there are also a number of "mixed benefit" schemes.

Apart from these public programs, social welfare services are also provided by a number of public organisations on a national level. Moreover, welfare services are provided through national networks by departments of various ministries. Welfare services are also provided at a local level by local public authorities, the Church and voluntary organisations. The municipalities have the following competences for the granting of welfare services: they can provide cheap housing, services for the elderly, public land for cultivation at low prices and finally they can provide food, clothing and small sums of money in case of extra-ordinary circumstances such as earthquakes or heat waves. As was already pointed out before, the Prefectural self-governing bodies also provide social services.

5. *Financing*

The various social insurance schemes are financed in a different way by contributions from employers and/or employees (or other insured people) from "social financing sources" (these are earmarked indirect taxes), from general or extraordinary state subsidies out of general taxation and from the proceeds of the exploitation of the capital owned by the social insurance institutions. Normally, the financing system is based upon the pay as you go principle.

The situation with regard to the methods of financing of each of the social insurance schemes is somewhat confused, which results in a strong diversification of the financing structures within the various schemes. The contribution rates vary, depending, among others, upon the type of enterprise, region and industrial branch. However for the social insurance of persons first insured after 1992, the situation is somewhat clearer. We shall first discuss persons already insured before 1993 and after that the way of financing social insurance for persons affiliated after 1992.

For persons already socially insured before 1993, contributions are levied upon the (real and fictitious) earnings from employment. The division between the contribution shares of the employers and the employees shows a diverse picture, even where the groups of insured persons bear a strong resemblance to each other. In the area of pensions the contribution rates for the employees are usually half as high as the rates which apply for employers. However, there are also schemes where the contribution shares of the employers and the employees are the same, or schemes where the employers contribute six times as much as the employees. A similar lack of uniformity applies in the area of sickness insurance (medical care and sickness benefit); sometimes the insured people pay more than the employer, sometimes they pay the same or less. The same applies with regard to the contributions for the supplementary social insurance funds. As from 1982 the employers who employ (unemployed) young workers, women or handicapped persons fall under a more favourable contribution system.

In respect of the schemes for the self-employed, contribution liability obviously rests only upon the insured people themselves. There is a great degree of inequality between the various groups of the self-employed with regard to the contribution/benefits relationship. The contribution rates within the schemes for civil servants and farmers are very minor. Contrary to the situation for employees, the failure by self-employed people to pay their contributions does affect their entitlement to benefit.

The 'social financing sources' constitute another source of financing. Sometimes these constitute a highly important source of financing. As an example we mention the social insurance fund for lawyers: the resources of this fund from social financing sources constitute 270% of the contributions paid by those involved. As another example we can mention the sum which each person must pay to the car owners fund when he wants to acquire a driving license; another example: a 1% tax on tabacco and lottery profits payable to the fund for assistance for the accommodation of employees. The 'social financing sources' were very much contested as they favour the stronger schemes and the richer groups of socially insured persons.

The State itself also contributes towards the financing of the social insurance schemes by means of periodical (mostly annual) subsidies to the social insurance institutions. Thus, the shortages of the *I.K.A.* are annually made up out of general taxation. In the last few years the state subsidies have gradually increased. The state finances most of the expenditure of the social insurance schemes for civil servants and farmers. The national health system, which is currently being set up, is financed entirely by the State. The public social assistance schemes and sometimes also the private assistance schemes are also financed out of general state means.

The reform of 1992 introduced a tripartite system for the funding of the *I.K.A.* social insurance. As far as pensions are concerned, employers pay 13,33%, the state 10% and the employees 6,67% of their gross cash earnings; as far as the sickness insurance is concerned, employers pay 5,10%, the state 3,80% and the employees 2,55% of the gross cash earnings; supplementary pensions are equally financed by the employers and the employees at a rate of 3% each.

Civil servants appointed after 1992 also pay contributions for the coverage of the risks of maternity and sickness (2,55%) and old-age, invalidity and the death of the breadwinner (6,67%). They pay contributions for the supplementary pension to their competent fund at an average rate of 5%.

The self-employed pay contributions for pensions and sickness insurance. Farmers who were formerly not obliged to pay contributions for basic pensions and sickness coverage should now pay contributions, after 1.1.1998, according to their entry in one of seven specific earnings classes.

The proceeds from the 'social financing sources' are no longer fed to specific social security schemes (of certain groups); they are now paid into a central 'solidarity account', which redistributes the money to the poorer social security schemes.

6. Judicial review

A person who wants to challenge a decision of a social insurance institution needs to bring forward proof of the illegality of such a decision; if not, the possible deficiencies in the decision are covered by the presumption of legality of legal actions under public law.

A decision of a social insurance institution can only be challenged before a court, when all the possibilities of internal administrative appeal have been exhausted.

All social insurance institutions have internal regulations which should enable the insured people to invite the administrative body to reconsider their case. Such reconsideration of the litigious decision may take place by a body which is higher in hierarchy than the body which has taken the decision, by the same body that took the litigious decision, or can be dealt with by a body within the same institution which is specifically set up for this purpose. The former two possibilities constitute hierarchical appeal, the latter constitutes a request for redress.

Special bodies for dealing with requests for redress are very exceptional. However, they do exist within the *I.K.A.* and the *O.G.A.* In most cases the requests for redress are dealt with by the Board of Management of the institutions concerned.

Internal administrative appeal mostly deals with an investigation into the facts upon which the decision was based, but sometimes also points of law are considered. It is possible that also opportunity arguments are dealt with. The procedures and principles of internal administrative appeal are laid down in internal regulations of the social insurance institutions. After the internal appeal procedure is finished, the old decision is substituted by a fresh one in which the litigious decision may be reaffirmed, nullified or modified.

If the insured person still has objections against the decision, he may appeal to the administrative courts. These courts consist of three judges. The administrative courts hear appeals, in first and in last instance, in disputes concerning contribution liability and benefits. Also the failure to act by an administrative body is subject to appeal. The administrative courts may confirm, nullify or modify the litigious decision. The judgement of the administrative court is final, although appeal (cassation) may be made to the Council of State; the Council of State then only decides on points of law, judging exclusively upon the legality of the litigious decision.

The citizen can also base legal protection against illegal acts of the administration on a claim for damages against the administrative body concerned. The administrative courts are competent to deal with such claims. Decisions of the administrative courts in damages proceedings are subject to further appeal to the Administrative Court of Appeal. Cassation to the Council of State is also possible.

Chapter Nine

IRELAND

1. Introduction: concept and sources of social security law

In Ireland, instead of the term social security, the term *social welfare* is used. This concept includes all income maintenance schemes. We distinguish three categories of schemes: social insurance schemes, social assistance schemes and also a residual category.
Social insurance schemes exist for the risks of old age, sickness and invalidity (with a special insurance scheme for industrial injuries and occupational diseases), maternity, survivorship, unemployment and, something which is peculiar to the Irish system, the risk of loss of maintenance following desertion by one's spouse.

In respect of all these risks (with the exception of the risk of industrial injuries and occupational diseases) there are also special assistance schemes. Special assistance schemes also exist for single parents. Then there is a general assistance scheme (*supplementary welfare allowance*) which acts as a safety net for the other specific schemes.

Besides the social insurance and assistance schemes, there is a residual category of income maintenance schemes. These are the *child benefit schemes*, a scheme for supplements to families on low income from employment (*family income supplement*) and a number of schemes providing benefits in kind, such as free travelling and free energy services.

The scheme for medical care falls outside the Irish concept of social welfare. However, in line with the framework chosen for this work, we shall, nevertheless, pay some attention to this scheme.

The Irish Constitution contains hardly any clauses of direct importance to social security. An exception to this could be made in relation to Section 41 of the Constitution, which includes fundamental rights clauses in connection with the family. According to the Irish Courts, the state's duty to protect marriage (as laid down in Section 41(3)(1) Constitution), prohibits the unfavourable treatment of married beneficiaries who live together vis-à-vis beneficiaries who are either cohabiting, or who are married, yet living apart.

The main source of Irish social security law is the Social Welfare (Consolidation) Act, 1981. This act contains all social security acts (except one) which existed at the moment of the introduction of the Act. However, it has not brought about any fundamental substantive simplification or reform. This explains why the act was explicitly referred to as a Consolidation Act.

The Social Welfare Act of 1981 is modified at least once a year. This follows from the fact that the rates of benefits are contained in the Act and that modification of these rates has not been delegated. As a rule, the new benefit rates are accompanied by some material changes in the Act. The modification acts are integrated within the Social Welfare (Consolidation) Act 1981, yet are in practice they are also individually quoted. Materially, there is really only one act, which is virtually all-inclusive. Besides this Act, only the Health Act of 1970 is of importance to us, offering a framework for the medical care system.

Thus, the applicable legislation is almost completely consolidated in to one act. However, this does not imply that it contains the entire body of social security law. This follows from the fact that the *Minister for Social Welfare* and the *Minister for Health* have issued a large number of *statutory instruments* (*regulations*) which provide further details concerning the Act. The legal basis for the *regulations* is contained within the Act itself. In some cases the prior approval of parliament is required. In other cases parliament has a certain period of time in which it can retrospectively nullify the *regulations*. Sometime, the Minister of Finance's approval must also be given to delegated legislation. Apart from *regulations*, internal guidelines may also play a role in the daily application of social security law. Mostly, these remain concealed from the citizen.

2. *Administrative organisation*

The administration of social security is fully state-controlled. Almost all social security schemes are administered on a central level. The competent department for the *income maintenance* schemes is the *Department of Social Welfare*, headed by the *Minister for Social Welfare*. The latter is in charge of the general supervision of the administration. The *Department of Health*, under the authority of the *Minister for Health*, is responsible for the medical care system.

Various civil servants from the department are involved in the routine administration of the *income maintenance* schemes. For example, *deciding officers* are in charge of taking decisions in individual cases. In the preparatory phase, *investigating inspectors* and *social welfare officers* collect the necessary information. For this they are equipped with far-ranging legal powers.

The residual social assistance scheme (*supplementary welfare allowance*), as well as some assistance schemes in respect of sickness and invalidity, are administered on a regional level by the *Health Boards*. These are the state bodies normally involved in the administration of the Health Act. They are composed of eight elected members of local institutions (representing the medical profession), as well as three members appointed by the *Minister for Health*. The fact that *Health Boards* are also administrating income maintenance assistance schemes is more the result of an historical development than of a carefully considered decision.

The unemployment schemes are administered on a local level by the *employment exchanges*, which constitute a part of the *Department of Social Welfare*. The means test is administered by the *Department* itself.
The schemes for (school) meals and energy services are administered on a local level.

The social security contributions are collected by the taxation service, in particular the so called *Revenue Commissioners* and are lodged in the *Social Insurance Fund*.

It has to be noted that Ireland in, recent years, has made a considerable effort to introduce informatics into the daily administration of social security.
Recently Customer Service Advisory Councils were also created.

3. *Personal scope of application*

In describing the personal scope of application we make a distinction between social insurance, social assistance schemes and other schemes.
Insurance can be both compulsory and voluntary. In principle, every person between the ages of 16 and 66 years, who is 'employed', as specified in the Act, is compulsorily insured. From the further statutory provisions, it appears that 'employment' must be paid and carried out on the basis of an apprenticeship or contract of employment within the Irish territory. Employment on an aeroplane or a vessel which is registered in the Republic of Ireland (or the owner of which is resident, or has its main place of business in the Republic), equally gives rise to compulsory insurance.
The basic principles are subject to a number of extensions. On the grounds of these extensions certain explicitly mentioned categories of people are compulsory insured. Here we can mention civil servants, military personnel, police officers, domestic workers, midwives and trainee nurses.

On the other hand, the basic principles are subject to a number of restrictions. Thus employment carried out for a spouse or for certain other family members does not lead to insurance. Another important restriction concerns secondary activities and activities of insignificant importance. Certain regulations define which activities are to be considered as secondary activities and consequently not as a primary source of living. According to other regulations, activities of insignificant importance are those remunerated with less than a fixed sum per week.
Recently, the self-employed were made compulsorily insured. The same age limits of 16 and 66 years also apply to self-employed persons. Furthermore, there is a minimum earnings limit, under which there is no compulsory insurance.
In respect of insurance for industrial injuries and occupational diseases, there are special rules, on the grounds of which there are limitations as well as extensions in relation to the definition of the group of insured people.

Compulsorily insured people are not equally insured for all social risks. With regard to certain categories, the Act provides a modified insurance scheme. This is regulated in delegated legislation, on the grounds of which there are thirteen insurance classes. The majority of compulsorily insured people are insured for all risks. Where coverage is limited to certain risks, this can be explained by the fact that, for example, there is no need for more extensive coverage. In principle, the self-employed, who have only recently become compulsory insured, are only insured for the risks of old age and death.

The Act also provides for the possibility of voluntary insurance. This possibility is open to those who have ceased to be compulsory insured on reaching pensionable age, and who have paid contributions over a minimum period of 156 weeks. The people concerned must make an application for voluntary insurance within 12 months after the year in which their compulsory insurance ended. Voluntary insurance offers coverage against only a limited number of risks, especially old age and/or death (optional). The benefits which are paid when these risks materialise are highly dependent upon the number of paid or credited contributions. These constitute the justification for the existence of voluntary insurance.

Almost all the assistance schemes in the Irish system are of a categorical character. Thus, for example, there is a right to *unemployment assistance* for every person between 18 and 66 years of age who lives in the Republic of Ireland and who is capable and willing to carry out suitable employment. A special scheme, *preretirement allowance*, is available to the long term unemployed over the age of 58. Blind people of 18 years or older have the right to a *blind pension* on the condition that they live in the Republic of Ireland. Those of 66 years or older are in principle entitled to *old age (non-contributory) pension*, provided they live within the Republic. Lone parents are entitled to *lone parents allowance*, while persons looking after a welfare pensioner may claim *carer's allowance*.

There are other assistance schemes directed towards certain groups of women. Thus, there is a *deserted wife's allowance* for the woman who is deserted by her spouse and who is younger than 40 years of age and has at least one dependent child. The *prisoner's wife allowance* provides assistance to the woman whose spouse is sentenced to prison for at least six months, provided she is younger than 40 years of age and has at least one dependent child. For all these schemes there are no residence or nationality requirements in respect of the women.

In order to be entitled to a *widow's (non-contributory) pension*, one must be a widow and live within the Republic of Ireland. The latter also applies to the guardian of an orphan who has a right to an *orphan's (non-contributory) pension*. Certain other people specified by the minister are also entitled to this orphan's pension.

Besides the categorical assistance schemes, there exists a general scheme: the *supplementary welfare allowance*. In principle, there is a right to this allowance for every person with insufficient means of subsistence, who lives in the Republic of Ireland. However, the Act contains a number of restrictions: people who follow full time daily education, people in full-time employment, or those who are involved in a trade dispute, are excluded from this right.

Beneficiaries to *child benefit* must live in the Republic of Ireland. The same also applies to the child for whom the right exists.

Obviously, in order to be entitled to the benefits in kind, one must also live within the Republic of Ireland. However, this requirement is not explicitly mentioned by statute.

In order to be entitled to *family income supplement* one must be a member of a family (not a child) in full-time, low paid employment. If two members of the same family satisfy the employment conditions, then the one with the highest income is considered to be the entitled person.

4. Risks and benefits

First, two remarks of a general nature must be made: one concerning the requirement for all benefits of a satisfactory *contribution record* and the second regarding the uniform structure of the various social security benefits.

All social insurance schemes, with the exception of the insurance against industrial injuries or occupational diseases, link the right to a benefit to *contribution conditions*. A person has the right to benefit on grounds of the following conditions:

a) he must have paid a certain number of weekly contributions (39 for short term benefits and 156 for long term benefits) in the period falling between the commencement of the insurance and the day before benefit is claimed; and
b1) in respect of *disability, maternity allowance* and *unemployment benefit* he must have paid or been credited with at least 39 contributions in the year before benefit is claimed (at least 13 of which, in the case of disability benefit, are paid contributions); while in respect of invalidity pension, 48 paid or credited contributions in the relevant year are necessary in order to qualify for the maximum pension; or
b2) in respect of *old age (contributory) pension, retirement pension, widow's (contributory) pension* and *deserted wife's benefit* he must have paid or been credited with an average yearly number of contributions over a fixed period, ranging from 20 or 24 to 48, with the amount of the basic benefit varying slightly in accordance with the claimant's insurance record.

As can be seen, in the contribution conditions under b, not only contributions actually paid, but also those credited, are taken into account. The latter are meant for those who are (or have been) insured and yet, for reasons beyond their control, are not in a position to pay sufficient contributions in order to satisfy the contribution conditions. Thus there are, for example, *pre-entry credits*, granted to those who are insured for the first time. Equally important are credits given during periods of unemployment or incapacity for work.

A record of all insured people (*contribution record*) is kept by the *Department of Social Welfare*.

The insurance schemes, as well as the assistance schemes, operate with a system of basic benefits and additions, both being flat-rate.
The basic benefits are granted to those who satisfy the relevant entitlement conditions. These are not the same for all schemes.
Additions to basic benefit are given for various reasons and in diverse situations. Thus, for example, there is an addition for adult dependants. Usually an adult dependant will be the spouse of the insured person. This person may only have limited means.
There are also additions for children younger than 18 years who usually live with the entitled person. When the child is following full time daily education, the age limit is extended to 21 years in the case of certain payments. The additions to assistance benefits are subject to the applicable general means test. In principle, additions to insurance benefits are not dependent upon the income or financial position of the beneficiary(ies). Recently, however the rule has been introduced that only one half of the additions is payable if the spouse of the entitled person is not considered to be an adult dependant. The reduction does not apply to married people who live apart.
As well as the two general additions described above, we can distinguish a number of additions intended for special situations. Thus, there is, under certain conditions, a right to an addition for the entitled person who is older than 66 years and living alone. An equally modest increase of basic benefit is granted to the entitled person who reaches the age of 80 years (*old age allowance*).
All the additions vary in level, depending upon the basic benefit to which they are attached.
Besides additions in cash, there is also a right to benefits in kind attached to certain social security benefits. These concern matters such as free travel, free energy and fuel supplies, free telephone connection and other such things. These benefits are granted mainly to people of 66 years or older.

No legal requirements with regard to the periodic adjustments of social security benefits exist. This situation allows the government to increase the amounts in a rather selective way. For example, although such adjustments are usually made annually in respect of both the basic benefits and the additions, during recent reforms the level of benefits schemes has been raised with higher increases for those on lowest payments. The inflation figures are taken as a point of reference.

4.1. Old Age

When a person reaches the age of 66 years, he may be entitled to an old age pension, either on the basis of insurance or on the basis of assistance.
Entitlement to an insurance pension (*old age contributory pension*) exists when the contribution conditions are satisfied and the insurance commenced before the person involved reached the age of 56 years.

When these conditions are not satisfied, an assistance pension (*old age non-contributory pension*) may be payable. This pension is subject to a means test.

At the age of 65 years, insured people are entitled to pension covering a one year period, preceding the entitlement to old age pension (*retirement pension*). For this pension similar contribution conditions apply, as for the (*contributory*) *old age pension*, albeit that the person's insurance must have commenced before the age of 55 years. Another condition is that a person of 65 years must have stopped his work. However, there are some important exceptions to this rule.

The so called *pre-retirement allowance* is a new assistance benefit payable to long-term unemployed people of 55 years of age and older who have not yet reached pensionable age. The level of benefit is equal to that of *unemployment assistance*.

4.2. Death

The Irish social security system provides an extended list of benefits in respect of death. There is an insurance pension for survivors, both widow and widower, as well as an assistance pension for the surviving widow.
The right to an insurance pension exists when the contribution conditions are satisfied. The basis for this can be either the insurance record of the deceased spouse or of the survivor.

When the insurance conditions cannot be satisfied, the widow can claim an assistance pension (*widow's non-contributory pension*). This pension is subject to a means test. Both schemes entail a definite loss of the right to a pension if the widow remarries. Benefit is suspended during a period of cohabitation.

As is the case for survivors, there is a distinction between an insurance and an assistance pension for orphans. For the one contribution conditions apply (which must be satisfied by the parent or the stepparent of the orphan), for the other a means test is applied.
In principle the right to orphan's pension exists until the orphan is 18 years of age. However, this limit is extended to 21 years when the orphan follows full-time day education.

The death grant covers funeral costs. This grant is payable on the death of an insured person, the spouse of an insured person, the widow(er) of an insured person or the child of an insured person. Again, contribution conditions apply. The death grant consists of a lump sum, flat-rate benefit which varies according to whether the deceased was a child of younger than 5 years, a child between 5 and 18 years or an adult.

Special rules apply in respect of a death resulting from an industrial injury or occupational disease. The survivor as well as orphans are entitled to a substantially higher pension and there are no contribution conditions. However, here

too remarriage or cohabitation of the survivor results in the loss, and respectively suspension of the pension.
Besides the surviving spouse and orphan, the parent of the diseased is also a potential beneficiary. The parent must have been fully or partly maintained by the deceased person.
There is also a right to a special flat-rate payment for the coverage of funeral costs.

To conclude it must be mentioned that most periodic social security benefits are payable to an adult dependant for another six weeks after the death of the beneficiary. During this period none of the death benefits, as described above, are payable.

4.3. Incapacity for work

In the area of social insurance a distinction is made between *disability benefit* and *invalidity pension*. The former benefit is for those who are incapable of suitable work and who satisfy the contribution conditions. During the first three days of incapacity there is no right to a benefit.
When someone is continuously incapable of working for one year, and the incapacity is permanent, there is a right to an *invalidity pension*. This benefit is more favourable than the *disability benefit*, and there are stricter contribution conditions.

When the incapacity to work is the result of an industrial accident or an occupational disease, the applicable rules are different from those mentioned above. In such a situation, there is the right to *injury benefit* during the first 26 weeks. Here too, there is a waiting period of 3 days. However, if the incapacity lasts longer than 4 days, benefit is payable from the first day. There are no contribution conditions.

The latter also applies for *disablement benefit*; this benefit is payable after the initial period of 26 weeks has expired, provided that at that time the right to injury benefit still existed. There must be an incapacity of at least 1% as a result of a loss of physical or mental capacity due to an industrial injury. The calculation of the degree of incapacity is carried out on a strictly medical basis; whether or not there is a loss of earning capacity remains outside consideration. The percentage of incapacity is rounded up to the nearest ten. If this percentage amounts to less than 20%, *disablement benefit* is paid as a flat-rate gratuity (*disablement gratuity*). However, when the incapacity is expected to last more than 7 years, the beneficiary may opt for a pension instead of a gratuity. In case of incapacity of more than 20%, *disablement benefit* is paid periodically at a rate related to the percentage of incapacity. In the latter case the beneficiary may also be entitled to two supplements. The first, an *unemployability supplement*, is payable to the beneficiary who, as a result of a loss of physical and mental faculty, is permanently incapable of work. The supplement can be granted for a limited period and may be withdrawn at any time. The latter applies equally to the so called *constant attendance allowance*, a supplement in-

tended for beneficiaries of a pension who are 100% incapable of work and who, as a result, are in need of constant care.
The benefits in respect of incapacity due to an industrial accident or an occupational disease are much more favourable than the benefits in respect of "normal" incapacity. The difference can sometimes reach 40%. Note though that in 1992 injury benefit was reduced to the same rate as disability benefit.

Within the area of assistance, the *disability allowance* provides a benefit for those who are incapable of work and who are not entitled to an insurance benefit. The incapacity must be substantial and likely to last for at least one year. It is measured against employment which, with regard to age, experience and training, is considered to be suitable. The allowance is means tested.

There is a separate scheme for blind people. Someone who is visually impaired to such a degree that he is either unable to perform work for which sight is essential, or unable to continue his activities, is entitled to a pension for the blind. This pension is subject to the same means test as the one which applies for old age pension assistance.
There are also separate schemes for two other categories of persons. Thus there is an *infectious diseases maintenance allowance* for those who are not capable of working due to the fact that they are undergoing treatment for an infectious disease. The *rehabilitation maintenance allowance* is payable to people who are substantially incapable of suitable employment and are undergoing rehabilitation treatment in an approved institution. For both the benefits the same means test applies as for the *disability allowance*.

There is a separate insurance scheme in respect of maternity. A woman who satisfies the contribution conditions and who can produce a statement of the date at which her baby is due (issued by a recognised practitioner) is entitled to *maternity allowance*. This allowance is payable for a period of 14 weeks, beginning no later than 4 weeks before the expected date of birth and ending no earlier than 4 weeks after the birth has taken place. This benefit amounts to 70% of the average weekly wage of the woman.

4.4. Unemployment

A person who is unemployed and who satisfies the contribution conditions is entitled to *unemployment benefit*, provided that he is able to and available for work. Among other things, the availability must follow from the fact that a person looks for employment which, in view of age, sex, physical state, training, useful work activities, place of residence and family, is considered to be suitable.
Those who are unemployed due to a strike are disqualified from entitlement to *unemployment benefit*, unless the person concerned is not directly involved in the industrial action.
Those who are unemployed because of their own fault are also disqualified from benefit, as well as, those who have turned down a job offer, who have not taken enough initiative in finding suitable employment and those, under the age

of 55, who have been made redundant and have received redundancy pay in excess of a prescribed limit. In the latter case the disqualification lasts for a maximum period of 9 weeks.

There are three waiting days for the right to *unemployment benefit*. The duration of benefit is dependent upon the age of the persons concerned. In respect of those younger than 18 years, benefit covers a maximum period of 26 weeks. For those between the ages of 18 and 65 the maximum duration is 65 weeks. If one reaches the age of 65 years during this period, benefit is continued for one year, provided that a minimum of 156 contributions have been paid.

After the first half year, benefit is payable at a lower rate. Two categories are exempted from this rule, i.e. those above 65 years of age who have paid at least 156 weekly contributions and those below 65 years of age who, in the year in which they become unemployed and in the 7 preceding years, have paid 280 weekly contributions.

An important opportunity is given to the long-term unemployed or unemployed lone parents by the so called *'Back to Work scheme'*. Under this scheme, they can continue to receive their unemployment benefits for a given period after they take up work in indigenous industries or while starting self-employed activities.

In the assistance unemployment scheme, unemployment benefit is payable in the form of *unemployment assistance*. Instead of contribution conditions, a means test is applicable. Furthermore, there is also a condition that the unemployed person is capable and available to accept any suitable employment. The same disqualification rules apply, albeit that the maximum period of disqualification is three months and that there is a minimum period of one week.

The duration of *unemployment assistance* is unlimited. After 65 weeks the level of the benefit is slightly increased.

All unemployed individuals have a regular duty to register with the *employment exchange*. The frequency of the registration duty varies from once a day to twice in two weeks. Benefit is often paid in cash on these occasions. There is also an opportunity to check whether a person has made sufficient job applications, or whether there are offers of employment.

4.5. Health care

The statutory provisions concerning medical care provide two packages of benefits in kind.

The widest range of benefits are payable to those who cannot be expected to pay medical care out of their own pockets because this would cause severe hardship.

An income limit determines which people fall within this category; thereby the situation of the entire family is taken into consideration. An increased income limit applies for those who are more than 66 years of age. The beneficiaries receive a so called *medical card*. The package of benefits for this group comprises of practitioner's treatment, specialist's treatment, medicine, dental care

and hospital care in a state hospital. A personal charge is only required for each day that a person stays in a hospital. The personal charges are subject to an annual maximum. Only those who have a contagious disease are exempted.
If a person (and possibly his spouse) has an income which exceeds the income limit all, practitioner's treatment must be paid entirely out of his own pocket. If a person's income exceeds a second (higher) income limit, all specialist treatment must be paid for as well. Hospital care is granted under the same conditions as those which apply for the above mentioned category. Dental care for children younger than 6 years of age and school children is free; also certain dental treatment to adults is free of charge, provided that certain contribution conditions are satisfied. Medicine is free to the extent that the costs thereof exceed a certain monthly level; for those who suffer certain listed diseases (long duration), all medicine is free of charge.

The scheme for medical care may be supplemented by voluntary insurance, which may offer varying benefit packages. Voluntary health insurance is administered by the *Voluntary Health Insurance Board*, set up by the competent minister.

Care is provided by self-employed practitioners on the basis of an agreement concluded between the national organisation of general practitioners and the competent department. The *Health Boards* employ dentists. The state hospitals also fall under the authority of the *Health Boards*. There are private hospitals in operation too.

4.6. Family

In the Irish social security system there are various forms of child support. Firstly, there is a general *child benefit* scheme, providing uniform benefits to all residents. In addition, the benefit structure of the income maintenance schemes provides child additions on top of the basic benefits (see below). Finally, there is a *family income supplement* scheme as a sort of equivalent for employees on low income.

Only people who actually live with the child are entitled to *child benefit*. When the child is staying in an institution, maintenance payments for that child are required. Entitlement only exists in relation to children below the age of 16. This age is increased to 18 in cases where the child is in full-time day education, when the child is on a training course for the unemployed or when the child is not able to sustain itself due to a physical or mental defect. *Child benefit* consists of a monthly amount, which varies, depending on whether it concerns the first 3 or subsequent children.
In addition to this *general child benefit*, a *child benefit supplement* has been established.

Family income supplements provide weekly payments to support families on low incomes. Thus, a *family income supplement* is payable to those with a full-time job who have at least one child for whom there is a right to *child benefit*, and whose income lies below a legally defined level. The benefit consists of 60% of the difference between the legally defined level and the family income, subject to a maximum. Under the condition that a person remains in work, the supplement is payable for a period of 52 weeks. During this period a change in the family income does not affect the level of benefit.

4.7. Need

Irish assistance is predominantly set up on categorial lines. Nevertheless there does exist an assistance scheme, which operates as a general safety net: the *supplementary welfare allowance*. This allowance is intended for those who have insufficient means to support themselves and their families. People following full-time day education, those who are in full time employment (except students working during their holidays under the '*Summer Work Scheme*' for a maximum of 10 hours a week for voluntary organisations or community groups) and those involved in a strike are excluded from the *supplementary welfare allowance*. A person should be registered as looking for employment.
The subsidiary character of the scheme follows from the fact that the beneficiary must do every thing possible to obtain other benefits.
The right to (possibly supplementary) benefit is subject to a means test. Alongside this benefit or as a supplement to an insufficient income, the administrative body can provide a supplement to cover extra costs. It is also competent to provide a lump sum benefit intended to cover exceptional expenses. Apart from this, the administrative body may, as an exception, provide benefits in kind. A lone parent's allowance is payable to unmarried single parents, separated parents and parents whose spouses are dead or imprisoned.

Two special assistance schemes are payable to women who are presumed to be unable to provide for themselves.
Women who have been deserted by their spouse are entitled to a *deserted wife's allowance*, provided that they are more than 40 years of age. The latter requirement also applies for the right to *prisoner's wife's allowance*, a benefit for women whose spouse is sentenced to prison for at least 6 months.
All these benefits are means tested. The level of the benefits is equal to that of the (non-contributory) *widow's pension*.

The *deserted wife's allowance* has an insurance equivalent, i.e. the *deserted wife's benefit*. Instead of a means test, there are contribution conditions. The woman can choose whether to rely upon the contribution record of her husband or that of herself. From 1992, however, this benefit will not be paid to claimants whose income is in excess of a prescribed limit.
In respect of all these benefits there is a so called *cohabitation rule*. On grounds of this rule benefit is suspended when a claimant lives together with another person as if husband and wife.

Finally, a carer's allowance is payable to a person providing full-time care and attention to certain categories of welfare claimants.

5. Financing

The social insurance expenditure, except for insurance against industrial accidents and occupational diseases, is financed from four sources. Apart from contribution payments from employers, self-employed and employees, there is an annual state supplement, which covers any shortage of the *Social Insurance Fund.*
There are varying contribution rates for compulsory and voluntarily insured people. The rates within these categories vary considerably, depending on the scope of coverage. The basis for contribution liability are the earnings from employment in the current year (compulsorily insured people), or the past year (voluntarily insured people) There is an upper earnings limit.
The employer is liable to pay contributions in respect of compulsorily insured people. He can deduct the amount of employees' contributions from their wages.

Employers hiring the unemployed as additional staff, benefit from considerable contribution advantages.

The expenditure for industrial accidents and occupational diseases insurance is financed entirely by the employers. There is a uniform contribution rate. Here, the earnings from employment are also the basis for contribution liability, subject to the same earnings limit as the one applying for the other insurance schemes.

The assistance expenditure is borne entirely by the state. The same applies in respect of *child benefits* and *family income supplement.* The costs of (school) meals are borne together by the central and local government.

The state also finances most of the medical care expenditure. The remaining costs are met by contributions.

6. Judicial review

With the exception of *supplementary welfare allowance,* all decisions in relation to insurance and contribution liability and the entitlement to benefit within the framework of the different social security schemes are taken by the so-called *deciding officers.* These are appointed by the Minister out of his own civil servants.
Within 21 days, the *deciding officer's* decision is subject to appeal before an *appeals officer.* The latter is also appointed by the Minister from his civil servants in the *Department of Social Welfare.* One of the a*ppeals officers* is appointed *chief appeals officer.*
The *appeals officer* has a range of semi-judicial powers; for example, he can call upon witnesses under the threat of penal sanctions and hear these under oath. He can follow a purely written procedure, which in fact happens in 60% of the cases. In certain cases the *appeals officer* can be assisted by laymen ex-

perts, for example a medical practitioner; the experts have no voice in the final decision.

The appellant is entitled to be accompanied by a member of his family. With the approval of the *appeals officer*, he can also bring another (third) person, such as a lawyer. Thus there exists no obligatory legal representation, let alone a legal assistance scheme.

Further aspects of the procedure are fully in the hands of the *appeals officer*. This constitutes one of the main points of criticism against the appeals system. However, the jurisprudence of the *High Court* and the *Supreme Court* (see below) increasingly recognise certain procedural guarantees.

The *appeals officers* judge the contested decision to its full extent, i.e. both on points of fact and points of law. There is no obligation for the *appeals officers* to motivate their decisions, nor are the decisions published.

In principle, further appeal is only open in disputes concerning contribution liability and disputes concerning the question of whether an accident resulted from the performance of an employment giving rise to industrial injuries insurance. This appeal is open to the *High Court*, an independent judicial body. The *High Court* only decides on points of law.

Perhaps due to the very limited possibility of further appeal, increasing use is being made of *judicial review*. This general remedy (that is to say not restricted to a certain legal area) is available against decisions which, according to the appellant, are either contrary to the Constitution, or taken without authority, or contrary to procedural requirements, or which are utterly unreasonable. The competent judicial bodies are the *High Court* and the *Supreme Court*.

The decisions of the administrative officers and tribunals, dealing with welfare schemes, are not made available to the general public. The small, but steadily growing number of High and Supreme Court cases dealing with welfare law are published.

There is a separate appeal procedure in respect of *supplementary welfare allowances*. This is solely a matter for the *Health Boards*. The procedure is even more unclear than the ordinary appeal procedure. Although the Act offers the opportunity to enact regulations on this matter, so far this has never happened.

A special appeal procedure exists for those who are refused *unemployment benefit* or *assistance* because of a strike. Further appeal against the decision of the *appeals officer* is possible to a judicial body which has been created especially for this purpose, the *Social Welfare Tribunal*. This body consists of five members, appointed by the Minister, two of whom are representatives of the employers and the employees. The decision of the *Tribunal* is open to appeal to the *High Court* on points of law. Furthermore, on the request of an interested party, the *Tribunal* can review its decision in the light of new facts and circumstances.

Chapter Ten

ITALY

1. Introduction: concept and sources of social security law

Italian social security traditionally distinguished between social assistance (*assistenza sociale*) and social insurance (*previdenza sociale*); since the Italian constitution of 1948 this distinction has become less relevant. We shall not embark upon the complicated adventure of trying to define the concept of social security (*sicurezza sociale*) as such, but limit ourselves to describing the contents of the most important schemes of social security as they are valid today in Italy. Two remarks have to be made here. First of all, in accordance with the general set up of the country reports, we shall not deal with transitory arrangements, although these may be quite important as, in the pensions area especially, fundamental reforms have occurred in the recent past. We shall also concentrate on the general system of social security, covering the wage earners and some assimilated groups of self-employed persons. Due to the complexity of all these special schemes, unless specifically mentioned, we shall only concern ourselves with the general system.

Within the general system there are social insurance schemes which cover a loss of income from work as a result of sickness, maternity and tuberculosis, as well as involuntary unemployment. Furthermore, there are pensions: invalidity benefits and pensions for incapacity for work, survivor's pensions and old age pensions. Industrial injuries and occupational diseases are the subject of a separate insurance scheme. A national health service is also in operation.

The principle of social security (which is understood to mean that every individual, being freed from need, may fully enjoy civil and political rights in the interest of the whole nation) is based upon article 3 Constitution: "It is the Republic's task to remove all economic and social obstacles, which limit the freedom and equality of the citizens and which stand in the way of the development of the people and of the effective participation of all active people in the political, economic and social organisation of the country'.

Article 32 Constitution regards health protection as "a fundamental right and of importance to the whole community", while article 38 Constitution gives further substance to the principle of solidarity, "Every citizen who is not capable of work and who has insufficient means of subsistence is entitled to maintenance and social assistance. Economically active people are entitled to the provision and insurance of means adjusted to their daily needs in case of injury, sickness, invalidity, old age and involuntary unemployment. People incapable of work and handicapped people are entitled to employment and vocational training. Bodies and institutions set up or integrated by the State will be responsible for carrying out the tasks determined within this article. Private assistance is free". Article 38(4) Constitution is of special importance: the State not only regulates the relations between and the constitution of the social security institutions, but also provides for their integration, as the social protection of the people concerned reflects a public interest.

It is the legislator who, by an evaluation of the necessities of life on the one hand and of the existing financial means on the other, determines how and on which level the benefits provided for in article 38 Constitution should be granted and adjusted to any change in circumstances. Yet the *Corte costituzionale* has reserved the right to ensure the minimum level of the constitutionally guaranteed benefits.

One of the results of article 36 Constitution, which recognises the right of workers to earnings which are "sufficient to insure for themselves and their families a free and decent existence", is that social insurance benefits must be sufficient not only for the necessities of life of the claimant himself, but also of his family.

On the grounds of the case law of the *Corte costituzionale* the social provisions of the Italian constitution should be considered as enforceable legal norms. The legal effect of these provisions varies from the granting of subjective rights to legally binding guidelines of interpretation. It follows that statutes, decrees and administrative decisions which are directly contrary to the social constitutional provisions can be voided. Many social constitutional provisions do require the mediation of the legislator to grant subjective rights to the legal subjects concerned. Whether or not article 38 Constitution requires such mediation is debatable, but article 36 Constitution is considered to be a directly applicable norm containing subjective rights.

The constitutional social security principles have been implemented by the legislator, albeit neither in a uniform nor a consistent manner. Nevertheless, if one considers the Italian social security system in the light of its constitutional principles, this system can be considered to be unitary.

For the sake of completeness it should be mentioned that the Statutes of the regions contain provisions concerning regional action for removing economic and social obstacles which hinder the free development of a person and the fundamental equality of citizens, as well as for the effective realisation of fundamental rights with regard to the family, social security, health, education and to labour. Although such provisions are moulded in various forms, it appears from their very wording that they are of a programmatic nature. Furthermore, as the provisions are situated on the same level as the provisions of statutes, the latter may be left out of consideration. Obviously, we can also not deal with measures in the field of social protection, especially of social and medical assistance, which have been taken by the different regions, municipalities and provinces.

The occupational (pension) schemes which supplement social insurance benefits are not the object of social security legislation, but are governed by private and labour law. They may take the shape of earmarked capital within the enterprise or of special funds. Below, the occupational (pension) schemes will in principle not be dealt with.

2. *Administrative organisation*

The Minister for Labour and Social Security is competent in the area of social security. The Minister of Health is responsible for health care.
The competent minister exercises control over the administrative institutions which are described below.

The National Social Security Institute (*Istituto nazionale della previdenza sociale, I.N.P.S.*) is competent in the area of benefits in cash for sickness and maternity, as well as for insuring the risks of old age, death, invalidity, family allowance and unemployment. It is also in charge of the collection of contributions. An Evaluation Committee has been established within the *I.N.P.S.* to control the pension expenditure and work towards the harmonisation of the contribution levels.
The *I.N.P.S.* has regional inspectorates, provincial, town and district services (which are also empowered to collect contributions) and local services and information centres.
The Ordinary and Extraordinary Loss of Earnings Compensation Funds (*Casse Integrative Guadagni Ordinaria e Straordinaria*) also operate within the I.N.P.S.

The majority on the board of governors of the *I.N.P.S.* has to consist of representatives of the wage earners; the same majority is required for the provincial commissions of the *I.N.P.S.*, which decide in first instance on appeals in respect of social security benefits. Furthermore, the employers and the personnel of the *I.N.P.S.*, of the competent departments, and of some other administrative bodies are also represented on the board of governors.

As was already mentioned, the *I.N.P.S.* also hosts separate boards governing the special systems of groups of the self-employed (e.g. the farmers, artisans and tradesmen). Other special systems are organically separate from the *I.N.P.S.* (mainly the various groups of free professionals). Their funds are constituted as private law bodies, with autonomous administration; however, their activities are regulated by law.

Social protection in case of industrial injuries or occupational diseases is entrusted to the National Institute for the Insurance against Industrial Injuries (*Istituto nazionale per l'assicurazione contro gli infortuni sul lavoro, I.N.A.I.L.*). The *I.N.A.I.L.* is also in charge of granting benefits and collecting contributions. The *I.N.A.I.L.* operates via central bodies, as well as via bodies organised on a regional or provincial level. Where medical care is involved, the administration of social protection lies with the local health units; tasks concerned with cash benefits, such as the determination of incapacity to work, lie with the *I.N.A.I.L.* With regard to some categories of workers, the protection against professional risks has been removed from the *I.N.A.I.L.* and entrusted to other specific bodies (e.g. the *Casse marittime* in respect of mariners and fishermen). Employees of the post office and the railway are insured for professional risks by their employers.

Health protection is entrusted to the National Health Service (*Servizio sanitario nazionale*), which operates via the local health units (*Unità sanitarie locali*). Each unit is responsible for the realisation of health protection for all citizens within a certain area. The local health unit is composed of a council, a president, a general manager and a Board of Directors. Although the unit is an administrative body under public law, its general manager bears financial responsibility for the operation of the unit. The responsibilities of each are defined by administrative decree of the responsible minister.

The organisation, administration and operation of the local health units are regulated in regional statutes which, for example, provide for the establishment of specific bodies of a technical nature within which the representatives of the health care providers and other co-operative persons also take part. The State has the task of determining the objectives of health care within the framework of the general economic policy. The level of benefits which are offered to citizens are also determined by national legislation. Managerial and structural experiments may be carried out in relation to private organisations, when these are able to guarantee a lower level of expenses combined with an adequate level of care.

3. *Personal scope of application*

We have already referred to the existence of special schemes for social security, in addition to the general scheme (which was initially developed for employees). These can be distinguished from the general scheme by their personal scope of application (self-employed, agricultural workers, employees of specific employers etc.). Here we will only deal with those insured within the general scheme.

Blue collar workers and those treated as such are covered by sickness and maternity insurance under the general scheme. White collar workers are not entitled to sickness benefit, but are entitled to continued wage payments from their employers for a period of at least three months. In case of tuberculosis, all family members of the insured person are also covered by the sickness insurance scheme. The scope of the invalidity benefit scheme, the pension scheme for incapacity for work, the old age pension scheme encompasses all employees. Incapacity for work and old age pensions as well as survivor's pensions, are subject to contribution conditions and thus to the previous employment record. In contrast, the pension for persons older than sixty five years of age, who find themselves in difficult economic circumstances, is merely subject to residence conditions. The employment insurance scheme applies to all employees; the benefits of the *Cassa integrazione guadagni* and the mobility benefits only cover certain categories of employees. People with no previous employment record are not eligible for unemployment benefit.

The industrial injuries insurance scheme covers those who carry out paid manual subordinate labour; the majority of white collar workers are, as a consequence, excluded from the industrial injuries insurance scheme.

All citizens are equally covered by the national health service. National health service insurance is compulsory, as is the payment of an annual contribution. Each person making use of the national health service receives a health card, which enables him to make use of the services of the national health service.

Subject to certain conditions, those not compulsorily insured, who do not or no longer carry out any professional activities, are given the opportunity of voluntary insurance (continuation of compulsory insurance) with the I.N.P.S. Housewives are also offered the possibility to insure themselves; in practice the latter possibility is of no great significance.

4. Risks and benefits

With regard to the up-rating of social security benefits, it may be observed that pensions are adjusted according to the real increases in the cost of living. Pensions above the minimum are only partly adjusted:
- for a pension with a maximum amount equal to twice the minimum pension, by 100%;
- for pensions amounting to between twice and three times the minimum pension, by 90%; and
- for those pensions amounting to more than three times the minimum pension, by 75%.

The annuities due on the grounds of the insurance scheme for industrial injuries and occupational diseases are annually, automatically adjusted to the evolution of wages within industry.

Where old age, survivor and incapacity for work pensions share many common features, we shall discuss these features under the heading 'old age', without repeating them under the subsequent headings. The pension schemes have undergone structural reforms, first in 1992 and then again in 1995; it is not unlikely that new fundamental reforms are to follow before the end of the transition periods provided for under the previous reforms. We shall, in principle, focus on the situation to be created after the end of the transition periods under the present legislation.

4.1. Old age

In the general system the risk of old age is first of all covered by the old age pension scheme (*pensione di vecchiaia*). Once the present old age pension scheme becomes fully effective, the pensionable age will be flexibilised between 57 and 65 years of age. The pension amount will vary according to the age when the pension is taken up. No age limits will be set and the full pension will be due after 40 years of contribution payment. Men and women will then be treated equally.

The pension will be calculated in function of the contribution record of the insured person (before it was in function of the previous average wage). The total amount of contributions paid are multiplied by an individual coefficient which is fixed according to the age of the insured person at the moment of retirement. It is required that contributions have been paid for at least five years. The first pension according to the new system will be awarded from 1.1.2001.

Contributions are levied upon wages. Wages below a certain amount are not taken into account; in order to promote the supplementary pensions the amounts of the wage exceeding an upper limit are also disregarded for the purposes of the contribution record.

Leave from work in case of maternity opens the possibility to apply for more favourable insurance coefficient in the pension calculation or for a reduction of the pension age by 4 months per child with a total maximum of 24 months.

As regards the requirement of effective retirement, it is to be noted that this fully applies to pensioners under the age of 65. However a partial accumulation with income from self-employed activities is allowed under certain conditions. For persons over the age of 65 partial accumulation with income from employment as a wage earner is also allowed.

The new calculation method on the basis of the contribution record entirely applies to employees who entered working life after 1.1.1996. For those employees who have completed at least 18 years of contribution on 31.12.95, the old calculation method remains. Pension amounts are than calculated as a percentage of the average salary received during the whole career. A mixed system applies to those persons with a contribution record of less than 18 years on 31.12.95.

The seniority pensions (*pensione di anzianità*), which were awarded to claimants of at least 52 years age, after 35 years of professional activity or irrespective of the age of the claimant after a 36 year contribution record, has been 'frozen' for a number of years (no new entitlements in some periods between 1992 and 1995) and will be progressively abolished in the framework of the reforms of 1995. The early pension possibility after 35 years of contribution will gradually be raised to 57 years of age and the minimum contribution record will be gradually raised to 40 years (in 2008) to coincide then with the requirement for a *pensione di vecchiaia* awarded without age requirement.

Measures have been taken to develop and promote collective supplementary pension schemes, such as by providing these schemes with a regulatory framework

The pension for elderly people in difficult economic circumstances (*pensione agli anziani in disagiate condizione economiche*) is not subject to conditions concerning previous professional activities. The pension is awarded to all citizens older than 65 years of age, who are resident in Italy and who have an income below a certain (indexed) minimum. The pension is flat-rate.

4.2. Death

Entitlement to survivor's pension (*pensione agli superstiti*) exists upon the death of a retired person or of a person satisfying the entitlement conditions for incapacity for work or old age pension. The level of the survivor's pension is expressed as a percentage of the pension of the deceased person. The surviving spouse receives 60% of the pension and each child 20% (40% where there is no surviving widow or widower or when the surviving spouse is not entitled to his/her own pension). In order to be eligible, the child must be younger than 18 years, incapable of work or a student.
As regards the survivor's pension, similar changes have been introduced in respect of the pension calculation and additional entitlement conditions as in the old age pension scheme.
Accumulation with earnings from activities as a wage earner is allowed under certain conditions.
Since 1995 the amount of the survivor's pension is made dependent upon the means of the beneficiary.

Survivor's pension is payable on the condition that the deceased person has paid contributions for a period of at least five years, at least two of which must fall within the period of the last five years. Privileged survivor's pension (this is a pension, paid due to a death while performing work in respect of which no pension is payable under the industrial injuries insurance scheme) is not subject to contribution conditions.
Survivor's pension is payable to the surviving widower as well as to the surviving widow. In cases of divorce the judge may decide that the ex-spouse, who formerly received alimony, should receive all or part of the widow's pension.
The right to survivor's pension ends upon remarriage, but the claimant receives a lump sum of twice the annual amount of the survivor's pension.
The total of all survivor's benefits may never amount to more than 100%. If this should appear to be the case, widow(er)'s pension is paid in full with the remaining amount being divided among the surviving orphans.
If there is no surviving widow(er) or orphan, the parents, brothers and sisters of the deceased person receive 15% of the pension to which the deceased person was entitled; here too the benefits may not exceed 100% of the deceased person's pension.

If the deceased insured person did not enjoy a pension, the survivors are awarded a lump sum amounting to 45 times the total number of contributions paid, subject to a minimum and a maximum level. This lump sum is payable, in order of priority, to the surviving spouse, the surviving children or the surviving parents.

If the deceased was a victim of an industrial injury or an occupational disease, survivor's pension is payable to the survivors. The level of this pension is expressed as a percentage of the benefit for permanent incapacity for work which the victim obtained or would have obtained, i.e. 50% thereof for the surviving spouse, 20% for each semi-orphan and 40% for each orphan; should none of these exist 20% is payable to each parent, grand parent, grand child, brother or sister. Again the total sum of the survivor's benefits may not exceed 100% of the annuity. In respect of a person liable for alimony after a divorce, who is deceased as a result of an industrial injury or an occupational disease, a court may grant the survivor's benefit fully or partly to the ex-spouse. A lump sum is also payable on the death of a victim of an industrial injury or occupational disease.

For the sake of completeness we mention that a death benefit is included within the sickness insurance scheme.

4.3. Incapacity for work

The scheme awarding sickness benefits in case of short term incapacity for work only applies to blue collar workers; the employers of white collar workers have to continue, for at least three months, to pay the salaries of their workers who are incapable of working.
In order to be entitled to sickness benefit, the concerned wage earner must be incapable of work and fulfil a waiting period of three days. The total duration of the benefit is six months per year. The benefit amounts to 50% of the lost wage; from the 21st day of sickness the benefit rate amounts to 66% of the wage. However, if the person who is incapable of work is hospitalised, benefit for a person with no dependants is reduced to two fifths of the wage.

The tuberculosis insurance, which is integrated within the sickness insurance scheme, is subject to derogating provisions; the benefit is paid without limits for the duration during treatment of the disease.

In case of pregnancy/maternity, maternity benefit is payable to the insured women, possibly also to the fathers, for two months preceding the estimated date of birth and for three months thereafter. The benefit amounts to 80% of the lost wage. Where the wage continues to be paid by the employer, no benefit is payable. The mother, or the father if the mother makes no request or if the father is solely responsible for the child, may subsequently claim benefit for a further six months. During the optional period benefit amounts to 30% of the lost wage.

In Italian law there is a distinction between an invalid and a person who is incapable of work. A person, whose ability to work in occupations suited to his capacity is reduced to less than one third, is considered as an invalid; people who are completely and permanently incapable of carrying out any work, are considered to be incapable of work.

Neither the invalidity benefit (*assegno di invalidità*) nor the normal pension in respect of incapacity for work (*pensione di inabilità*) are granted for life; an affirmation of benefit entitlement must be requested every three years. Yet after the third consecutive affirmation benefit is automatically extended.
In order to be entitled to benefit for invalidity or incapacity for work, the person incapable of work must have paid contributions for at least five years, three of which must have been in the last five years. However, if the invalidity or in-

capacity for work is due to circumstances at work other than those covered by the industrial injuries insurance scheme, the contribution conditions do not apply (professional incapacity for work).

Invalidity benefit amounts to as many times a percentage of the average annual income from work over the entire career as there are insurance years (with a maximum of 40 years). Transitional rules apply in respect of years worked before 1993. The percentage used varies in the way that the invalidity benefit is proportionally reduced according to the amount of the income obtained from work.

The pension in respect of incapacity for work is calculated in the same way, albeit that not only the actual insurance years are taken into account, but also the years between the granting of a pension and the attainment of pensionable age.

The average annual income which is taken into account, both for the invalidity benefit and the inability pension is subject to a maximum limit.

Those who are fully incapable of work and who need help in order to move or who need permanent assistance in carrying out tasks necessary for daily life, are entitled to an extra monthly flat-rate benefit; a further supplement of 5% is payable in respect of each dependent child.

Special rules apply if incapacity for work is due to an industrial injury or an occupational disease.

Temporary benefits in respect of professional risks are only payable from the fourth day after the industrial injury; for the day on which the injury occurred the claimant receives 100% of his wage paid by the employer, for the three following days he is given 60% of his wage. The benefit continues until the damage to health is cured or consolidated. For the first ninety days temporary benefit in respect of a professional risk amounts to 60%, thereafter 75% of the average wage during the fifteen days preceding the occurrence of the professional risk.

The degree of incapacity for work is determined according to a table of permanent percentages of incapacity for work concerning industrial injuries. In respect of occupational diseases, the degree of incapacity for work is determined on the grounds of an estimation by the advisory doctor to the *I.N.A.I.L.* The degree of incapacity for work may be annually reviewed over a period of four years after the first diagnosis; afterwards revision is only possible every three years. After ten years further review is not possible. Incapacity for work of 10% or less does not give rise to entitlement to any benefits.

Benefit for permanent incapacity for work due to an industrial injury or occupational disease is calculated on the basis of the average wage during the year preceding the termination of work, albeit that the amount of this average is reduced according to a scale of percentages. A minimum and a maximum basis of calculation are used. The basis of calculation determined in this way is then multiplied by the degree of incapacity for work.

In case the help of a third person is necessary, a supplement will be granted as it is for the people totally incapable of work.

In respect of some cases, special provisions allow for a conversion of the pension into a flat-rate amount.

If the industrial injury or the occupational disease results in total permanent incapacity for work, an extra flat-rate benefit is payable to the claimant.

4.4. Unemployment

A distinction must be made between the real unemployment insurance scheme and the special unemployment supplement. The latter is only payable to employees who do not fulfil the conditions under the unemployment insurance scheme.
Entitlement to benefit on grounds of the unemployment insurance scheme is subject to the condition that the claimant has been insured for at least two years and has paid contributions for at least 52 weeks during the preceding two years. Entitlement to unemployment supplement is subject to the condition that the claimant has paid at least ten monthly contributions. People who have never worked (such as school leavers) are therefore neither entitled to insurance benefit nor to the supplement.
Under both unemployment schemes the unemployed person is required to register as looking for employment with the labour exchange.
No waiting period applies to get the benefits. The unemployment insurance benefit is payable for 180 days. Unemployment supplement is payable for 90 days per year (with a possible extension in case of a national economic recession). The unemployment insurance benefit amounts to only 30% of the average pay during the last three months. There is a upper limit to the amounts of both the unemployment benefit and the unemployment supplement.
If unemployment is the result of dismissal due to the closure of an enterprise or a reduction in staff, a special unemployment benefit is granted. This benefit amounts to two thirds of the previously earned wage; it is payable over a period of 180 days. The minimum contribution condition is reduced to thirteen weeks.

An enterprise reducing or ceasing its activities for reasons of its own, or that temporarily reduces or stops its activities, may apply for the intervention of the *Cassa integrazione guadagni ordinaria*. If the *I.N.P.S.* gives its authorisation, the worker can claim a supplement to his wage, payable by the *Cassa integrazione guadagni ordinaria*. This supplement amounts to 80% of the wage which would have been earned in the hours in which work is not performed.

A benefit of the same amount will be paid for maximum of 6 months by the *Cassa integrazione guadagni straordinaria* in case of temporary unemployment due to the restructuring, reorganisation or conversion of the enterprise (or due to certain other reasons such as e.g. the destruction of the enterprise by a natural disaster). The exceptional situation may not last for longer than three years.
The payment of the benefits by the *Cassa ordinaria* or the *Cassa straordinaria* is only possible after a procedure in which the full effects of the economic problems under consideration are verified and in which the trade unions and the *I.N.P.S.* play an important role.

When an enterprise which does not fall under the scope of application of the *Cassa* but still employs at least 15 people, is facing major, irreversible economic problems, it may decide to make a collective dismissal.
The employees who are victims of such a collective dismissal will receive a mobility benefit for a period up to 24 months (or 36 months for persons of at least 60 years of age).

They will also be put on a mobility list which is controlled by the regional employment board. This board has the duty to take all possible initiatives to find new jobs for the dismissed employees. Employers who have previously been forced to implement a collective dismissal are obliged, when later hiring new workers, to give priority to those on the mobility list.

In 1995 a special indemnity has been introduced in favour of workers who are not enjoying the benefits of the *Cassa* or the mobility lists, and who fulfil useful social work after they have lost their jobs.

4.5. Health care

The national health service constitutes the realisation of the principle of article 32 Constitution. The improvement, maintenance and recovery of the physical and mental health of the whole population is entrusted to the national health service. The national health service provides prevention, diagnosis, recovery, as well as rehabilitation. Furthermore, it is responsible for the determination and the removal of the health risks which exist in the living and working environment. The objective of the national health service is the maintenance of the health of the entire state community.

All residents (including all foreigners, at their request), are covered by the national health service. Medical care is provided for an unlimited duration from the beginning of sickness. The national health service operates with doctors who have a contract with the region, the public and recognised private hospitals and other co-operating bodies.
The general practitioners receive a fixed monthly payment for each patient registered with them. This amount is determined in accordance with a scale which is laid down in an agreement between the Minister of Health, the regions and the practitioner's organisations. The fixed amount per patient is dependent upon the age of the patient as well as upon the experience of the doctor. Each general practitioner may register a maximum of 1,500 persons.
Hospital physicians receive a fixed monthly wage. Individual agreements are concluded with specialists who are not bound to a hospital; such agreements provide compensation on the basis of a fixed amount per hour of consultation.
Public hospitals, as well as recognised private hospitals, are managed on a regional basis.

Patients enjoy freedom of choice with regard to their general practitioner, recognised specialist or (recognised) hospital.
The visits to a general practitioner and hospital treatment are free of charge.
A personal contribution is charged for clinical tests and laboratory tests, i.e. at the level of 25% of the official tariff (subject to a minimum and a maximum; in case of multiple tests the maximum is doubled).
The assistance of a specialist medical doctor is to be paid by the patient up to a certain maximum.
Pharmaceutical products (medicine) are classified into three groups:

- group A, consisting of essential medicine and medicine necessary for the treatment of chronic diseases, where no personal contribution is required, except a (low) fixed sum per prescription;
- group B, consisting of medicine 'of remarkable therapeutic value', where the patient has in principle to pay half of the retail price;
- group C, consisting of 'comfort' medicine, in principle fully at the charge of the patient.

However certain categories of persons are totally free of any personal contributions and others only have to pay a fixed amount per prescription. Yet other categories are only freed from personal contributions in respect of medicine and specialist fees in relation to certain pathologies; and they still have to pay the fixed amount per prescription.

Pregnant women are eligible for the services of a midwife; their hospital stay and medicine are free of charge.

The cost of artificial aids are refunded by the national health service, provided that the purchase of these aids was previously approved; the payment of the refund takes place in accordance with an official scale.

Under the threat of loss of benefit, the victims of an industrial injury or an occupational disease must make use of the services of physicians appointed by the *I.N.A.I.L.* and act in accordance with their instructions and also, where applicable, their possible recommendation for surgical intervention. The benefits are paid by the *I.N.A.I.L.*, which also pays all personal contributions which would have been due for medical care.

4.6. Family

Family allowances must ensure that, in accordance with article 36 Constitution, the income of the employee is sufficient not only for himself but also for his family. The family allowances (*assegno per il nucleo familiare*) are borne by the *I.N.P.S.*

The payment of the *assegno per il nucleo familiare* depends upon the number of members of the family unit and the income of the family unit. Are considered to be members of the family: the husband and wife, any children who are younger than 18 years of age, as well as any invalid brothers and sisters of one of the spouses until the age of 18 and without age limit in cases of total incapacity to work, are all considered to be members of the family.

Every family unit registered with the local authorities is eligible for the *assegno*, even if the unit consists of only one person, on condition that the income of the unit does not exceed a fixed amount.

4.7. Need

The granting of support to citizens in a situation of need due to a lack of individual economic resources is a competence, not of the central state, but of the regions. Each region exercises this competence in its own way. However, one can generally say that the region will require from its residents that they must be ready to participate in activities to improve their situation. The amount of the assistance will vary according to the composition of the family and the level of family earnings. The duration of the assistance will, in principle, be limited. Some regions provide special housing and energy support.

5. *Financing*

The basic principle with respect to the financing of social security is based upon national solidarity. This solidarity has been realised and co-ordinated by the State by means of the imposition of contribution liability (the contributions have a parafiscal nature) and direct financial support. The financing of Italian social security is based upon the "pay as you go" system. However in the area of industrial injuries and occupational diseases the system of financing is mixed; here certain mathematical reserves are construed which express the actual value of pensions.

Contributions constitute a certain percentage of earned wages. In principle contributions are levied upon unlimited wages. However, since the pension reform, contributions for the new pension scheme (not for the old) are only due up to an upper limit; the amount of the wage exceeding this limit is not subjected to contributions and is, consequently, not taken into account for the calculation of the pension. A minimal wage for the payment of contributions has also been introduced.
Employees pay contributions in respect of the risks of maternity and sickness, invalidity, old age and death, as well as a special solidarity contribution. The solidarity contribution is levied upon wages between a lower and an upper wage limit.
Employers pay contributions in respect of the risks of maternity and sickness, invalidity, old age and death, unemployment and family allowances. Furthermore, the employers also pay a part of the solidarity contribution.
The employer's contributions vary in accordance to whether the employer is involved in industry or trade. The contributions from employees are the same in both sectors.
Although the contributions are established separately for each branch of social insurance, transfers between branches may occur, as was the case for the contributions for maternity and tuberculosis insurance and also for financing part of the new pension scheme.

Some categories of employers pay lower contributions for the branches of family allowances and old age, for example certain mining enterprises, exporters and certain enterprises providing services (such as transport or tourism).

In respect of the insurance scheme for professional risks, employers pay contributions, the level of which is dependent upon the degree of risk within their branch of industry. This percentage varies between 3 and 5%. Furthermore, the employers are liable to pay an additional contribution, which is equal to 20% of the total sum of (other) social security contributions.

The National Health Service is financed by contributions from the sickness insurance fund and from contributions from the regions, the provinces, the municipalities and other legal persons under public law.

Some pensioners also pay a contribution for the National Health Service. For people who are voluntarily affiliated to the National Health Service there are special contribution rates.

Annual subsidies are granted for the unemployment insurance scheme and the family allowance scheme. The industrial injuries and the occupational diseases scheme is not subsidised. The State guarantees the benefits from the *I.N.P.S.* Benefits from the *Cassa integratizione guadagni* are financed for a major part by the State.

6. Judicial review

Judicial review in respect of social security is divided into two phases, an administrative phase and a judicial phase.

In the administrative phase the claimant must inform the administrative body of his complaint concerning a decision made by that body. This body has ninety days in which to respond to this complaint. If the body remains silent this is considered as a rejection of the complaint (silence is seen as a negative decision). Once the administrative phase is completed (without result), the claimant may turn to a court, in first instance the *pretore del lavoro* (judicial phase). Employees may be represented and assisted by "institutions of patronage and assistance" which are financed by the State and the labour unions.

Chapter Eleven

LUXEMBOURG

1. Introduction: concept and sources of social security law

Although it is difficult to describe the concept of social security in a way which is endorsed by everybody, some unanimity regarding the scope of this concept does exist. Thus, social security (*sécurité sociale*) encompasses:

- social insurance schemes (*assurances sociales*), within which a distinction is made between sickness and maternity insurance schemes (*assurance maladie-maternité*), a pension insurance scheme (*assurance pension*) and an injuries insurance scheme (*assurance accidents*). The sickness and maternity insurance schemes include benefits in kind (medical care), benefits in cash in case of incapacity for work due to illness and funeral grants. The pension insurance scheme covers old age, invalidity and survivor's pensions. The injuries insurance scheme includes medical care, grants in cash and pensions; it covers industrial injuries as well as occupational diseases and some other risks (e.g. injuries sustained at school and injuries sustained when going to or coming from the work place or when carrying out rescue operations);
- family allowances (*prestations familiales*) composed of a maternity supplement (*allocation de maternité*), a birth supplement (*allocation de naissance*), a monthly family benefit (*allocation familiale mensuelle*) an education allowance (*allocation d'éducation*) and a beginning school allowance (*allocation de rentrée scolaire*);
- unemployment benefits (*prestations de chômage*).

Within the broader concept of social security, the following benefits are included as well:

- the guaranteed minimum income (*revenu minimum garanti*) and
- social assistance (*aide sociale*).

From its beginning, social security in The Grand Duchy was influenced by German law; therefore, the Luxembourg social insurance schemes are still mainly set up along professional lines. Nowadays, family benefits have lost their professional character. Unemployment benefits, as well as the guaranteed minimum income and assistance, do not, in principle, distinguish between the various occupational groups. An enumeration of the most important professional groups with their own social security status includes: blue collar workers, white collar workers in the private sector, civil servants and white collar

workers in the public sector, municipal white collar workers and civil servants, artisans, traders and industrialists, self-employed intellectual occupations and agricultural occupations. Furthermore, for employees of specific employers there are separate social security schemes, e.g. for blue collar workers of Arbed (a steel plant), for white collar workers of Arbed and for employees of the National Railway Company.
An important degree of harmonisation of the various professional insurances has been realised in the last decade; nowadays a single social protection system applies to all workers of the private sector, both as far as pensions and benefits in kind of the sickness insurance are concerned.

It must be noted that apart from the social security schemes referred to above, occupational insurance schemes also exist, concluded with *mutuelles* or on an enterprise level.
As such, occupational social insurance schemes offered by enterprises are not controlled by specific regulations, legislative rules merely provide a favourable regime for the taxation of these schemes. Next to that, the general rules of collective labour law and insurance law must be applied. The occupational insurance schemes offered by the enterprises are primarily aimed at providing additional old age and survivor's pensions and additional invalidity pensions.

The activities of the mutual assistance societies (*sociétés de secours mutuel/ mutuelles*) are regulated by legislation and a High Council for the mutual societies exists (*Conseil supérieur de la mutualité*). The numerous assistance societies grant their members benefits in respect of risks such as death as well as, for example, additional benefits for injuries other than industrial injuries. In addition, compensation to members of the mutual assistance societies may also be payable in respect of any medical costs which are not covered by (statutory) social security. The mutual guarantee funds enjoy support from the State as well as a favourable taxation regime.

In 1948 the constitution of Luxembourg laid down a number of provisions which are of importance to us:
- article 11.4 Constitution: "The statute organises the social security, the protection of the health and the leisure of the workers and guarantees trade union freedom";
- article 11.5 Constitution: "The statute guarantees the right to work and the realisation of this right for every citizen".

Although these constitutional provisions may be regarded as the legal basis for all social security legislation, the real significance of the provisions for positive law remains minimal. Perhaps the constitutional clauses have no role other than to require the intermediation of a formal statute for the development of social security rules (that is to say, to offer a statutory framework for such rules); specially subject to this requirement, are, for example, rules with regard to granting compensation for not being able to exercise the right to work, i.e. unemployment benefits.

Each branch of social security is based upon at least one formal act; these are usually further elaborated by decree. It must be noted that the social insurance act (*Code des assurances sociales*), which was introduced in 1925 and subsequently frequently modified, contains a codification of social insurance law: in the last decade only a few newly introduced social insurance acts and important decrees were not integrated in the act; the latter relate to unemployment insurance, family benefits and the guaranteed minimum income.

2. *Administrative organisation*

The Minister for Social Security is competent in respect of social security and in respect of all social security institutions, the mutual assistance societies, the *Conseil supérieur* and the *Conseil arbitral des assurances sociales*. The Minister for Family and Solidarity is, among other things, competent in respect of family benefits, the guaranteed minimum income and social assistance. The Minister for Labour is competent for unemployment benefits as well as for employment policy and labour exchange.

A supervisory body, the *Inspection générale de la sécurité sociale*, was established within the Ministry of Social Security and under the authority of the Minister. It carries out policy and supervisory functions in respect of social security as a whole. There is also a separate board, *le Contrôle médical de la sécurité sociale*, which is charged with tasks related to medical evaluation, e.g. the recognition of invalidity, the determination of work incapacity in case of illness, the assessment of the work incapacity in case of professional disease.

The Common Social Security Centre (*Centre commun de la sécurité sociale*) is competent for the compilation and the processing of computerised data, the registration of insured people and the receipt and collection of contributions.

The sickness and maternity insurance scheme, which has been unified in 1992, is administered by the sickness funds (*caisses de maladie*), which all come together within he *Union des caisses de maladie*, a legal person under public law. This *Union* has been given an important task in the negotiations with the health care providers and in the development of health care policy.
The sickness funds themselves are legal bodies under public law. The following sickness funds are active:
a) the Sickness Fund for white collar workers in the Private Sector (*Caisse de maladie des employés privés*) which is competent in respect of all white collar wage-earners as well as self-employed people who are primarily engaged in an intellectual activity;
b) the Sickness Fund for blue collar workers (*Caisse de maladie des ouvriers*) which is competent for people with a mainly manual professional activity as well as for the voluntarily insured persons;
c) the Sickness Fund of the self-employed (*Caisse de maladie des professions indépendentes*) which is competent for the artisans, traders and industrialists;

d) the Agricultural Sickness Fund (*Caisse de maladie agricole*) which is competent in respect of people active within the agricultural sector;
e) the Sickness Fund of the civil servants and the public sector employees (*Caisse de maladie des fonctionaires et employés publics*) competent for civil servants and employees of the state;
f) the Sickness Fund of the civil servants and the employees of the municipalities (*Caisse de maladie des fonctionaires et employés communaus*) competent for civil servants and employees of the municipalities; and
g) three sickness funds on an enterprise level: the sickness funds of the blue collar workers of Arbed (a steel plant), of the blue collar workers of Arbed and the Medical Mutual Society of the Luxembourg Railways.

The institutions of the sickness funds for wage earners (except for those funds which belong to only one enterprise) are composed on a parity basis of representatives of the employers and representatives of the insured people. The position of chairman rotates. All members of the enterprise's sickness funds, except for the chairman-manager (or his deputy), are elected representatives of the insured people. The institutions of the sickness funds for self-employed people and for agricultural occupations are composed only of representatives of the insured people.

The pension insurance scheme, which was made uniform in 1987, continues to be administered by bodies whose powers are determined by the professional category of the insured person, i.e.:
a) the Pension Fund for white collar workers in the Private Sector (*Caisse de pension des employés privés*), which is competent in respect of all insured people, white collar workers as well as self-employed people who are primarily engaged in an intellectual activity;
b) the Pension Fund for Artisans, Traders and Industrialists (*Caisse de pension des artisans, des commerçants et industriels*) which is competent in respect of these categories of self-employed people;
c) the Agricultural Pension Fund (*Caisse de pension agricole*) which is competent in respect of people active within the agricultural sector;
d) the Insurance Institution for Old Age and Invalidity (*Etablissement d' assurance contre la vieillesse et l'invalidité*), is competent in respect of blue collar workers and other remaining insured persons.

The management of each pension fund is charged to a board of directors. This board is chaired by a chairman-civil servant. The remaining members are appointed by the Commission of the Pension Fund. The board of directors is responsible for taking decisions regarding affiliation, contributions, administrative fines and the concerned statutory benefits. The commission of the Pension Fund operates as a representative body: it drafts the internal regulations of the Pension Fund as well as the annual budget and accounts. The chairman of the board of directors also chairs the commission and has the right to vote.

In both the Commission and the board of directors of the Pension Fund for Employees of the Public Sector and in that of the Insurance Institution for Old Age and Invalidity, there is parity between representatives of the employers and of the insured people. Elsewhere, these bodies are composed entirely of representatives of the insured people. All representatives are directly elected, re-

spectively by the insured people and the employers, for a period of five years. In order to be eligible as a candidate, the same conditions as for the local elections apply.
Meetings of the board of directors and the commission are attended by a governmental commissioner, who, just like the chairman of the board of directors, is competent to suspend decisions taken by these bodies which are in his opinion contrary to the relevant statute; the competent minister then decides the case, after a recommendation of the inspectorate.

Enterprises which are subject to the injuries insurance scheme have associated themselves within a mutuality, i.e. the Injuries Insurance Association (*Association d'assurance contre les accidents*). The management of this association is entrusted to a management committee, the chairman of which is appointed by the government. Some affairs must be dealt with by the general assembly of the association. The association is composed of two sections; the industrial section and the agricultural and forestry section. The supervision of both sections rests with separate general associations and management committees, but takes place according to the same principles.

The National Fund for Family Benefits (*Caisse nationale de prestations familiales*) is responsible for the administration of family benefits.

All in all, there are more than twenty administrative bodies involved with the administration of the social insurance schemes. It is true that a certain degree of administrative concentration was ensured by the services of the two sections of the Injuries Insurance Scheme Association and the Insurance Institute for Old Age and Invalidity, being united to form the Social Insurance Service (*Office des assurances Sociales*). Moreover, the four previously existing family benefit funds, which were organised on a professional basis, have merged into one single National Family Benefits Fund. Also, the following institutions have pooled their administrations:
- the Sickness Fund for the Self-Employed and the Pension Fund for Artisans, Traders and Industrialists, under the name *Administration commune des caisses de sécurité sociale des classes moyennes;*
- the Agricultural Sickness Fund and the Agricultural Pension Fund, under the name *Administration commune des caisses de sécurité sociale de la profession agricole;*
- the National Fund for Family Benefits and the Pension Fund for white collar workers in the Private Sector.

The National Solidarity Fund (*Fonds National de Solidarité, F.N.S.*) is a legal body under public law, with financial autonomy. The Fund is charged with the administration of the guaranteed minimum income and is managed by a board of directors, the members of which are appointed by the government.

In each municipality there is a social service (*office social*), composed of five members, voted for in secret elections by the municipal council. One member is re-elected each year. The office is responsible for the payment of the minimum income, the supervision of benefits for the relief of the poor, and with tasks of social assistance. The office is supervised by the Council of Mayor and Aldermen.

3. Personal scope of application

All persons professionally active in Luxembourg are compulsorily covered by the social insurance system. However, as the social insurances are still administrated on the basis of distinct professional groups, it remains necessary to distinguish between various groups of professionally active people, in order to know to which fund they are compulsorily affiliated.

All persons receiving a replacement income from social insurance are also compulsorily affiliated with the social insurance funds (sickness funds), provided their benefit has been subjected to a contribution for the Luxembourg sickness insurance. The beneficiaries of the guaranteed minimum income are also covered if they are not otherwise socially protected. Students who are not protected as dependent family members are also compulsorily insured.

The spouse and all direct descendants of the insured person are co-insured, subject to the condition that they are dependent upon the insured person and are themselves not covered against the same risk. Adopted or foster children are treated as descendants. Close relatives who, in the absence of a spouse care for the household of the insured person are also insured.
All people older than eighteen years of age, who loose the quality of insured or jointly insured person may continue the affiliation with their sickness fund within three weeks (continued insurance). All people resident in the Grand Duchy, who are not otherwise insured against sickness, can voluntarily affiliate themselves to the sickness insurance scheme. This results in the sickness and maternity insurance schemes covering virtually all residents, although they are still strongly established upon a professional basis.

Nowadays, there is a uniform pension insurance scheme. All people in the Grand Duchy who are gainfully employed, be it for another person or on their own account, or who can demonstrate periods which are treated as periods of professional activity, are compulsorily insured under the old age, invalidity and survivor's pension insurance scheme. Periods treated as periods of professional activity include the following: periods of enjoyment of income maintenance benefits which gave rise to pension insurance contribution liability, periods during which a person has been a helper for a self-employed person, periods of employment in relief work and periods of military service. On the request of one of the parents of a child, (made within twenty four months of the birth or adoption of the child), a period of twenty four months (the so called baby years) may count as a period of professional activity, subject to the condition that the claimant was insured for a pension for at least twelve months during the three years preceding the birth or adoption and that this period does not fall under one of the above periods (e.g. continuation of wages or the enjoyment of income maintenance).

Apart from compulsory pension insurance there exists the possibility of 'optional continued insurance'. The latter possibility is open to those who were insured for a pension for at least twelve months preceding the loss of status as an insured person. A request for continued insurance must be made within six months. Periods of continued insurance are counted as periods of compulsory insurance.
Civil servants and white collar workers of the government and of the railway are not insured on the grounds of the pension insurance scheme; for these categories separate pension schemes exist, which we shall not discuss here

People who have attained the age of sixty five are no longer admitted to the pension insurance scheme.

The members of the Injuries Insurance Scheme Association are the enterprises. Benefits from the injuries insurance scheme are payable to all employees, domestic personnel and self-employed master artisans, as well as the dependent family members of the latter. The heads of the enterprises who are subject to the injuries insurance scheme can take out voluntary insurance for themselves and for other people who are not compulsory insured. Furthermore, the injuries insurance scheme covers people working for a governmental body or the army, as well as free intellectual occupations. Also pre-schooling, schooling (including universities) and after schooling of those following education in the Grand Duchy is covered, as well as all help and rescue operations for the benefit of a third person in danger and the theoretical and practical activities of people who take part in volunteer corps involved with help and rescue.
Below, we will not discuss the particular features of the injuries insurance scheme for government personnel, members of the military service, students and rescuers/helpers Equally, we will not discuss the special injuries insurance scheme for people employed in the agricultural and forestry sector (called *assurance accidents agricols et forestiers*).

All pregnant women and women who have just given birth, whose legal place of residence at that time is in the Grand Duchy, belong to the scope of people who are eligible for maternity allowance and prenatal birth allowance. In order to qualify for the benefits they have to visit a medical doctor regularly.
All children brought up in the Grand Duchy are eligible for the post natal birth allowances.
Each child that has regularly been brought up in the Grand Duchy and who has his legal place of residence there, is entitled to the monthly family allowances from his birth until he attains eighteen years of age. The claimant is eligible until the age of twenty seven if he follows higher education and for an unlimited time if he is incapable of providing for his own needs due to a chronic illness or disability.
Employees, as well as young people whose training is finished (subject to a 'waiting period'), and self-employed people who have had to cease their activities due to sectorial or general economic problems, are eligible for benefit as full time unemployed people.

In order to be able to enjoy the guaranteed minimum income, the claimant must be resident in the Grand Duchy; he must also have resided in the Grand Duchy for at least ten of the last twenty years. With respect to the allowances for handicapped persons, it is also required that a claimant's legal place of residence is in the Grand Duchy and he must have resided in the Grand Duchy for at least ten years. In order to be able to receive an advance on the payment of alimony from the F.N.S., the claimant must have his legal place of residence in the Grand Duchy and must have resided there for at least five years.

4. Risks and benefits

4.1. Old age

Every person insured for a pension, who can demonstrate that he has been insured for at least 120 months, is entitled to an old age pension (*pension de vieillesse*) from the age of 65 onwards. Every insured person who can demonstrate that he has been insured for 480 months is entitled to an early retirement pension from 60 years of age onwards (*pension de vieillesse anticipée*). In order to satisfy the latter requirement, not only the actual periods of insurance are taken into account, but also periods during which an invalidity pension was received, periods of study as well as waiting time for school leavers in the scheme for unemployment compensation and periods during which a parent has raised one or more children under the age of six in the Grand Duchy. The latter periods may not amount to more than eight years on the birth of the second child, nor to more than ten years on the birth of the third child. If the child is physically or mentally handicapped and is not brought up in a specialised institution, the above maximum age limit is eighteen. Periods of caring for a dependent person requiring help for daily living are also taken into account.
The insured person can enjoy an early retirement pension from as young as 57 years of age on the condition that he has effectively been insured for 480 months (i.e. without taking into account the above mentioned assimilated periods).
A person who is enjoying an early retirement pension must forego all significant or non-incidental occupational activities. If paid employment is exercised for which monthly earnings exceed one third of the minimum income, the pension is reduced by half.
It is also possible to postpone the pension until the age of 68 years; in such case the pension amount is increased by an actuarial coefficient.

The old age pension consists of two elements, the proportional increases and the flat-rate increases. The amount of the proportional increases is mainly a function of income from work on which contributions are payable throughout the recipient's whole career. The proportional increase is 1.78% per annum of the total, re-valued income from work, which is taken into account for the payment of contributions. The amount of the flat-rate increases is exclusively dependent upon the duration of the period of insurance. For each year of insurance a flat-rate amount is payable, up to a maximum of 40 years. The old age pension, which is based upon at least 40 years of insurance and periods treated as such, is subject to a minimum limit; if the claimant can demonstrate at least 20 years, but not 40 years, the amount of the minimum pension is reduced by as many fortieths as there are years less than 40. The old age pension is subject to a maximum limit.

A person who is insured for a pension and who, at the end of his 65th year, does not satisfy the minimum conditions with regard to the duration of insurance, is entitled to repayment of all contributions which he has paid himself and which his employer has paid on his behalf; these contributions are indexed when they are repaid. Repayment excludes any entitlement to benefit.

The above conditions with regard to old age pension also apply mutatis mutandis to the invalidity and survivor's pensions described below.

4.2. Death

The surviving spouse of the beneficiary of an old age or invalidity pension, as well as the surviving spouse of a person insured for a pension for at least twelve months during the three years preceding his death, is eligible for a survivor's pension (*pension de survie*). If the death of the insured person was due to an injury or to a recognised occupational disease, the above minimum insurance requirements are not relevant. It is required that the spouse was married to the deceased person for at least one year, except when they had a common child.
The ex-spouse of the deceased insured person, who has not remarried, is also entitled to a survivor's pension. If there is no surviving spouse, subject to further conditions, parents and relatives in the ascending line and relatives twice removed in the side line, are entitled to a survivor's pension.
If several people satisfy the conditions, the survivor's pension is divided equally between them. In cases where there is also an ex-spouse who is eligible, the survivor's pension is divided pro rata temporis between the ex-spouse and the remaining eligible persons.

The survivor's pension terminates upon remarriage. If the beneficiary is younger than 50 years of age at the time of his remarriage, he receives five times the amount of pension of the preceding year as a lump sum. If remarriage takes place after the age of 50, the beneficiary is only entitled to three times the above amount of pension.

Children of the insured person are entitled to a survivor's pension, subject to the same requirements regarding the employment record, as for the spouse's survivor's pension. This survivor's pension is payable until the child attains 18 years of age or 27 years of age if he is studying. The survivor's pension of an orphan is terminated upon marriage, unless he is studying.
Widow(er)'s and orphan's survivor's pensions are related to the old age or invalidity pension which the deceased insured person received or would have received. The surviving spouse receives two thirds of the proportional increases and, in specified instances, of the special proportional increases, plus all the

flat-rate increases and, in certain circumstances, the special flat-rate increases. An orphan receives one fourth of the proportional increases and, in specific cases, of the special proportional increases, plus one third of the flat-rate increases and in specific cases, of the special flat-rate increases. When special flat-rate or proportional increases are payable, they are determined in an analogous way as for the invalidity pensions (see above). If both parents of the orphan died and the orphan is entitled to a pension both in the father's and mother's name, the higher of the two pension amounts is doubled.

To the extent necessary, a supplement is payable to the survivor's pension of the widow(er) and the orphan of an insured person or pensioner, provided that the latter satisfied the conditions regarding insurance and periods treated as such with respect to a minimum pension; the supplement is two thirds in respect of the widow(er) and one fifth in respect of the orphan.

The maximum survivor's pension is determined in the same way as the maximum old age pension.

On top of the old-age pension of the deceased or a survivor's pension for the spouse, being paid for the month in which the death occurred, the survivors get an amount equal to three months of the pension the deceased would have received.

A funeral grant (*indemnité funéraire*) is payable on the grounds of the sickness and maternity insurance scheme, on the death of the insured person or of one of his family members. The grant is payable to the person who is responsible for the funeral. The grant is reduced respectively to half or one fifth of the standard amount, if the deceased was younger than six years old or was dead at birth. However, in the voluntary scheme there is a waiting period of three months before a person is entitled to a funeral grant.

If death was due to an injury covered by the injuries insurance scheme, a funeral grant equal to one fifteenth of the annual income from work is payable together with a pension to the relatives of the deceased person. The surviving spouse receives a pension equal to 42.8% of the annual income; if she is at least 53.5% incapable of work and has been so for more than three months, she receives 50% thereof. Upon remarriage, the survivor loses his right to pension. If, upon remarriage, he is younger than 50 years, he receives 60 times the monthly pension as a lump sum; if he is 50 years old or more, he receives 36 times this amount.

The widow of a person who was at least 50% incapable of work due to an insured professional risk, but whose death was not caused by this risk, receives a lump sum of 40% of the annual income from work as a roughly estimated compensation.

To the extent that it gives rise to entitlement to family allowance, a dependent child of the deceased person receives a pension equal to 21.4% of the annual income from work of the deceased person. The ascendants of the victim, who shared the same household as the victim, and whose maintenance was largely dependent upon the victim, receive a pension equal to 32.1% of the annual income from work of the victim (however, the amount as well as the duration of this pension may be reduced in accordance with the real damage suffered). The same pension is payable to the father or mother, father-in-law or mother-in-law, step-father or step-mother of the victim, as well as to his brother or sister or unmarried son or daughter, who at the time of death were at least 45 years of age, subject to the condition that they cared for the household of the victim for the five years preceding his death. The pension is terminated upon the marriage or remarriage of these people. The total survivor's pensions may not exceed 85.6% of the annual income from work of the deceased person.

4.3. Incapacity for work

We can distinguish here:
- the cash benefits under the sickness and maternity insurance;
- the invalidity pensions ; and
- the pensions under the injury insurance.

Benefits in cash on grounds of the sickness and maternity insurance scheme in case of maternity are only payable if the claimant was affiliated with the sickness fund for at least six months in the year preceding the birth.
The schemes for wage earners include benefits in cash in case of illness and benefits in cash in case of maternity. These compensations always amount to the equivalent of what the insured person would have earned by continuing his work, although benefits payable under the scheme for white collar workers in the private sector may not exceed the maximum limit. Benefits in cash in case of illness are payable from the first day of incapacity for work for a maximum duration of 52 weeks. Benefits in cash in case of maternity are payable during at least eight weeks before and eight weeks after the birth. A four week supplement is granted for nursing mothers and in case of premature birth or multiple birth.
However, cash benefits are not payable if the claimant's wages continue to be paid on the grounds of legislation or agreement (e.g. this is determined in the act for white collar workers in the private sector: they are entitled to a continuation of their wage during the course of the month and the following three months).
People insured under the scheme for self-employed occupations receive cash benefits only from the fourth month of incapacity for work due to illness; this cash benefit equals the income the self-employed person declared and on which contributions were levied.

On the grounds of the pension insurance scheme, each insured person younger than sixty five years old, who can demonstrate that he has been insured for a pension for twelve months during the three years preceding the determination of invalidity by the controlling physician or after the sickness compensation in cash has expired, is entitled to an invalidity pension (*pension d'invalidité*). The required minimum period of insurance is not applied if the invalidity was due to an occupational disease or injury, which arose during a period of insurance.
An insured person is treated as an invalid when his capacity for work has, as a result of a long duration of illness, a defect or weakening, been reduced to such a degree that he can no longer carry out his former occupational activity nor

any other profession which reflects his strength and ability. The recipient of an invalidity pension may not carry out any substantial paid work. The pension is suspended if the self-employed activity of the claimant is carried out by another person on his account. Until the age of fifty, the insured person must attend all rehabilitation and retraining projects which are offered to him.

Invalidity pension consists of proportional increases and flat-rate increases (as in the old age pension), increased by special proportional increases or special flat-rate increases. The special proportional increases supplement the proportional increases until 55 years of age; they equal a yearly amount of the total income from work for which contributions were paid between the age of 25 and the time when invalidity occurred, divided by the number of civilian years in this period. The special flat-rate increases supplement the flat-rate increases by an identical amount until 65 years of age. If the insurance record of the claimant between the age of 25 and the time when invalidity occurred is interrupted, the increase is only payable in relation to the number of effectively covered years as a proportion of the total number of civilian years that this period includes.

There is a minimum invalidity pension which is calculated in the same way as the minimum old age pension, albeit that the years between the moment of entitlement to pension and the 65th year are treated as insurance years. However, if invalidity occurs after the age of 25, the above years are only counted as a proportion of the claimant's length of insurance to the number of years between his 25th birthday and the occurrence of the risk.

The maximum invalidity pension is determined in the same way as the maximum old age pension.

A person insured on the grounds of the injuries insurance scheme is entitled to a pension (*rente d'accident*) from the thirteenth week of incapacity for work and for as long as the complete or partial incapacity for work lasts. The pension in respect of complete incapacity for work amounts to 85.6% of the average income from work over the previous year, or a part thereof in respect of partial incapacity for work. The basis of calculation is subject to a maximum limit in the same way as the basis of calculation for the payment of contributions.

If the person who is partially incapable of work due to an injury is involuntarily without employment, the pension is increased up to the amount of the pension in respect of full incapacity for work, but for no longer than three months while possible unemployment benefits are deducted.

If the victim of an insured injury is not only completely incapable of work, but his capacity is reduced to such an extent that he needs the continuous help of another person, the pension is increased in proportion to the degree of incapacity with a maximum limit equal to the annual income from work.

For as long as the insured person receives a pension for incapacity for work of at least 50%, he is granted an allowance of 10% for each dependent child for whom he receives child allowance. The pension and pension allowance may not exceed the annual income from work.

The degree of incapacity for work can only be reviewed within three years after the determination of the pension, except in respect of a worsening of the incapacity for work by at least 10%.

On the grounds of the injuries insurance scheme, pension payable in respect of incapacity for work of less than 10% is, after a period of at least three years, payable as a lump sum; the pensions can be paid off on the request of the claimant, if his incapacity for work due to an injury is higher than 10% but not higher than 40%.

4.4. Unemployment

People belonging to the scope of application of the unemployment scheme are entitled to unemployment benefit (*indemnité de chômage*) subject to the condition:
- that they are between sixteen and sixty four years of age;
- that the waiting period is completed (if they are school leavers);
- that they are capable of work and living in the Grand Duchy;
- that they are registered as seeking employment and submit a claim for unemployment benefit;
- that they are involuntarily unemployed, such implying that no benefit is due when the worker left his last job without good reason, i.e. when no exceptional, valid and convincing reasons are present.
- that all suitable work is accepted.

The beneficiary must sign on at the registration office or during a control on the appointed days and hours. He must participate in the occupational training or general training programs to which he is invited by the competent administrative authority. The granting of benefit can be made dependent upon carrying out work which is declared by the government to serve the public interest. Unemployment benefit is payable for a maximum duration of 365 days within a two year period; however, the director of the employment authority can, on request, decide to include a further period of 182 days. For this it is required that the unemployed person appears to have little chance on the labour market due to his age, physical or mental afflictions, or any other serious circumstances. The benefit will also be payable for a longer period if the unemployed person is at least 50 years old and satisfies a certain number of insurance years. The right to benefit is terminated at an earlier stage if the entitlement conditions are no longer satisfied, e.g. by unjustifiably refusing an offer of employment.

Unemployment benefit amounts to 80% of the average gross wage of the three months preceding the occurrence of unemployment, without the amount thus calculated exceeding two and a half times the social minimum wage or exceeding two times the social minimum wage if the unemployment has already lasted for longer than 182 days during a period of twelve consecutive months. In case the unemployment benefit is paid for more than 365 days, the amount of the benefit should not exceed one and a half times the social minimum wage. The percentage of the gross wage is raised to 85% when the unemployed individual has children at charge; it is reduced when he is living together with a partner earning more than two and a half times the social minimum wage.

Unemployment benefit for younger school leavers amounts to 70% of the social minimum wage in respect of an uneducated blue collar worker of the same age. However, young people of 16 or 17 years of age who cannot produce a certificate of completion of school age or of termination of technical training, only receive 40% of the social minimum wage. Elderly self-employed people receive 80% of the social minimum wage that would be payable to them as skilled workers.

4.5. Health care

The sickness and maternity insurance scheme covers the costs of medical care due to illness or maternity. These benefits in kind are payable from the time of affiliation with a sickness fund (exception: the voluntary insurance scheme includes a waiting period of three months). They are payable as from the time of occurrence of the illness and for the entire duration of the illness, provided that the claimant remains affiliated with his sickness fund. In case the patient ceases to be affiliated to a sickness fund, the right to benefits in kind of the sickness insurance is maintained for the current month and the three subsequent months, upon the condition that the concerned person had been insured for at least six months immediately before the end of the insurance. Moreover the right to benefits in kind is maintained for three months if the concerned person was receiving medical treatment at the moment of the termination of the insurance. An additional prolongation of the benefit in kind is awarded to beneficiaries of a full pension of the injury insurance, whatever the duration of the previous affiliation was.
Benefits in kind cover medical and dental care, travel and ambulance costs of the ill person, pharmaceutical costs, costs of curative aids and aids (artificial aids etc.), radiological examinations, hospital costs and birth costs.

Medical care may be provided by any of the physicians who are recognised by the state. The physician's fees are determined by collective agreement or, failing this, by arbitration via the *Commission de conciliation et d' arbitrage*. In the latter case, the solution agreed upon requires ministerial approval. Tariffs are annually adjusted. Hospital tariffs are determined on the grounds of an agreement with the *Entente des hôpitaux*.
The insured person has freedom of choice in respect of his doctor and hospital and, with the approval of his sickness fund, may be treated abroad. The fees are reimbursed by the sickness fund. Services of medical doctors which are officially listed, are covered for the full amount agreed upon in the collective agreement. However when visiting a general practitioner, the patient is charged a personal contribution of 20% of the minimum fee; this contribution can, however, only be charged once in a period of 28 days. For all other visits to a medical doctor, a personal payment of 5% is requested. In case of hospitalisation, no personal contribution is required; a contribution is merely payable towards the 'hotel costs' of the stay in a hospital. Refunds of the costs of dental care are made in accordance with collective agreements. A personal contribution of 5% is charged for dental consultations; for artificial dental prosthesis, the personal contribution may not exceed 20% of the tariffs established for decent and useful care. Other artificial aids are, after the approval of the sickness fund, compensated according to the tariffs determined by an agreement. Medicine is divided into four categories: non-refundable medicine; drugs subject to

reduced reimbursement, the costs of which are refunded for 40%; normal medicine, the costs of which are refunded for 80% (except in cases of hospitalisation when a refund of 100% is payable) and prioritarian medicine which is fully refunded.

The costs of hospitalisation are payable directly by the sickness fund; the patient only pays the part of the cost for which he is liable. This also applies for medicine. Medical care costs made for the victim of an injury within the meaning of the injuries insurance scheme are borne directly by the association of the injuries insurance scheme. Victims of an insured injury pay no personal charges; personal contributions which would have been payable regardless of the occurrence of such injuries are borne by the association of the injuries insurance scheme.

4.6. Family

Entitlement to maternity allowance (*allocation de maternité*) arises from the eighth week before the estimated date of delivery with a maximum duration of 16 weeks. Similar provision applies in respect of an adoption. Maternity allowance is reduced by the amount of maternity or sickness benefit in cash payable under the social insurance schemes, by the wage that the claimant continues to enjoy, and by the amount of unemployment benefit of the claimant.

In order to be entitled to birth allowance (*allocation de naissance*) in the period preceding the birth, the mother must undergo five medical examinations and a dental examination. In order to be entitled to the actual birth allowance, the mother must undergo a post-natal examination within ten weeks of the birth. For post natal-birth allowances, the child must be subject to two pre-natal examinations and it must have at least four medical examinations before the age of two years.

The amount of the monthly family allowance (*allocation familiale*) varies according to whether it concerns the first, the second or the third child; for each subsequent child the same amount is payable. The allowances are increased when the child has attained the age of respectively 6 and 12 years. Handicapped children under the age of 18 are entitled to an additional, special allowance. This allowance is continued, without an age limit, for people who are incapable of providing for their needs due to a defect or chronic illness.

The education allowance (*allocation d'éducation*) is paid to the parent residing in the Grand Duchy who cares at home for one or more of his children who are younger than two years of age. The beneficiary does not exercise a professional activity or, if he does, his income and that of his spouse do not exceed a certain maximum.

A beginning school allowance (*allocation de rentrée scolaire*) is paid in September for all school going children.

4.7. Need

The guaranteed minimum income (*revenu minimum garanti*) is an assistance benefit awarded under the following conditions:
a) actual residence in Luxembourg and residence in Luxembourg for at least 10 years in the last 20 years;
b) availability for the labour market and readiness to accept any suitable job pointed out by the employment administration;
c) at least 30 years of age;
d) readiness to participation on courses, training courses or other measures to prepare, initiate or prepare him for professional life; readiness also to do temporary public works for the state, the municipalities, public institutions or non-profit institutions.

Adults who, because of their bad health, are unable to earn their own living will also qualify for the guaranteed minimum income, without having to satisfy the above mentioned conditions of availability for work and of age. The same goes for the following categories of persons, who are also free of the condition of readiness to undertake social integration activities (condition d):
- persons of 60 years of age or older;
- the person educating children, for which family allowances are being paid and under the condition that the child is younger than 6 years old; or the child is between 6 and 15 years old and it is against the interest of the child that the concerned person works or participates in social integration activities; or the child is handicapped;
- the person taking care of a seriously handicapped person requiring constant attendance.

The guaranteed minimum income consists of a differentiated amount between the poverty line established in function of the composition of the common household and the income out of work, social security and capital of that household.

Once a year a heating allowance may be paid. The amount of this allowance is determined each year with reference to the number of people concerned. In order to be eligible, the claimant must have no income in excess of a certain limit (the ratio of the annual heating allowance to the income limit equals two to five).

Furthermore, the beneficiaries of a solidarity pension who are not already affiliated with a sickness fund, are affiliated with the *Caisse nationale d' assurance maladie*.
For the sake of completeness we mention that the *Fonds National de Solidarité* is also empowered to grant advances on alimony payments.

The municipal welfare offices are responsible for the municipal duty of providing social assistance. This duty consists of providing the necessary means for assistance to the needy. Assistance may be paid in cash, but can also involve measures in order to allow poor people to carry out useful work or to help them find paid work.

5. *Financing*

The sickness and maternity insurance scheme is mainly financed from contributions. The system of financing is based upon the pay as you go principle. A distinction has to be made as to the health care insurance branch and the income replacement branch of this insurance.

In the schemes for employees, insured people who are gainfully employed pay half of the contributions, their employers pay the other half. In the schemes for self-employed occupations, agriculturists and intellectual free professions, as well as in the voluntary insurance scheme, the contributions are entirely borne by the insured people themselves. Half the contributions of beneficiaries of pensions are payable by the beneficiaries and the other half by the body responsible for paying the pension. If the wage or pension falls below the lower contribution limit, the insured person is merely liable to pay contributions over the actual amount of his wage or pension; the remainder is the responsibility of the employer or pension institution.
The health care branch of the maternity and sickness insurance is financed out of a uniform contribution by all socially insured persons. This contribution is established in function of the total expenditure to be covered, taking into account that the state pays an 'over-contribution' of 250% of this uniform contribution rate upon the total sum of the pensions for which contributions are due to the sickness insurance and that the state pays also an 'over-contribution' of 10% of the uniform contribution rate on the total sum on which other socially insured persons pay contributions.

The contribution rates of the sickness insurance amount to 5% for health care; 0,2% for the cash benefits to be paid to the self-employed and to the wage earners benefiting of the continued payment of their wages during the month the work incapacity emerges and the three subsequent months; and 4,2% of the cash benefit of the wage earners who cannot benefit from the continued payment of wages.

The pension insurance scheme is financed by contributions amounting to 24% of the gross income from work; one third of these are borne by the insured person himself, one third by his employer or the institution which pays his income maintenance, and one third by the State. In the same way as the in the sickness insurance, the State does not act as subsidiser, but as contributor. Insured people who are active on their own account pay a personal contribution of 16% and the State pays 8% this is also the case in the voluntary insurance scheme.

Income from work which is used as a basis for calculation of contribution liability is determined at minimally the social minimum wage for an unskilled employee of at least eighteen years of age and maximally four times this amount. In the continued insurance scheme, contributions are flat-rate (determined by decree) and not calculated as a percentage of the income from work of the insured person. Some periods of insurance, for example the so called baby years (see above), are financed fully by the state budget.

The income giving rise to contribution liability for the schemes in respect of old age, invalidity and survivor's pensions is indexed; it is also annually adjusted to increases in the standard of living. Pensions are not only regularly price indexed, but also adjusted to increases in wages. The latter takes place by a special act; at least every two years there is a government inquiry into whether or not it should take the initiative for such an adjustment.

The costs of the injuries insurance scheme are entirely borne by the heads of enterprises. Their contributions are determined in relation to the degree of risk of the particular type of enterprise and the total sum of wages which are payable. The administration costs of the association of the injuries insurance scheme are paid half by the association itself, and half by the State.

Benefits which are payable on grounds of the injuries insurance scheme are not only price indexed, but also adjusted to the level of wages (at least every two years according to the increase in the standard of living). The State assumes the responsibility for one third of the costs of adjustment to the standard of living of pensions, as well as the indexing of pensions.

The monthly family allowance is half financed by contributions, and half by the State. According to the law, contributions are due by the employers and the employees (as a rule, at a rate of 1,7% of the wages, subject to an upper limit) and by all tax paying residents who are not employees, not older than sixty five years of age and who do not enjoy retirement, invalidity or orphan's pension. The latter category is again divided into various professional categories, for which there are different contribution rates. In reality the employer's contribution of 1,7% is not paid by the employer but taken over by the state, in order to lower the cost of labour.

Maternity allowance and birth allowance, as well as the costs of administration of the family benefits, are borne entirely by the State.

Unemployment benefits are payable by the Employment Fund.
The financial resources of this fund proceed from:
a) a special contribution to be paid by private sector employers in the years the Fund is to be replenished (in 1996 the contribution was established at 0% of the salaries on which social security contributions are to be paid);
b) a solidarity tax calculated as 2,5% of the personal income tax and 4% of the income tax of the collectivity;
c) a contribution due by the municipalities and divided between these according to the commercial revenue they generate;
d) a contribution by the state to be fixed in the yearly budget statute; and
e) an excise tax on gasoline and petrol.

Furthermore, a special contribution can be charged from employees in the private sector over the sum of the wages which give rise to contribution liability for the pension insurance scheme.

If the unemployment fund remains without sufficient means, the money is advanced by the State; however, the fund must pay this money back.

The means needed for financing the guaranteed minimum income and the other assistance benefits derive from an annual government subsidy, part of the lottery and lotto proceeds and from gifts and personal income.

The means of the municipal welfare offices are derived from the income from property belonging to these offices, gifts, fund raising, lotteries, taxation on theatre performances ... and, to the extent necessary, from State subsidies.

6. Judicial review

In first instance, disputes between insured people and the administrative bodies of the social insurance schemes are dealt with by the *Conseil arbitral* and in case of a higher appeal by the *Conseil supérieur des assurances sociales*. In cases of violation of the law or of violation of substantial procedural requirements, judgements in the last instance of the *Conseil arbitral*, as well as judgements of the *Conseil supérieur des assurances sociales* are open to cassation to the *Cour supérieur de justice*, operating as a *Cour de cassation*.

The *Conseil arbitral* sits with a chairman and two delegated assessors (*délégués assesseurs*); the *conseil* can be assisted by one or more doctors who appear as experts during the oral proceedings of the case. The chairman and deputy chairman of the *Conseil arbitral* are lawyers, having the status of civil servants. The delegated assessors and their substitutes are referred to respectively as delegated employer and delegated insured person.
The *Conseil supérieur des assurances sociales* consists of a chairman and two assessors, to be chosen from among the magistrates, one delegated employer and one delegated employee. The chairmen, the assessors and their substitutes are appointed for a period of three years. The appointment of the delegated person and his substitute takes place in the same way as is the case for the delegated assessors in the *Conseil arbitral*.

Appeal is possible within forty days of the publication of the contested decision; this period is considered to be respected when the appeal or higher appeal was instituted by another (not competent) Luxembourg state authority or social security institution.

Disputes with regard to family benefits and the guaranteed minimum income are dealt with in first instance by the chairman of the *Conseil arbitral*, in higher appeal by the *Conseil supérieur des assurances sociales*, consisting of a chairman and two magistrates.

Decisions of the board of employment concerning unemployment benefit are subject to appeal with the *Commission nationale de l' emploi*, a body established on a tripartite basis; the *Conseil arbitral* decides in last instance.

All costs concerning social security disputes are borne by the State, but the administrative bodies which instigate and subsequently lose a case must pay a certain amount. The procedure is free for insured people.

Chapter Twelve

THE NETHERLANDS

1. Introduction: concept and sources of social security law

The financial memorandum concerning social security, which the Ministry of Social Affairs and Employment presents annually to parliament, makes a distinction between four main categories of social security schemes, i.e. social insurance schemes, 'complementary' social services, schemes for civil servants and occupational pension insurance schemes.

The social insurance schemes are divided into general insurance schemes and employee insurance schemes. This division is based upon the personal scope of application. There are employee insurance schemes with respect to the risks of unemployment, temporary and permanent incapacity for work and medical care. The general insurance schemes cover the risks of old age, death, permanent incapacity for work (hereafter: invalidity), dependent children and medical care (serious medical risks).

The 'complementary' social services are distinguished from the social insurance schemes by virtue of the fact that they are entirely financed out of general taxation. The most important complementary social service is assistance. Furthermore, a number of other services exist, the purpose of which is to supplement social insurance benefits (up to the relevant social minimum), or to offer coverage to people whose right to benefit has expired (or, as may be the case, who were never insured at all).

For the moment, civil servants and people treated as such generally still fall outside the scope of the employee insurance schemes and the general insurance scheme against incapacity for work. They are covered by separate schemes. Some schemes for civil servants have a general character, others cover special groups of civil servants (e.g. military personnel, railway personnel). Since 1996 civil servants' schemes regarding temporary and permanent incapacity for work have been harmonised with the employee insurance schemes. From 1998 on, all employee insurance schemes will be applicable to civil servants. Consequently, all civil servants' schemes should be abolished by that date. Civil servants will be covered by the employee insurance schemes and by 'extra legal benefits' negotiated per sector.

In addition to the general pension schemes which are contained within the general insurance schemes, there is an opportunity to build up an occupational pension with industrial and enterprise pension funds, or by collective agreement with life insurance companies. These private pension schemes are not obligatory by law. However, on the request of a sufficiently large group of people, the Minister of Social Affairs and Employment may make participation in such a pension scheme obligatory for a branch of industry or occupation. The majority of employees and self-employed people are guaranteed an occupational pension, usually linked to their previous income.

For the sake of completeness, we also refer to a number of other occupational schemes. These schemes are the result of negotiations between employers and employees and are usually embodied in collective labour agreements. Thus they offer 'extra legal benefits', in addition to the benefits provided by the employee insurance schemes. Some employees in the private and public sector may enjoy an early retirement benefit *(VUT)*, whereby the beneficiary is offered the opportunity to withdraw from his professional life before he attains pensionable age. Until he attains pensionable age the employee receives a wage-related benefit.

In this work we will focus upon the social insurance schemes and the complementary social services. The remaining schemes will receive only marginal attention.

Article 20 (chapter 1 "fundamental rights") of the Dutch constitution provides:
"1. The security of existence of the population and the distribution of prosperity are subject to the care of the government.
2. The statute provides rules concerning social security rights.
3. Dutch nationals in the Netherlands, who cannot provide for their own existence, are entitled to assistance provided by the State and regulated by the statute."

The legal importance of the social fundamental rights to social security benefits is disputed. Most of the arguments put forward to Parliament in favour of the adoption of such rights were of an ideological or political nature. Their legal importance, i.e. the duty of the government to protect social legislation against possible revocation, seems irrelevant in practice. In this respect it must be borne in mind that according to article 120 of the constitution, the judiciary is not allowed to judge the contents of formal statutes on their compatibility with the constitution. In other words, although the constitution is the highest source of social security law, in practice it has very little to offer.

The formal social security acts either contain the contents of the social security schemes, or are restricted to a framework for the creation of schemes which are not primarily entrusted to the Government. In almost all social security acts some material legislative powers have been delegated, albeit not always to the same extent or to the same subordinate legislator (Crown, Secretary of State, administrative body). Some regulations issued in pursuance of delegated powers to the crown are important and voluminous. By or on the grounds of the formal statute, powers are also often delegated to the Minister and to the Social Insurance Council *(Sociale verzekeringsraad)*. When powers are delegated to an administrative body, the exercise of such powers is often subject to the prior approval of the Minister or that of a supervisory body.

Sometimes legislative powers are not delegated to an administrative body, but rather a certain degree of discretionary powers with respect to the application of the social security acts is provided for. As the exercise of discretion may not result in arbitrary decisions, the administrative body must make its own rules with regard to the use of such powers. To this end, internal directives, etc. are made and possibly issued to the public. Such directives do not have any legal basis in the constitution, nor in delegated powers in formal statutes. Hence, they do not constitute material legislation, but 'pseudo legislation'.
The judiciary is not directly bound by it. However, if an administrative body deviates from pseudo legislation, it must do so for particular reasons. When these do not exist, the administrative body may violate the so called 'general principles of proper administration', such as the principle of equality, the prohibition of arbitrary decision making and the principle of trust. These principles are important guidelines for the judiciary, in determining the validity of acts of the administration. The importance of pseudo legislation in the area of social security law must not be underestimated.

In many areas of social security law an important (factual) source is case law. This is not only due to the complexity of social security law, but also to the fact that the legislator has sometimes deliberately adopted 'open' concepts, the application of which is, as it were, delegated to the judiciary.

2. *Administrative organisation*

The employee insurance scheme is, as far as the collection of contributions and the granting of benefits are concerned (with the exception of benefits granted in the framework of the insurance scheme for medical care), administered by the National institute of social insurance *(Landelijk instituut sociale verzekeringen, Lisv)*. The *Lisv* is a legal person, whose board is composed on a tripartite basis. The board of governors is composed of ten members. Three of the members are appointed on the recommendation of the representative employee organisations, and three on the recommendation of the representative employer organisations. The president of the board and the other three members are independent members. The *Lisv* is assigned the task of administering employee insurance schemes through contracts with independent administrative institutions. The *Lisv* is charged with the co-ordination of the administrative tasks. This co-ordination is notably important as far as the medico-ergonomic assessment of incapacity for work is concerned. The *Lisv* is responsible for the improvement of the co-operation between the administrative institutions and other actors in the field of social legislation, such as social services in the municipalities, the labour mediation services, etc. The *Lisv* is further responsible for the administration and management of the central and sectoral funds. Furthermore, the *Lisv* advises the Minister on items concerning the administration of social insurance law. The statute provides the *Lisv* with the competence to make rules which are binding.

Lisv is authorised to entrust the preparation and implementation of its decisions to regionally organised administrative institutions *(uitvoeringsinstellingen, UVI)*. The *UVI* are functionally independent from the *Lisv* and carry out their tasks on the basis of an agreement with the *Lisv*. The *UVI* enjoy legal personality and need recognition from the Minister. Although a number of other *UVI* exist, approximately two thirds of the former industrial councils (succeeded by *Lisv*) have entrusted their administration to the Communal Administration Office *(Gemeenschappelijk Administratiekantoor, GAK)*. The actual administration of the social security acts is then carried out by the regional GAK offices, supported by the head office. Until the year 2000 the number of *UVI* is de facto limited to five *(GAK, GUO, SVB, Cadans* and *USZO)*. After this date, new *UVI* should be able to enter the market. The *UVI* can be entrusted with other tasks, provided these are approved of by *Lisv*. Nevertheless, in spite of the fact that the actual administration is in the hands of the *UVI*, the *Lisv* remains legally responsible for its own policy and decisions. Furthermore, the social partners can establish sectoral councils *(sectorraden)* for each branch of industry. These sectoral councils have an advisory function vis-à-vis the activities of the *Lisv*.

Apart from the above employee insurance schemes, the *Lisv* also administers, in view of the similarities with the corresponding employee insurance scheme, the general insurance scheme with respect to incapacity for work as well as the Supplements Act *(Toeslagenwet, TW)*; the allowances granted in the framework of this act supplement inadequate employee insurance benefits.

Where the granting of benefits is concerned, the general insurance schemes for the risks of old age, death and dependent children, are administered by the Social Insurance Bank *(Sociale Verzekeringsbank, SVB)*. The *SVB* is a legal person under public law. The Board of governors of the *SVB* is composed of twelve members and twelve substitute members, all of which are appointed by the Minister for Social Affairs and Employment. One third of the members are appointed on the recommendation of the representative employee organisations, and one third on recommendation of the representative employer organisations. The others are independent members. Under the responsibility of the Board, a directorate of four persons is charged with the day-to-day management of the *SVB*. An important part of the competencies of the Board are entrusted, through mandate, to the directorate. The *SVB* operates with a system of regional offices. The collection of contributions for the general insurance schemes takes place via the Inland Revenue *(Rijksbelastingdienst)*. Contributions are levied both through wage and income tax.

The granting of benefits within the framework of the sickness costs insurance schemes is entrusted to the sickness funds *(Ziekenfondsen)*, as well as, where it concerns the general insurance scheme against serious medical risks, to private insurance companies and bodies which administer sickness costs schemes under public law. The sickness funds are foundations or mutual societies which are recognised as such by the Minister. Their task is to ensure that insured people can successfully claim medical benefits. For this purpose they conclude agreements with persons or institutions which provide medical care. A reasonable degree of influence of the members over the boards of the Funds must be ensured. As far as the general sickness cost insurance is concerned, an important role is also played by the so-called 'connecting offices' *verbindingskantoren)* and the Central Administration Office *(Centraal Administratiekantoor, CAK)*. The regionally operating connecting offices are responsible for the administration of and the control on the services that are delivered by the medical practitioners under the general sickness costs insurance scheme. On a national level, the *CAK* plays a role. One of its tasks is carrying out the payments to medical practitioners on behalf of the connecting offices.

A number of funds (of diverse importance) play a role in the governing of the finances of the various insurance schemes, for example the Departmental Fund for the sickness insurance scheme and the General Unemployment Fund for the unemployment insurance scheme.

Control over the administration of the social insurance schemes, except with regard to medical care, as well as over the administrative bodies concerned (including the funds) is in the hands of the Board of supervision on social insurance *(College van toezicht sociale verzekeringen, Ctsv)*. The administrative bodies of the medical care insurance schemes are supervised by the Sickness Fund Council *(Ziekenfondsraad ZFR)*. The *Ctsv* consists of three members which are appointed by the Government on the recommendation of the Minister. The *ZFR* is composed of five groups of seven members, appointed by the Minister and by the representative organisations of employers and employees, sickness funds and participants (medical practitioners etc.). Two more members are appointed by organisations which represent the insured people.
Both *Ctsv* and *ZFR* are legal persons under public law.

The main task of the *Ctsv* is the control of the lawfulness and the efficiency of the administration of social insurance law by the *Lisv*, the *SVB* and the administrative bodies. In order to carry out this task the *Ctsv* uses a number of means by which to control the above mentioned bodies and eventually to revise their policy. When decisions of lower administrative bodies are found to be illegal or contrary to the general interest, the *Ctsv* can ask the Government to suspend or annul them. Apart from its controlling function, the *Ctsv* also has a task in providing information and carrying out research. It has to provide data which can be used in connection with, the financing of social security, the preparation of social security policy, statistical information and scientific research. Furthermore, the *Ctsv* advises the Minister concerning the costs involved with the implementation of social insurance law.

The *ZFR* is charged with the control of the sickness funds, both for the administration of the employee sickness costs insurance and the general sickness cost insurance. The *ZFR* has important means to exercise this control and to influence the policy of the sickness funds. The *ZFR* is also responsible for the management of the departmental funds and for the payments to the *CAK* and the connecting offices.

The *Ctsv* and the *ZFR* are responsible to the competent minister, who can issue guidelines regarding the performance of tasks. The Minister for Social Affairs and Employment is competent both in the field of social insurance and in the field of complementary social services. The Minister for Welfare, Public Health and Sports is competent in the field of the medical care insurance schemes.

The complementary social services are financed out of general taxation. The distributive function for all the services, except for the *TW*, is entrusted to the Councils of Mayor and Aldermen *(Colleges van Burgemeester en wethouders)* of the municipalities. In larger municipalities the administrative tasks have often been delegated to special commissions, in which people other than members of the municipal council may also sit. Decisions are prepared and implemented by a special civil servant or by the Municipal Social Service *(Gemeentelijke Sociale Dienst, GSD)*. Recently, the municipalities have been given broader discretionary powers in the implementation of social assistance law. They are expected to develop proper policies in the field of social assistance and reintegration. The municipalities are controlled by the competent Ministers. It should also be mentioned that there are a number of advisory bodies both on a local or national level, some of which have been made obligatory by the statute.

Finally, it must be pointed out that, apart from the administrative structure as determined in social security legislation (formal), there is also an organisational structure which is commonly referred to as informal. The informal structure includes certain associations within the administrative bodies e.g. the Federation of Industrial Councils *(Federatie van Bedrijfsverenigingen, FBV)*, the Association of Dutch Municipalities *(Vereniging van Nederlandse Gemeenten, VNG)*, and the Association of Dutch Sickness Funds *(Vereniging van Nederlandse Ziekenfondsen, VNZ)*. These are organisations under private law which have established themselves in practice. Their activities range from consultation and advise to the co-ordination of administrative policies. Notwithstanding their lack of power, they exercise considerable influence.

3. Personal scope of application

As the personal scope of application constitutes the difference between the general insurance schemes and the employee insurance schemes, the two types of insurance will be dealt with separately.

People residing in the Netherlands, as well as people not resident in the Netherlands but who are subject to taxation with respect to work which is carried out within the Netherlands, are obligatorily insured for the general insurance schemes. This is the basic starting point.
Resident means every person who is living in the Netherlands. Whether or not a person lives in the Netherlands is a question of fact which is to be judged in the light of circumstances. The important question is whether someone has established a permanent link with the Netherlands, or whether this country constitutes the genuine centre of his personal activities.

Those people who work in the Netherlands and for that reason are liable for wage and income tax but are not resident there, are nevertheless insured under the general insurance schemes.

Each general insurance act provides the possibility of derogation from the starting point by subordinate legislation. The extension and limitation of the personal scope of application of the general insurance schemes with regard to specific groups of people generally purports to draw a demarcation line between those, who, in view of their income, are subject to the Dutch general insurance schemes on the one hand, and to those who are subject to foreign schemes on the other.

The general insurance schemes with regard to the risks of old age and death offer limited possibilities of voluntary insurance. Voluntarily insured people pay the same contributions and receive the same benefits as obligatorily insured people.

In discussing the personal scope of application of the employees insurance schemes we will pay separate attention to the insurance scheme for medical care. However, firstly we will discuss the sickness, invalidity and unemployment insurance schemes. The starting point is that each natural person, under the age of 65, who has a contract of service under public or private law, is obligatorily insured as an employee within the employee insurance scheme. People who carry out a contract of service abroad are not considered to be employees, unless they live in the Netherlands and their employers are settled or resident in the Netherlands (or whose main seat of business or permanent representative is in this country). A contract of service under private law is considered to be a relationship between the employee and the employer which exists on the grounds of a contract of employment within the meaning of the civil code. The courts which are competent in social security disputes will, more than the regular civil courts, disregard the legal status of a contract of service and judge the employment relationship in the light of the specific facts of the case. Three main criteria are considered essential, i.e. personal service, wage as a consideration for labour and subordination to the authority of the employer.

Here too, there are exceptions to the fundamental starting point: the scope of application of all the statutes with respect to the employee insurance schemes is explicitly extended to a number of people who do not (or do not easily) satisfy the fundamental criteria, for example travelling salesmen, apprentices and, subject to further conditions, home workers, musicians and artists. On the other hand, some persons who do satisfy these criteria are excluded. According to the respective acts those who are no longer employed under a contract of service are nevertheless treated as employees within the meaning of the employee insurance acts (e.g., those who receive sickness or unemployment benefit). Subject to certain conditions relating to the minimum period of insurance, a person whose sickness or invalidity benefit has expired and who becomes incapable of work within a number of days (maximally one month) is nevertheless entitled to benefits on the basis of the employees insurance schemes (the so called after-effect of insurance). The three insurance acts also provide a (limited) opportunity for voluntary insurance.

In principle, the personal scope of application of the obligatory sickness costs insurance scheme for employees is the same as the one which applies for the sickness insurance scheme. The most important restriction is a corollary of the determination of the insurance wage limit: those, whose annual income arising out of one or more contracts of employment exceeds a certain amount, are not obligatorily insured. Here also there are a number of extensions; thus, for example, railway personnel are also affiliated to the sickness fund.

The sickness costs insurance scheme provides an opportunity for joint insurance. The following people are jointly insured:
- the spouse of the insured person, if he or she belongs to the same household and the insured person is considered to be the breadwinner; and, subject to further conditions, the unmarried partner of the insured person who is treated as a spouse;
- the natural and unmarried children and foster children of the insured person, for whom the insured person is the breadwinner, to the extent that children are younger than 16, 18, 21 or 27 years of age according to the case.

Insured people (both directly and jointly) belong to the personal scope of application of the sickness costs insurance scheme; however, if they want to make a claim on the basis of this scheme they must be registered with a recognised sickness fund; this requirement is of a purely administrative nature.

The Netherlands is the only country in the European Community, whose law contains provisions for persons who have conscientious objections against insurance in general and consequently also against social insurance. Those who have conscientious objections, of whatever nature, may be exempted from contribution liability for the general insurance schemes; however, they are liable to pay wage or income tax at the same rate as that applying for the general insurance contributions. If the risk covered by the general insurance scheme materialises, the conscientious objector is entitled to benefits; due to it's character, only the old age insurance scheme knows a separate payment arrangement. There is a different arrangement for conscientious objections in the employee insurance schemes. Those with objections may be exempted from contribution liability. If the risk materialises, the insured person (and the jointly insured person) is not entitled to benefit.

In describing the personal scope of application of the complementary social services, we will only make some general remarks. The coverage of the General Assistance Act *(Algemene bijstandswet, Abw)* is very wide: any Dutch person in the Netherlands who is in such circumstances (or may be so in the near future) that he cannot meet the necessary costs of subsistence, is granted assistance by the municipality in which he resides. Foreign nationals who remain legally in the Netherlands are eligible for social assistance under the same conditions. The *Abw* has a general scope of application, but contains specific arrangements for certain categories of people. These have a categorical character; for example, there is a special arrangement for unemployed employees, which includes unemployed school leavers. These special arrangements have less severe means tests than the general assistance arrangement requires.

The personal scope of application of the Supplements Act *(TW)* and the income scheme for elderly and unemployed employees, who are partially incapable of work *(Wet inkomensvoorziening oudere en gedeeltelijk arbeidsongeschikte werkloze werknemers, IOAW)*, follows the insurance scheme on which these are grafted. The scope of application of the income maintenance scheme for the elderly and formerly self-employed people, who are partially incapable of work *(Wet inkomensvoorziening oudere en gedeeltelijk arbeidsongeschikte gewezen zelfstandigen, IOAZ)*, reflects the image of the scope of the *IOAW*, but is aimed at people who were previously self-employed.

4. Risks and benefits

Before we deal with the various risks and benefits, we shall first discuss a subject of a more general nature, namely, the level of income maintenance benefits. In the general insurance schemes and in the complementary social services, the income maintenance benefit levels are based upon the relevant social minimum, which is expressed as a percentage of the minimum wage. In the employees insurance scheme these are generally wage-related in a first period, and based upon the minimum wage in a second period.

The level of wage-related employee insurance benefits is expressed as a percentage of the daily wage of the insured person. Generally, the daily wage is the wage that the person earned in the period immediately preceding the materialisation of the risk. There are maximum daily wages; since the introduction of the *TW*, the minimum daily wages have been abolished.
In order to answer the question of how the daily wages are determined in practice, we need to consult the daily wage regulations, as implemented by the *Lisv*. The system of the various daily wage regulations is largely identical. The wages which give rise to contribution liability (the contribution wages) constitute the basis for the calculation of daily wages. There are special rules for certain groups of employees, such as musicians, artists and seasonal workers.

The level of benefits from the general social insurance schemes are based upon the relevant social minimum. Except for some disregards, this implies that the beneficiary will be guaranteed a (net) income equal to:
- 100% of the net minimum wage for the beneficiary and his or her spouse (or 50% thereof for each of them)
- 90% of the net minimum wage for the beneficiary with a child younger than 18 years of age, who gives rise to entitlement to child benefit (single parent family);
- 70% of the net minimum wage for the unmarried beneficiary (single person).

The level of the minimum wage is contained in the Minimum Wage and Minimum Holiday Allowance Act *(WMM)*. Every half year social benefits, the minimum wage and pensions must be adjusted to wage developments within the market sector (indexing). The contribution wage limit is also linked to the index of wages.

The level of benefits, as far as general assistance is concerned, under the *Abw* is contained in the statute and differs according to the family situation and the age of the beneficiaries.

In Dutch social security law unmarried partners of the same or of a different sex, constituting a stable common household, are in principle put on the same footing as married people.

4.1. Old age

Every Dutch resident who attains the age of 65 is entitled to an old age pension. When a person has been resident in the Netherlands for 50 years, he is entitled to the full amount of pension, i.e. a monthly amount of 50%, 70% or 90% of the net minimum wage, depending upon whether he is married, single or the head of a single parent family. For each year in which one has not been insured or has culpably failed to pay contributions, there is a pro-rata reduction in the pension.
Married people with a partner who is below 65 years of age, are, subject to further conditions, entitled to a supplement which brings the benefit up to 100% of the net minimum wage. In such a case the income of the partner may not be in excess of a certain limit.

According to various legal techniques, in addition to the statutory old age pension, there is an occupational pension scheme for the majority of civil servants, employees and people carrying out a self-employed occupation. Generally the amount of this pension is related to the previously earned income from work, as well as to the length of time that a person has been affiliated to the occupational pension insurance scheme. The full occupational pension and the full statutory old age pension together often reach 70% of the previously earned wages.

Sometimes employees and civil servants are offered the opportunity to retire before they attain pensionable age (65), i.e. from the age of 60, or sometimes even earlier. Those who accept this possibility may receive a preretirement pension *(VUT)* until they attain 65 years of age, at a level of 80% 90%, or sometimes even higher, of the previously earned salary.

4.2. Death

The death of a person may deprive the survivors of their income. The death of the insured person can, under specific conditions, give rise to entitlement to survivor's pension for widows or widowers and their children, and for full orphans. The former General Widow's and Orphans insurance *(Algemene Weduwen- en Wezenwet, AWW)* was abolished recently and replaced by a new General Survivor's insurance *(Algemene nabestaandenwet, Anw)*. Since the new law contains important transitional arrangements concerning the beneficiaries under the old *AWW* we will discuss both arrangements here.

Under the old arrangement *(AWW)* all women of 40 years or older were entitled to a widow's pension on the death of the insured person; younger women were only entitled to this pension if they had unmarried children, or were incapable of work. Widows who did not meet these conditions were only entitled to benefit on a temporary basis. Also unmarried divorced widows (pseudo-widows) were eligible for benefit. Benefits to widows were terminated when they attained 65 years of age; when a widow remarried she received a lump sum. The widow's pension and the temporary widow's benefit amounted to 70% of the net minimum wage; if the widow had a child under the age of 18 this was 100%. The level of orphan's pension depended upon the age of the orphan. As a result of a judgement by the Central Court of Appeal *(Centrale Raad van Beroep, CRvB)*, widowers can now claim a survivor's pension subject to the same conditions as widows.

The new survivor's insurance *(Anw)* puts widows and widowers on the same footing. But under the new arrangement the personal scope of application of the arrangement has been reduced and the conditions upon eligibility have been severely toughened. Moreover, benefits under the *Anw* are subject to a wage income test. The following people are now entitled to a survivor's benefit: the survivor with children under 18, who live in his household; under certain conditions, the survivor who is incapable for work; and the survivor who was born before January 1 1950. The benefit is lost when the survivor marries again or forms a new household. The survivor's benefit is equal to 70% of the net minimum wage. This benefit is reduced with part of the wage income of the beneficiary and can therefore disappear altogether if income from labour is high enough.

Survivors with children under 18 years of age are, under further conditions, also eligible for a so-called 'half-orphan's benefit' *(halfwezenuitkering)*. The half-orphan's benefit is equal to 20% of the net minimum wage. Orphans under the age of 16 are entitled to an orphan's benefit *(wezenuitkering)*. Under certain conditions orphans under the age of 18 or 21 can also be entitled to orphan's benefits. The amount of the orphan's benefit depends on the age and is calculated as a function of the survivors benefit. For children under 10 this is 32% of the survivor's benefit, for children between 10 and 16 this is 48%, and for children between 16 and 21 this is 64% of the survivor's benefit. These benefits are not subject to a income test.

According to the transitional arrangements in the *Anw* a number of former beneficiaries of the *AWW* can still be eligible for survivor's benefits even if they do not satisfy the conditions under the *Anw*, depending, among others, upon their age.

The occupational pension schemes usually provide survivor's benefits to the survivors of the participants. The amount is deducted from the amount of occupational retirement pension which the deceased person enjoyed or would have enjoyed. Sometimes there are schemes for divorced couples and, increasingly, for cohabiting partners.

Under most social insurance schemes death benefit is payable to the relatives at the usual benefit level. As a rule, the level of this is equal to the entitlement to benefit of the deceased person, and covers a period of two months plus the remaining days of the month in which death occurred.

4.3. Incapacity for work

There is an important difference between, on the one hand temporary incapacity for work and, on the other hand permanent incapacity. With regard to temporary incapacity for work, there is no general insurance scheme, but only a scheme for employees; with regard to permanent incapacity there is both a general insurance scheme and an employee insurance scheme.

The employee insurance for temporary incapacity for work or sickness insurance *(Ziektewet, ZW)* covers the first year of incapacity. In principle, the insured employee, who is not capable of carrying out his work due to illness, is entitled to sickness benefit. The concept of illness includes physical defects, pregnancy and birth (from six weeks before the birth to six weeks after the birth there is irrefutable evidence of incapacity for work). Recently, the *ZW* has lost much of its importance as a consequence of the introduction of a prolonged obligation of the employers under civil law to continue paying wages to sick employees *(Wet Uitbreiding Loondoorbetalingsplicht bij Ziekte, WULBZ)*. According to the *WULBZ*, employers have the obligation under civil law to continue paying wages to employees with a permanent employment contract, at a rate of 70%, during the first 52 weeks of sickness. The period and the amount correspond with the entitlement that sick employees had under the *ZW*. It is expected that the employers will take out private insurance to cover the risk of sickness of their employees. Therefore, the *WULBZ* is often said to have 'privatised' sickness insurance. However, the *ZW* still has some purpose. Evidently, employees who continue receiving wages from their employer are no longer entitled to sickness benefits. But sickness benefits will still be paid to certain groups of employees. These include mostly employees with temporary employment contracts. Furthermore sickness benefits can be paid to people who are not under an employment contract, but who still are employees in the meaning of the employee insurance schemes; people who receive unemployment benefits; and people confronted with an employer who is bankrupt. Periods of sickness due to pregnancy or delivery are still covered under the *ZW* for all employees. People who were formerly entitled to invalidity benefits and who re-entered a permanent employment contract, and people who have donated an organ, are also eligible for benefits under the *ZW*. Sickness benefit is payable over a maximum period of one year. Sickness benefit amounts to 70% of the gross daily wages of the insured person (subject to an upper wage limit).

Those who are completely or partially incapable of work are, after a waiting period of one year, entitled to invalidity benefit on the grounds of the general insurance scheme *(Algemene Arbeidsongeschiktheidswet, AAW)*. Furthermore, employees are entitled to an invalidity benefit on the grounds of an employees insurance scheme *(Wet op de arbeidsongeschiktheidsverzekering, WAO)*. Under the employee invalidity insurance a person is considered incapable of work if he, as a result of illness or a physical defect, has lost earning capacity in comparison with healthy people with the same education and experience. In order to calculate this loss of earning capacity, the individual's remaining capacity for work is assessed. In this test 'work' is any generally acceptable form of employment. As a result the remaining earning capacity is found. The difference between the original earning capacity and the remaining earning capacity equals the degree of incapacity for work. The benefit is calculated in relation with the degree of incapacity for work. In order to be eligible for invalidity benefit on the grounds of the general insurance scheme, a person must have earned an income from work in industry or from an occupation or have been handicapped at an early age in the year preceding the moment that he became an invalid, or became handicapped.

The level of the benefit provided by the general insurance scheme and the employees insurance scheme amounts to, respectively, a certain percentage of the gross minimum wage, and a percentage of the previously earned wages up to an upper wage limit. With a degree of incapacity of 80% or more, this percentage equals 70%. When the degree of incapacity is less than 15%, invalidity benefit is not payable; with a degree of incapacity between 15% and 25% no benefit is payable on the grounds of the general insurance scheme, but under the employees insurance scheme benefit is payable at a level of 14% of the last earned wage (subject to an upper limit).

The general insurance scheme in respect of incapacity for work does not only provide invalidity cash benefits, but also a number of benefits in kind for people who are incapable or who are likely to become so. Examples of such benefits are aids to maintain or to cure the incapacity, or for the improvement of living conditions, and medical services (training, mobility services, family help, etc.).

Over the last few years, several statutory measures have been taken to reduce the (high) number of people receiving a benefit for incapacity for work. These measures encourage employers to keep invalid people in employment or to hire invalid people, and to penalise employers whose employees become invalid.

4.4. Unemployment

The employee who becomes unemployed is entitled to unemployment benefit, if he has worked at least 26 weeks in a period of 39 weeks immediately preceding his unemployment. The employee who has lost at least 5 or at least half of his normal working hours per week, who is not entitled to a continuation of his wages and who is willing to accept employment, is considered to be unemployed.

All beneficiaries of unemployment benefit receive a wage related benefit for a period of half a year; this period may be extended by one or more periods, if the beneficiary satisfies the requirements with regard to his past employment record, i.e. he must have worked for at least 4 years in employment of at least 52 days per year during the last 5 years. Periods, during which the person was entitled to the full amount of invalidity benefit, are taken into account, as are periods in which the person has taken care of children under the age of 6, if the children are between the ages of 6 and 12 these periods are counted for 50%.
In determining the employment record, the 'actual' employment record over the last five years and the 'fictitious' employment record (this is the period between the eighteenth birthday and the day five years before the occurrence of unemployment) are added together. With an employment record of 5 years, the duration of the wage related benefit is extended by three months, with an employment record of 10 years, the benefit is extended by half a year, and for each further period of five years, by another half year. Those with an employment record of 40 years or more are eligible for the maximum extension of four and a half years, implying a total duration of benefit of five years.
When the period of the wage related benefit has expired, an entitlement to a so-called 'continued benefit' exists. The duration of which is 2 years for people under the age of 57,5 years, and 3,5 years for people above that age. The wage-related benefit amounts to 70% of the last earned wages (subject to an upper wage limit); the 'continued' benefit is equal to 70% of the minimum wage.

Some groups of unemployed people who are no longer entitled to unemployment benefit can claim complementary social services which guarantee an income equal to the level of the social minimum which is relevant for them (see section 4.7).

Unemployed people between 16 and 20 years of age, as well as unemployed school leavers up to the age of 26, who have been unemployed for half a year, are entitled to a job offer by a municipal service created for that purpose *(Jeugdwerkgarantie organisatie, JWGO)*. The employment lasts 6 months with the possibility of prolongation by a further 6 months. These people are paid the relevant minimum wage. People who have been unemployed for more than three years, regardless of their age, are eligible for a job in the so-called job-pool *(Banenpool)*. They receive minimum wages but have a 'normal' employment contract. Recently, also other specific arrangements have been taken to offer subsidised jobs to the long-term unemployed.

4.5. Health care

Employees and people treated as such, who are obligatorily insured under the sickness costs insurance scheme *(Ziekenfondswet, ZFW)*, are entitled to medical benefits in kind, provided that such benefits are not already covered by the general insurance scheme for serious medical risks *(Algemene Wet Bijzondere*

Ziektekosten). People who are jointly insured (usually the spouse and children) are also entitled to benefits. The package of benefits includes medical, curative, maternal, dental and pharmaceutical help, (artificial) aids, nursing in a hospital, ambulance services, home care and psychiatric treatment.

All residents are covered for the most serious health risks on grounds of the general insurance scheme, created for this purpose. The package of benefits includes treatment and nursing in an institution for the handicapped from the first day (e.g. nursing homes) and in psychiatric hospitals from the 366th day. Vaccinations and wheel chairs are also compensated for by the general insurance scheme for the length of stay in an institution. As a rule, a personal contribution is required from the claimant, which is sometimes dependent upon the ability to pay.

As mentioned before, the sickness funds themselves do not provide any benefits. The granting of benefits takes place via competent practitioners, for example doctors and dentists, as well as via recognised institutions, for example hospitals and nursing homes; the procedure for recognition is laid down in the statute. Agreements are concluded between the sickness funds on the one hand and those providing care on the other, or between their respective representative interest organisations. The statute contains a number of rules which *inter alia* provide a system of model agreements, deviation from which is only possible with the approval of the Sickness Fund Council. The tariffs which are agreed by the parties must be approved by the Central Body for Health Care Tariffs *(Centraal Orgaan Tarieven Gezondheidszorg)*, established by the government.

4.6. Family

Every person who is resident in the Netherlands is entitled to child benefit for his own children, his children through marriage and foster children for whom he cares or who are maintained by him, provided that they are under the age of 18. A child younger than 18 years of age, not residing in the household of the insured person, but financially depending on him, counts for two children.
Children of 18 years and older do not, in principle, create any right to child benefit, as they qualify for other social benefits themselves.

The child benefit is calculated on a basic amount, determined in the statute. The basic amount is equal for all children and does not increase with the number of children. But the amount of child benefit does increase with the age of the child. Thus, 70% of the applicable basic amount is payable, if the child is under the age of 6; if the child is between the ages of 6 and 12 years, 85% of the basic amount is payable; for children between the ages of 12 and 18 years the rate is 100%.
Entitlement to child benefit is determined quarterly.

4.7. Need

Here we shall discuss a number of social security schemes which are designed to provide minimum subsistence to people without sufficient means. These schemes all have something in common, the fact that the award of benefit is subject to a means test.

Every person who is in such circumstances (or who may be so in the near future) that he cannot meet the necessary costs of subsistence, is awarded assistance. The level of the necessary costs of living (for those who do not stay in an institution) are laid down in statutory instruments. Here, it should be borne in mind that benefit is payable on a family basis to married couples (with or without minor children) and to one parent families with minor children. The level of benefit differs depending on whether benefit is awarded to married couples, one parent families, single persons, and depending on the age of the beneficiaries. The level of assistance benefits is contained in the statute. People under 21 years of age get lower benefits than people above that age. Couples in which one of the partners is above 21 have a benefit that is in between. The amount of benefit for single parent families and single persons is respectively 70% and 50% of the amount of the benefit for a couple. Special rules apply to those who reside in mental or physical institutions. In some cases, and under a number of conditions, these amounts can be supplemented by the municipality. Assistance should take into account the personal circumstances and the capacities of the beneficiaries. The municipalities have some discretionary power in granting the supplements, but they should do this on the basis of a coherent and proper policy.

House owners and tenants, who are not yet entitled to housing benefit, are entitled to a housing costs addition to the extent that these costs do not exceed a certain statutory amount. The beneficiary who is unemployed, and whose subsistence depends on labour under a contract of employment, receives assistance under a special arrangement which is contained within the *Abw*. The benefit levels correspond with those of the general assistance scheme, but the beneficiary's duties differ. No right to assistance exists for those who have not yet reached 18 years of age. Special rules apply to the self-employed who have a business or carry out a profession and who are in need of assistance.

Apart from assistance for the 'general necessary costs of subsistence', subject to certain conditions assistance may also be payable for 'special necessary costs of subsistence'. The benefit for the general necessary costs of subsistence should cover all costs, including special expenses. Benefit is not necessarily in the form of free periodical or incidental payments, but can also take the shape of a loan or a security.
The legislator thought it desirable that some groups of people should be guaranteed a minimum subsistence without having to rely upon the general assistance legislation and the extensive means test which is a characteristic of the *Abw*. At the present time, there are a number of special benefit schemes which offer a minimum income to certain groups whose income has fallen below the relevant social minimum, i.e.:

- beneficiaries under the employee insurance schemes and under the general invalidity insurance schemes;
- elderly and partially incapable unemployed employees; and
- elderly and partially incapable, formerly self-employed people.

By virtue of the Supplements Act *(Toeslagenwet, TW)* sickness benefit, unemployment benefit and invalidity benefit are, if necessary, supplemented up to the relevant social minimum (corresponding to the levels applying to the general assistance scheme: 100%, 90% or 70% of the minimum wage, albeit that those under the age of 21, who are unmarried and living with their parents, are not entitled to any supplement). This benefit is subject to a means test.

The income scheme for elderly and partially incapable unemployed employees *(IOAW)* guarantees benefit on the level of the relevant social minimum (twice 50%, 90% or 70% of the net minimum wage) to:
- unemployed persons under the age of 65 who became unemployed between the ages of 50 and 57.5 and whose right to continued unemployment benefit has expired;
- unemployed persons, under the age of 65, who became unemployed after the age of 57.5 and who received wage-related unemployment benefit but not a continued unemployment benefit;
- unemployed persons, who became unemployed after their 50th birthday and whose right to unemployment benefit has fully expired, while they remained entitled to an invalidity benefit, calculated on the basis of a degree of incapacity of less than 80%;

This benefit is also subject to an income test.

The income scheme for elderly and partially incapable, formerly self-employed persons *(IOAZ)* contains an analogous arrangement for persons under the age of 65 and their co-operating spouses, who were formerly dependent upon their own business or profession, subject to the condition that they either stopped their gainful activity before the age of 55, or stopped their activities as a result of incapacity for work on the grounds of which there is entitlement to invalidity benefit, calculated on the basis of a degree of incapacity of less than 80%.

5. *Financing*

At the present time, social insurance benefits are financed almost entirely out of contributions. The central government guarantees the benefits, in case it should appear that the funds do not possess sufficient means of financing.

The basis for charging contributions is the income (general insurance schemes) or the wage (employee insurance schemes) of the insured persons, both of these are subject to upper limits. Nowadays employee insurance benefits and extra legal benefits also give rise to employee insurance contribution liability. Contributions must be paid on income or wages up to a maximum limit.

The contribution rates are set periodically by the competent Minister or by the administrative body, sometimes these are subject to the approval of the former. The rates normally apply for the whole country. However, for sickness and unemployment insurance they differ per branch of industry, depending on the 'weight' of the risk. The contribution rates are set annually in respect of the expected expenditure in the next year (pay as you go); some schemes are obliged to create a reserve but, in fact, most of the other schemes also maintain reserves.

The employers pay their own contributions, as well as those of their employees (both for the employee and the general insurance scheme), to the competent administrative body. For this purpose they deduct the amount of the contribution liability from the wage of the employee. The division of contributions between employers and employees is obligatory prescribed by law. The employer bears the financial risk of a wrong judgement as to the insurance obligation of the employee. The self-employed pay all their general insurance contributions themselves, provided their income exceeds the minimum limit; the contributions are charged as an assessment.

The child benefit scheme is financed out of general taxation.
The contributions which are collected are normally transferred to the funds created by the various social security schemes.

The complementary social services are financed entirely out of general means, which are brought under the yearly budgets of the central and local governments. Most complementary social services are financed by the central government; this is the case for 100% of the *TW*, while 10% of the costs of the *Abw*, the *IOAW* and the *IOAZ* are borne by the municipalities.

6. Judicial review

Those who want to contest decisions in the area of the employee insurance schemes and the *TW*, or in the area of the general insurance schemes, must appeal to the Section Administrative Law of the arrondissemental tribunals. Social security cases are heard here by a single professional judge. Further appeal is possible with the Central Appeal Court *(Centrale Raad van Beroep, CRvB)*. The *CRvB* consists of three judges who are appointed for life. In order to contest a decision before the arrondissemental tribunal, such a decision must have the status of 'subject to appeal' *(voor beroep vatbaar)*. In order to appeal against a refusal to grant benefits in kind or compensation on the grounds of the insurance schemes for medical care, prior application for a non-binding recommendation of the Sickness Fund Council is required, this must be done within 30 days after a 'decision subject to appeal' has been received.

The judges of the administrative jurisdiction have to determine whether or not the contested decision is compatible with the law. The procedure is almost entirely free from procedural requirements and there is no obligatory representation. In this way it is attempted to promote access to justice.

The so-called 'permanent-expert procedure' is a special procedure which should be followed in a number of statutorily determined disputes of a medical nature. Here, the judge relies heavily upon the opinion of the permanent expert, who is a general practitioner. The procedure normally ends with a reasoned decision of the chairman, which, in principle, is not subject to appeal. Disputes concerning contribution liability for the general insurance schemes are subject to the judicial procedure for income taxes, respectively wage taxes. This procedure will not be discussed.

No specialised machinery exists for the settlement of disputes concerning the complementary social services (except for the *TW*). There is merely a general administrative review procedure. This implies that the case is referred to a higher (political) administrative body, i.e. the executives of the provinces *(Gedeputeerde Staten, GS)*, with a possibility of further appeal to the Crown.

Crown appeals are dealt with by the Department for Administrative Disputes of the Council of State *(Afdeling Geschillen van Bestuur)*. However, the role of this body has been altered. In order to comply with the requirements formulated by the European Court of Human Rights, the *Afdeling Geschillen van Bestuur* has changed from an advisory body into a judicial body; the grounds on which the validity of decisions are judged are the same as those which apply for the regular administrative courts.

In case a beneficiary has grievances, not so much about the contents of a decision, but about the attitude (activities or lack of any activity) of an administrative body, he can lodge a complaint with the national ombudsman.

The civil court, more specifically the president of the high court in immediate judgement, may play a role in cases in which there is no jurisdiction for the administrative courts. For example, the civil court is competent if an administrative body does not implement a judgement of the appeal court. The civil court can use means of coercion to force parties to comply with a judgement.

Judgements of the *CRvB*, as well as judgements of the Court of Appeal in matters of contribution liability for the general insurance schemes, are open to cassation to the Supreme Court, but only in so far as the disputes concern the interpretation of concepts like 'wage', 'resident', etc. Here the legislator has aimed to establish a uniform interpretation throughout the entire body of social security and tax law.

Chapter Thirteen

PORTUGAL

1. Introduction: concept and sources of social security law

Social security (*segurança social*) is a relatively new concept in Portugal. The use of the term social security constitutes an expression of the transition from the dichotomy social assistance/social insurance, connected with the corporative state, to social security as a leading principle of the social constitutional state. Thus, the starting point for our treatise on social security in Portugal can only be article 63 Constitution, which provides in its first paragraph: "All people are entitled to social security" and which specifies in its third paragraph: "The social security system must protect citizens in case of sickness, old age, invalidity, widowhood, orphanage, unemployment and in all other cases of a loss or reduction of the means of subsistence or of the ability to work".

Within this meaning, the term social security refers to contributory and non-contributory schemes which provide cash benefits, which together are often referred to as social security in the narrow sense, and the forms of social protection organised by benefits and schemes for children and young persons, as well as for the elderly and the handicapped. These benefits are often collectively described by the term social action. The benefits from social security in the narrow sense, provide subjective rights to beneficiaries; subjective rights to (certain forms of) social action are not recognised.

The contributory schemes provide:
- family benefits. The following family benefits exist: family allowances for children and young people, birth benefit, benefit for the care of sick minors, maternity benefit (also for fathers) and adoption benefit;
- benefits in respect of a temporary loss of income due to sickness or unemployment, i.e. sickness benefit, tuberculosis benefit, two unemployment benefits (an insurance benefit and a social benefit) and compensation in respect of occupational diseases;
- benefits in respect of old age or invalidity, i.e. old age pension, invalidity pension, constant attendance allowance and pension for occupational diseases;
- benefits for specific needs of handicapped people i.e. the increase to a family allowance due to a handicap, special education benefit, monthly annuity benefit, invalidity pension, constant attendance allowance;
- benefits in respect of death, i.e. funeral benefit, death benefit and the survivor's pension.

There are non-contributory schemes which guarantee a minimum protection to each person who finds himself in a social-economic position of need and who has not paid any or insufficient contributions. These are:
- social invalidity and old age pensions;
- constant attendance allowance;
- family allowances and other family benefits;
- widower's/widow's pension; and
- orphan's pension.

As mentioned above, the Portuguese concept of social security, in its broad sense, also encompasses organised forms of social action aimed at young people, the elderly and the handicapped. These include child care facilities, leisure centres and protected housing for the elderly.

The right to health care is autonomous from the right to social security and does not depend upon the link to the social security system. The National Health Service is universal and general, covering all residents.
Furthermore, work injuries are not yet included in the social security system. The duty to protect against this risk belongs to the employers who may transfer their responsibility to the insurance companies.
However, the main act concerning social security of 1984 provides for the future integration of work injuries into the general social security scheme.

The Portuguese constitution of 1976, which is based upon the revolution of the 25th of April 1974 and reviewed in 1982, in 1989, in 1992 and in 1997, lays down the framework within which social security within Portugal was to develop. Apart from article 63 (concerning social security as such) and 64 (concerning health care); articles 67 to 72 Constitution are also relevant here; the latter provisions are dedicated respectively to the family, paternity and maternity, children, young persons, handicapped individuals and those who have retired.
The most important sources of Portuguese social security law are the formal statute (adopted by parliament) and the decree (originating from the government); both sources have equal legal value. According to article 165, (n° 1, sub f) Constitution the determination of the principles of the social security system and the national health care service belong to the relative legislative competence of parliament; in other words this subject matter falls under the domain of the statute, unless parliament empowers the government to enact legislation in this area.

The main act concerning statutory social security announces special provisions concerning supplementary schemes of statutory social security, which would be introduced in order to provide a better coverage of the social risks which are already covered by social security or in order to provide social protection of risks which are not yet covered by social security.
In the past there has already been a lot of support for a codification of the various legislative measures in one social security statute. The main statute regarding social security (act number 28/84 of 1984) constitutes a first step in this direction.

2. Administrative organisation

The administrative organisation of social security is laid down in the second and fifth paragraphs of art. 63 Constitution:
"2. It is the responsibility of the government to organise, co-ordinate and subsidise a unified and decentralised social security system, with the participation of the unions, the other organisations representing employees and the representative associations of the beneficiaries themselves.
5. The Government supports and supervises, in terms of the law, the activity and operation of the particular institutions of the social solidarity and other non-profit making institutions of recognised public interest with a view to carrying out the objectives of the social solidarity encompassed namely in this article and in articles 67(2)(b), 69, 70(1)(e), 71 and 72."
It appears that the organisation of social security is characterised by: unity of the system, decentralisation and participation.

The intended organic unification of social security and the integration of the various existing social security systems in the general system have still to be completed.

The administrative organisation of social security is decentralised. There are three levels of organisation: the central bodies, the regional bodies and the local bodies.
On the central level there are the general directories under the responsibility of the Minister for Solidarity and for Social Security, through the Secretary of State for Social Security, unemployment schemes fall under the domain of the Institute for Employment and Vocational Training of the Secretary of State for Employment of the same Ministry.

Apart from these services, which are integrated in the central administration, the following are also on a central level:
- the Department for International Relations of Social Security (*Departemento de Relações Internacionais de Segurança Social*);
- the Institute for the Financial Administration of Social Security (*Instituto de Gestão Financeira da Segurança Social*);
- the National Pension Centre (*Centro Nacional de Pensões*), which is not only concerned with pensions but also with the data banks of social security; and
- The National Centre for Protection against Professional Risks.

These four bodies have a legal person status and enjoy administrative and financial autonomy.

The actual administration of social security is entrusted to the regional social security centres (*Centros regionais de segurança social, C.R.S.S.*), which are public law bodies, autonomous from the central government. The latter retains administrative control; the *C.R.S.S.* are obliged to follow the orientations and general guidelines of the central administration.

All or almost all contact between social security and the citizen, takes place via the *C.R.S.S.* within the region of the citizen. The *C.R.S.S.* are governed by a board of directors, set up by the state department for social security. These directors get advise about the matters which are of importance for the administration of the *C.R.S.S.* from their Regional Social Security Council (*Conselho regional de segurança social*), consisting of representatives of the local authorities, the unions, the employers and the governing boards of private social security institutions. Within each *C.R.S.S.* there is a commission for the verification of cases of permanent incapacity for work, as well as an appeals commission. The system of control over permanent incapacity for work (*S.V.I.P.*) serves both the contributory and the non-contributory invalidity scheme, the allowance scheme for severe invalidity and in certain cases also the pension scheme for survivors.
The *C.R.S.S.* have local points of contact to which insured people can turn within their immediate environment.
On a regional level, although separate from the *C.R.S.S.*, there are regional employment centres, which, together with the *C.R.S.S.* are responsible for the administration of the two schemes for unemployment.
A whole range of non-profit making private institutions of social solidarity, work together with the *C.R.S.S.* in the field of social action. The *C.R.S.S.* cooperate with and supervise these institutions.

The public organisation of health care, which, as already mentioned, is strictly speaking not part of the social security system, is entrusted to the National Health Service (*Serviço Nacional de Saúde*) under the Ministry for Health.

The evaluation of medical criteria throughout the different schemes has been co-ordinated between the Ministry for Health and the Ministry for Social Security.

The work injuries insurance scheme is administrated by private insurance companies and is supervised by the Minister of Finance.

3. Personal scope of application

We have seen above that article 63 of the Portuguese Constitution proclaims the universality of social security. However, this does not alter the fact that the compulsory contributory schemes of social security only cover people and their families who carry out, or who have carried out, paid work. Traditionally, contributory social security encompassed a general scheme and various special schemes.

Nowadays, and according to the main act, Portuguese social security consists of the general social security system (the contributory scheme) and the non-contributory system.
The general social security system covers, compulsorily, the employed and self-employed people in agriculture, trade, industry and services of the private sector of activity. The general system also includes the voluntary social insur-

ance, open to people who exercise an activity not covered by the compulsory system nor by another system of social protection.
Special systems exist covering the civil servants and the military.

Unless it is otherwise stated, we shall deal only with the compulsory general scheme here after.

The non-contributory social security scheme protects all persons who do not fall under a contributory scheme; but not all risks are covered.

We can summarise the personal scope of application of the various schemes as follows. Each person carrying out work on account of another person as well as the self-employed, are covered by the schemes for maternity, paternity and adoption benefits, by the old age and invalidity pensions; these people also give rise to entitlement to death benefit and survivor's benefit for the surviving relatives.
Only wage earners are covered by the schemes for sickness, the schemes for occupational disease benefits, by the benefit scheme for assistance to sick minors, by the unemployment benefit scheme and by the social unemployment benefits.
Self-employed people may be covered by the scheme of occupational diseases benefits if they want so.

Family benefits are granted to two large groups of beneficiaries, i.e.:
a) people who are wage earners, or are retired or unemployed, as well as their spouses; and self employed people may be covered if they so wish, and
b) people not covered by any social security scheme, and whose monthly income does not exceed 40% of the national minimum wage or whose family income per capita does not exceed 30% of this national minimum wage.

Both categories are equally covered by the increases to family allowance due to a handicap, by the special education benefit scheme and by the constant attendance allowance.
Only people mentioned under a) are insured for funeral and monthly annuity benefits. Only people mentioned under b) receive orphan's benefit.
The social pension covers all Portuguese citizens (and people treated as such) who are resident in Portugal, do not fall under another contributory social security scheme, or who, although affiliated to a scheme, do not fully satisfy the relevant contribution requirements for entitlement to a contributory pension and whose monthly income does not exceed 30% of the national minimum wage if alone, or 50% of the same wage for a couple. People in receipt of an invalidity, old age or survivor's pension from the contributory scheme, may also receive a (supplementary) social pension, if the amount of the contributory pension is lower than that of the social pension.
The constant attendance allowance may be granted to any beneficiary of an invalidity, old age or survivor's pension, the beneficiaries of social pensions included.

All residents are covered by the national health service.

All wage earners are covered by the industrial injuries insurance scheme of his employer.

4. *Risks and benefits*

Old age, survivor's and invalidity pensions under the non-contributory as well as the contributory scheme, are, as a rule, revalued once a year by decree. The mechanism of adjustment of benefit rate applies also for the other benefits which are flat-rate, and for family benefits. The permanent compensations for professional risks are also adjusted by government decree.

4.1. Old age

There are two old age pension schemes, i.e. old age pension under the contributory scheme and the social old age pension.

Contributory old age pension (*pensão de velhice*) is payable to people who have paid contributions during at least 15 calendar years and who can demonstrate 120 working days for each year taken into account. The beneficiary must have reached the age of 65 years if he is a man. For women the system used to require 62 years of age. However, in the context of the non-discrimination rule a transitional arrangement has been introduced. The pensionable age will therefore be raised by 6 months each year until the year 1999. The amount of old age pension is equal to as many times 2% of the average wage over the ten most favourable years during the preceding fifteen active years, as there are years of contributions. There is a minimum and a maximum pension. Old age pension may be cumulated with a salary; this salary gives rise to contribution payments and the pension is increased by 2% per extra year of activity.
Early pension can only be claimed by the unemployed individual who is aged 60 or more, or from the age of 55 onwards when having performed heavy or unhealthy work.

The beneficiary of an old age pension provided under the legislation in force until 31st December 1993 with a spouse, whose income is lower than a statutory limit, is entitled to an dependent spouse addition. The possible income of the spouse is deducted from the allowance.

Social old age pension (*pensão social*) is only payable to people with a monthly income not in excess of 30% of the national minimum wage or not in excess of 50% thereof in cases where the pension is granted to the head of a family. Social old age pension is only payable from the age of 65.

4.2. Death

Death benefits, within the broad meaning of the term, may be divided into funeral benefit, death benefit and the survivor's benefit as well as, within the non-contributory schemes, widower's pension and orphan's pension. Furthermore special benefits exist if the death was caused by a work injury or an occupational disease.

Funeral benefit (*subsidio de funeral*) is payable on the death of the following members of the family of the worker or pensioner: the spouse, the dependant children, the descendants who are entitled to a monthly annuity benefit and the dependant ascendants.

Death benefit (*subsidio por morte*) is in principle due to the same people as those qualifying for a survivor's pension (see hereafter); however, the death benefit is payable without the requirement of a minimum qualifying period. Death benefit consists of a lump sum payment equal to a half year's average wage of the two most favourable years during the preceding five insured years of the deceased person. This average wage can not be lower than the national minimum wage. The surviving spouse receives at least 50% of this amount when benefit is also payable to descendants. A supplement is paid to severely disabled people who are permanently incapacitated for work and require constant attendance from a third person.

Survivor's pension (*pensão de sobrevivência*) is payable, on the condition that the deceased person has paid contributions for at least 36 months to:
- the surviving spouse and, under certain conditions, the surviving ex-spouse. It may be worthwhile mentioning that the person who lived together with the deceased for the two last years as if they were husband and spouse, will also be considered to be a widow(er);
- the descendant or people treated as such who are less than 18 years of age, 25 years of age if they are students of secondary, complementary or higher levels of study, or 27 years of age as long as they are undergoing a master's or a post-graduate course; without age limit if they are handicapped and entitled to family benefits and,
- the ascendants, in the absence of a spouse and descendants, if they were dependant upon the deceased person.

The above people receive a percentage of the pension that the deceased person would have received if he had been an invalid at the moment of his death. The percentage varies according to the category to which the surviving beneficiary belongs (60% for the spouse, 20% for one child, 30% for two children and 40% for three or more children).
If the survivor is a widow, she is entitled to survivor's pension on the condition that she:
- was married to the deceased person for at least one year, unless there are children from the marriage or unless the death was due to an injury; and
- is at least 35 years old; if she is younger the duration of the pension is limited to five years, unless the widow has dependent children or suffers permanent incapacity for work.

The widow loses her survivor's pension if she remarries.

Divorced and separated spouses who fulfil the above conditions are entitled to survivor's pension if, as rarely happens, she received alimony from the deceased person.

The rate of calculation of survivor's pension for orphans of the father/ mother varies, depending upon whether the pension is granted to one, two or more children who are not older than 18 years (increased to 25 or 27 in case of secondary or higher education or attendance of a post-graduate course); there is no age limit with respect to permanent and complete incapacity for work. The amount of pension is doubled if the insured person does not leave behind a spouse or ex spouse.
Together, the total amount of the survivor's pensions may not exceed 100% of the amount of reference.

Widow(er)'s pension (*pensão de viuvez*) is granted to the surviving spouse of the person who received a social pension. The beneficiary of the widow(er)'s pension may not be entitled to another pension and must satisfy the means test for a social pension. The widow(er)'s pension amounts to 60% of the social pension.

The orphan's pension (*pensão de orfandade*) is a non-contributory pension which, subject to a means test, is payable to orphans until they come of age (18 years old or earlier if the child is no longer dependent upon a guardian). The amount of pension is calculated on the basis of the same percentages as those for the survivor's pension for descendants, but it takes into account the social pension rate as the basis of calculation.

There are derogating rules if death was due to an industrial injury or an occupational disease. In these cases survivor's benefit is payable to:
- the widow/widower of the deceased person, at a level of the 30% of the basis of calculation until retirement age and 40% from that age onwards or immediately if the widow/widower suffers from physical or mental illness which reduces his/her capacity for work,
- the ex-spouse of the insured person, subject to the condition that he was entitled to an alimony pension and that he satisfies the same conditions as the spouse; if so, the same amount is payable as that to a widow or widower, although the amount is never higher than the amount of the alimony pension;
- the orphan of the mother or father, at respectively 20, 40 or 50% of the basis of calculation for one, two or more children until they attain the age of 18 years of age (22 or 25 in case of secondary or higher education; there is no age limit in cases where the child is permanently fully incapacitated);
- the orphan of the father or mother, at respectively 40, 80 or 100% of the basis of calculation for one, two or more children under the same conditions as for the orphan of the father or mother, but subject to a total amount of 80% of the previous salary of the victim;
- the dependent parents or ascendants of the insured person, at 15% of the basis of calculation for each ascendant until retirement age, and at 20% of

the basis of calculation from these ages onwards or if they suffer a physical or mental sickness which makes them incapable of work. If there is a spouse or orphan who is equally entitled to a pension, each ascendant receives 10% of the basis of calculation.
It is provided that the total benefits paid to beneficiaries may never exceed 80% of the basis of calculation.
There is also a benefit for funeral costs, amounting to thirty days wages; the amount of this benefit is doubled with respect to the possible transportation of the deceased person.

4.3. Incapacity for work

The insured person, who suffers temporary incapacity for work, is entitled to sickness benefit (*subsidio por doença*), subject to the condition that he:
- can demonstrate that he carried out paid work during at least six months, as well as during at least twelve days, in the four months preceding the determination of the incapacity; or
- if he is self-employed, can demonstrate that he has paid contributions over a period of six months.

Sickness benefit amounts (in general) to 65% of the average daily wage during the first six months prior to the second month preceding the beginning of the incapacity, and to 70% of this reference salary after a continuous period of 365 days of incapacity for work.
The first three days of incapacity for work of paid workers and the first thirty days of incapacity for work of the self-employed are waiting days and thus do not give rise to entitlement to benefit.
This benefit is payable during a maximum period of 1095 days and 365 days in respect to the self-employed.

If incapacity for work is due to tuberculosis the duration of benefit is unlimited and benefit amounts to 80 or 100% of the reference wage, depending upon the individual case.
Maternity benefit (*subsidio de maternidade*) is payable to female employees who are temporarily prevented from working due to a birth or an abortion. The conditions of benefit are similar to those with respect to sickness benefit. Maternity benefit amounts to 100% of the average income from work that would be considered when calculating sickness benefit. Maternity benefit is payable for 98 days, at least 60 of which being after the birth; in the case of an abortion or a stillbirth maternity benefit is payable for a maximum of 30 days; in case of the death of a child who was born alive, benefit is payable for at least 30 days, to be counted from the date of the birth.

The paternity allowance (*subsídio de paternidade*) may be granted to the father, whether he is a self-employed man or a wage earner, in cases of the death, physical injury and mental incapacity of the mother or the joint decision of the parents, for the period the mother would still have been entitled to the maternity benefit and, in cases of the death of the mother, for no less than 14 days.

Paternity allowance amounts to the reference salary for the first 6 months preceding the second month prior to the risk. This amount cannot be less than 50% of the minimum earnings set for the worker's activity sector.

The invalidity pension (*pensão de invalidez*) is payable is payable to an invalid person who has paid contributions for at least the last five calendar years and who can demonstrate 120 working days for each year taken into account. To be "invalid" means that a worker who, due to a physical or mental permanent incapacity (which is not the result of an industrial injury or occupational disease), is unable to earn more than a third of the earnings corresponding to the normal practice of his occupational activity. The incapacity for work is considered to be permanent where it may be presumed that the worker shall not become considerably better within three years time and will therefore not be able to earn more than 50% of the earnings corresponding to the normal practice of his work. The amount of invalidity pension and minimum invalidity pension is calculated in the same way as old age pension. Here too there is the possibility of entitlement to a dependent spouse addition, if the pension was provided under the legislation in force before 31st December 1993. The invalidity pension is granted from the first day of the month in which the claim can be submitted or from the day determined by the medical board. Invalidity pension is converted into an old-age pension after the pensioner has reached the retirement age. It should be mentioned that there is no scale of degrees of incapacity; a person is either invalid or not invalid. The social invalidity pension belongs to the non-contributory social security system.

The social pension is only payable to people with a monthly income which does not exceed 30% of the national minimum wage, or 50% thereof with respect to the head of a household. Social invalidity pension is payable to those who are at least 18 years of age and are recognised to be unfit for full-time work and who are not covered by a contributory scheme. The social pension is paid at a flat-rate.
The constant attendance allowance (*subsídio por assistência de terceira pessoa*) is granted to the beneficiary of an invalidity, old age, survivor's or social pension, in respect of whom the medical advisors are of the opinion that he cannot autonomously and successfully carry out his basic needs and is in need of the constant attendance of a third person. The allowance is paid in addition to the pension. The allowance varies according to whether it is payable as an addition to an invalidity, an old age, a survivor's or a social pension.

A number of social security benefits meet the specific needs of handicapped people: the increase in the family allowance due to a handicap, the special education benefit, the lifetime monthly benefit and the invalidity pension. The final benefit on this list, invalidity benefit, has already been dealt with above.

The increase in the family allowance due to a handicap (*bonificação por deficiência do subsidio familiar*) is payable to people below the age of 24, who satisfy the entitlement conditions under the non-contributory scheme or who are dependent upon a person insured under the contributory scheme, on the

condition that the child cannot maintain himself, that he attends a special education institution and that he needs individual therapeutic treatment.
The level of increase in the family allowance due to a handicap varies according to whether the person is less than fourteen years of age, between fourteen and eighteen years of age or between eighteen and twenty four years of age.

Special education benefit (*subsídio de educação especial*) is payable to handicapped people below 24 years of age who fulfil the entitlement conditions under the non-contributory scheme and to the descendants of persons who are treated as insured workers. The benefit covers the costs of special education, subject to a personal contribution of the family of the handicapped person. This personal contribution is determined in relation to the costs of the special education and the financial position of the family.

A lifetime monthly benefit (*subsídio mensal vitalício*) is payable to descendants and people insured under the contributory scheme and persons treated as such, on the condition that the descendants are at least 24 years of age and that they are not entitled to an invalidity pension or to a social pension.

If the incapacity for work is due to a work injury or an occupational disease, different provisions apply. A benefit for total temporary incapacity is paid provided that the victim is undergoing medical treatment or rehabilitation therapy. The benefit is calculated on the basis of 70% of the lost wages which exceed the national minimum for the applicable branch of industry (i.e. the basis of calculation). The victim receives two thirds of the basis of calculation. However, the victim only receives one third of this amount in the first three days following the injury, when he is admitted into hospital or when the medical costs and maintenance are borne by the responsible institution, except if there are people dependent upon the claimant.
In the case of a work injury, the degree of permanent incapacity is determined by the labour courts and in case of occupational disease by either the labour courts or by the National Centre for the Prevention of Professional Risks. The degree of incapacity can be reviewed on the initiative of the competent institution or of the victim himself.
The basis of calculation for the pensions is determined in the same way as for temporary incapacity; however, if the incapacity is less than 50%; if the incapacity is equal to, or lighter than, 50%, the benefit is calculated on the basis of 80% of the previously earned wages which must exceed the national minimum wage for that individual's branch of industry.
In case of permanent incapacity for all work, an annuity pension is payable at the level of 80% of the basis of calculation. In case of permanent incapacity for the usual work, the annuity pension varies between one half and two thirds of the basis of calculation, according to the degree of the remaining capacity to carry out another suitable occupation. In case of permanent partial incapacity, the annuity pension amounts to two thirds of the general reduction of the earning capacity.
If the victim requires the assistance of a third person, the amount of pension is increased by 25% (subject to an upper limit). If the victim is completely and permanently incapable of carrying out any work, his annuity pension is in-

creased by 10% of the basis of calculation (subject to an upper limit) for each dependent family member.

There are special provisions which allow a person to pay off certain pensions on the request of the pensioner or the competent institution. Paying off is compulsory if the degree of invalidity is equal to or lower than 10% and if the amount of benefit does not exceed a certain percentage of the national minimum wage.

A pension for permanent incapacity may be enjoyed together with a new salary.

4.4. Unemployment

On the grounds of the contributory scheme, full or part-time employees are entitled to unemployment benefit (*subsidio de desemprego*) if they satisfy the following conditions. They must
- be involuntarily unemployed;
- be fit for work;
- be available and willing to work;
- be registered as a job seeker with the Employment Centre of their area;
- have been employed for 540 days within a period of 24 months immediately prior to the date of unemployment.

The amount of the unemployment benefit is equal to that of sickness benefit; however there is a lower and an upper limit. Unemployment benefit may not exceed three times the national minimum wage of the insured person's branch of industry.

Unemployment benefit is payable for 10 to 30 months, depending upon the age of the claimant (minimum for those under 25 years of age; maximum for those over 55 years of age).The employees are entitled to social unemployment benefit (*subsidio social de desemprego*) if they fulfil the following conditions. They must:
- have worked and paid contributions for the general contributory scheme of social security for at least 180 days in the last 12 months;
- be involuntarily unemployed;
- the monthly per capita income of the beneficiary's family cannot exceed 80% of the minimum guaranteed wage in the relevant sector; and
- have reached the end of the period in which the unemployment benefit was granted and still remained unemployed.

Thus all employees who have exhausted their right to contributory unemployment benefit, or do not fulfil the relevant conditions with respect to previous periods of work and contributions, are entitled to social unemployment benefit.

Social unemployment benefit amounts to a certain percentage of the national minimum wage for the employee's branch of industry. This percentage varies between 70% and 100% according to the number of dependant persons.

However, the amount of social unemployment benefit may never exceed the average wage of the employee, as it is calculated for sickness benefit.

The benefit is due for the same period of time as the unemployment benefits, except when it is following the payment of such an unemployment benefit. In the latter case, the period of payment of the social unemployment benefit equals half the period of payment of the unemployment benefit.

4.5. Health care

There is a national health service in Portugal. No fees need to be paid for medical services. There is freedom of choice of physician between the general practitioners and specialists of the health centres and the recognised physicians. The government has introduced a variable personal contribution. Beneficiaries of invalidity pension, old age pension, survivor's pension or those entitled to benefit on the grounds of the occupational diseases insurance scheme (for permanent incapacity of at least 50%), as well as their spouses and minor children, are not required to pay any personal contribution regarding consultations with a physician, treatment in a public hospital or a health centre, or treatment by a recognised physician. A similar exemption applies for pregnant women and their children below 12 years of age as well as for those with certain young dependent handicapped persons and for specific categories of socially and economically vulnerable persons.

Physicians working for the national health service are either civil servants of the regional health boards, or civil servants of the hospitals. The physicians may also have remained self-employed, but recognised on the grounds of an agreement between the order of physicians and the Ministry of Health. The latter doctors may be consulted by people who cannot reach a public health centre within a specific time for reasons of distance. The physicians who are civil servants receive a salary, the amount of which is determined by the government and which varies according to the occupational category of the physician. The recognised physicians receive a flat-rate sum per consultation.

Entry into public hospitals as well as into health institutions approved by the Minister of Health, is free of charge. No personal contributions towards the costs are required for care in a public ward, nor for care in a private room if this was prescribed by the physician. Entry into private hospitals and clinics is, according to the law, also free if the public hospitals cannot offer the required health care within three months.

Both dental and medical care are provided within health centres. If a private, approved dentist is consulted, the fee may be reimbursed according to a tariff determined by the government.

Depending upon the type of the disease the claimant must pay between 30% and 60% of the costs of medicine which appears on an official health service list. No personal contribution is required from the beneficiary if he suffers from one of the diseases contained within in a specified list. A personal contribution of 20% is required for artificial aids which appear on the official list. For optical and dental aids prescribed by a health centre, a personal contribution of 25% is required. If the optical and dental aids are prescribed by a recognised private specialist, the beneficiary must pay the full price and the health service will offer a refund of 75%.

Transport costs are only reimbursed to patients who live in a remote district and even then, only under certain conditions.

Health care with respect to victims of an industrial injury or an occupational disease is financed in the former case by the concerned private insurance company and in the latter by the national health service. No personal contributions are required from the victim.
It seems necessary to mention that the system of health care, as described above, presupposes an ideal situation more than it reflects the current practice. In practice, admittance to free health care is very difficult; this state of affairs can, among others things, be explained with reference to the fact that the physicians working for the national health service also maintain, at the same time, a private practice, which provides them with a much more attractive income.

4.6. Family

Family allowance for children and young people (*subsidio familiar a criances e jovens*) is granted subject to the following conditions:
- the child may not carry out any paid activity;
- from the age of compulsory school onwards, the child must be enrolled in a school of the following level:
- from 16 to 18 years of age, in basic or equivalent education;
- from 18 to 21 years of age, in secondary or equivalent education;
- from 21 to 24 years of age, in university or equivalent education. However there is no age limit with respect to handicapped people who are entitled neither to lifetime monthly benefit nor to a social pension;
- the child must, in principle, reside in Portugal.

Family allowance consists of a monthly amount which is determined according to the income of the household and to the number and age of the eligible descendants.

An adoption benefit (*subsidio por adopção*) is payable to the insured worker who has adopted a child younger than three years old. The requirements with respect to the employment and contribution record are the same as those for sickness benefits. Adoption benefit is payable for 60 days, in order to support the arrival of the adopted child within the family. The amount of the adoption benefit equals that of the average income from work, which serves as a basis for the calculation of sickness benefit.

Wage earners who stay away from their work in order to give necessary assistance to their children who are under 10 years of age and are ill or handicapped, may be eligible for a benefit for assistance to minor children, provided that:
- they fulfil the entitlement conditions for sickness benefit, except for the requirement regarding incapacity for work;

- the child is part of a single parent family.

The amount of the benefit is equal to that of the sickness benefit which the beneficiary would have received should he become ill himself. The benefit for assistance to minor children is payable for a maximum period of 30 days per year, except in case of the child entering hospital, when it is paid for the whole period of hospitalisation.

The dependent spouse addition is payable to the beneficiary of an old age or an invalidity pension under the contributory scheme, who has a dependent spouse with an income which falls below the amount of the allowance. Any possible income of the spouse is deducted from the allowance.

4.7. Need

In 1996, a guaranteed social minimum income scheme was introduced. The scheme aims to integrate the socially excluded population back into society and the labour market. The introduction of the minimum social income has been combined with the enhancement of the social responsibility of both the state and the benefit recipients. The state has to provide the claimants with vocational training and the claimants are obliged to accept employment or to enter insertion programmes.

5. *Financing*

The contributory schemes of social security are almost entirely financed by their own resources. The government does not participate in the financing.

In the general scheme, a flat-rate contribution for social security is levied upon wages; approximately one third of these contributions are borne by the employees, approximately two thirds by the employers. However, recently a VAT rise was used in order to cope with the growing expenditures for the old age and unemployment schemes and to allow for a lowering of the employer contributions. The flat-rate contribution as well as it's division between employees and employers is determined by the parliamentary discussion concerning the social security budget.

Employers of handicapped people (people with a capacity for work of at least 20% below the normal capacity of an employee carrying out the same activities) only pay half the employer's contribution in respect of their handicapped employees.

A special wage contribution is levied upon the employers in respect of the occupational diseases insurance scheme.

Under the special contributory schemes there are special contributions rates; however, these are never in excess of those of the general scheme and are often remarkably lower.

The *C.R.S.S.* collect the contributions for social security and deposits these with the Institution for the Financial Administration of Social Security. This institution provides the *C.R.S.S.* with the financial means necessary for the payment of the benefits.

In Portugal the collection of social contributions is an enormous problem. Despite special legislative measures to enable a flexible collection of the debts which many enterprises have with respect to social security, the application of these legislative measures remains extremely difficult in a context of economic crisis. Many enterprises, which have social security debts do not have enough financial means for them to propose a plausible plan for the repayment of these sums. Recently, measures were taken in order to strengthen sanctions in respect of enterprises which are not prepared to present a plan for the regular repayments of their debts; thus, among other things, these enterprises will be excluded from every public contract, neither will they be able to register their stocks and shares with the exchange, nor can they pay any dividends. Furthermore, penal sanctions are also provided for.

The non-contributory social security scheme is totally financed by the State.

In respect of the work injury insurance scheme, the employers pay insurance contributions which vary in accordance with their risk. The financing system of the work injuries insurance scheme is mixed (both pay as you go and capitalisation).

Social action is financed by State subsidies, as well as the yield from sanctions due to social fraud within the contributory scheme, and by the payable, but not yet paid social security benefits which are superannuated.

6. Judicial review

People who have an interest in the granting of social security benefits (in the broad sense) and are of the opinion that their rights have been violated, can lodge a complaint or a petition with the administrative body which is empowered to grant these benefits. This is related to the constitutionally guaranteed right of petition, which enables people who have allegedly sustained damage as a result of maladministration to refer their case to the higher hierarchical, or supervisory bodies of the competent administrative institutions, as well as to the President of the Republic. Such people can also refer their case to the *Provedor de Justiça*. This ombudsman takes on complaints regarding improper acts or omissions of public authorities. He has no adjudication powers, but can direct necessary recommendations to the competent authorities, in order to induce them to prevent or repair the established injustices.

The act also provides a right of appeal to the administrative courts to people who were refused affiliation to the social security scheme or a benefit. In practice claimants hardly ever make use of their right to judicial review in respect of social security.

Chapter Fourteen

SPAIN

1. Introduction: concept and sources of social security law

Chapter III, title I of the Constitution of the democratic Kingdom of Spain, 27 December 1978, ("concerning fundamental rights and duties") is devoted to the "guiding principles of social and economic policy". In contrast to the provisions in the previous chapter, concerning classic rights and freedoms, the rights contained within chapter III cannot be directly invoked by the citizen in legal proceedings. The recognition, respect and protection of these guiding principles should be manifest within all legislation, jurisprudence and administration. They can only be invoked in court in so far as they are implemented in statutory provisions (cf. article 53, section 3 Constitution).
Article 39 Constitution concerns the social, economic and legal protection of the family. Article 41 Constitution is explicitly devoted to social security, it states: "The government shall maintain a public system of social security for all citizens, which guarantees sufficient social benefits and assistance in case of need, especially in case of unemployment. The additional benefits and assistance are free". Article 43 Constitution recognises the right to health care and attributes the organisation of this to the government. Article 49 Constitution is devoted to social services for the handicapped. Finally in article 50 Constitution it is provided that "the government (...) guarantees sufficient economic means to elderly citizens, by means of adequate and periodically adjusted pensions. Equally, the government promotes the welfare of the elderly, independent of their family duties, by means of a system of social services, which takes care of their special health, living, leisure and cultural problems".

It is rather difficult to define the Spanish concept of "social security" (*seguridad social*) in terms of positive law. This complication relates to, among others, the difficulty in establishing the legal relationship between social security and the fields of employment policy, education and social services, which belong more within the concept of public services than within the limited framework of social security benefits. This pretension of the State is seen by some constitutional lawyers as confirmed by the separate adoption in the constitution of, on the one hand, an article concerning social security (article 41 Constitution), and on the other hand, articles concerning the family, health care, services for the handicapped and pensions.
So, strictly speaking, do the benefits in respect of unemployment, social services and health care belong to social security? From the above it would appear not. But, on the other hand, unemployment is the only social risk that is explicitly mentioned in the constitutional provision concerning social security, (article 41 Constitution) and the competence in the area of social services is

distributed between the State, the autonomous communities and local government. It can also be pointed out that the conditions and financing of the health care system are barely integrated. In the light of article 41 Constitution there is also some doubt as to whether the free occupational benefit schemes should be excluded from the concept of social security.

In the light of the rather dogmatic debate between experts in constitutional and social security law about the exact scope of the Spanish concept of social security, we shall adopt a pragmatic approach, taking as a starting point the general Social Security act. This act defines the goals of social security; it guarantees an adequate protection in the events enumerated within the act, as well as a progressive improvement of the standard of living on a medical, economic, and cultural level to those who, due to their professional activities, fall under the scope of application of social security, as well as to their dependent family members and those considered as such. According to article 38 of the same act, the protection offered by the social security system includes:
a. specialist care in respect of maternity, sickness or occupational disease, a normal injury or an industrial injury;
b. the return to working life after these events have occurred;
c. benefits in respect of temporary incapacity for work, invalidity, retirement, unemployment, death and survival, as well as other special situations, specifically provided for;
d. family benefits in cash; and
e. social services.
So, the concept of social security in principle does not include social assistance.

The assistance schemes cover mostly the same risks as the social insurances. The degree in which "rights" to social assistance or to social services may be enforced as "subjective rights", varies. Assistance benefits are also subsidiary to the other social security benefits. They are only granted when a person is not (or no longer) entitled to social security benefits stricto sensu. In view of the decentralised powers which exist in this area (to be discussed below), social assistance and social services will not be dealt with here.

In Spain, since 1963, a general system exists which operates to some degree as a model (general system for employees of the industry and services), as well as a series of special systems. The scope of application of the special systems depends upon the sector of activity (e.g. special systems for agriculture, for coal mining or for people working at sea) or upon the sort of activity done (e.g. systems for self-employed people, for civil servants, for domestic personnel, for students). In recent years there has been a certain degree of harmonisation of these systems (e.g. in the area of financing and the determination of entitlement conditions for an old age pension).

A new range of non contributory benefits has recently been introduced in Spain. They cover the risks of old age, invalidity, and family. They are available under certain conditions to those people who cannot benefit from the contributory schemes.

The statutes which regulate Spanish social security are, to a certain extent, codified by the General Social Security Act, although many other statutes concerning social security exist alongside the General Social Security Act. Here we note that, on a statutory level, the basic schemes to a large extent still date from before the entry into force of the Constitution (29 December 1978).

The legislative basis for social security was extended further by means of governmental decrees and ministerial orders; the majority of these do not have a general application, but cover specific parts of social security law, such as the scope of application of social security, contributions or pensions.

The General Social Security Act declares that the compulsory social protection for which it provides may be supplemented; supplementary schemes are most likely to be found within collective labour agreements. The supplementary (occupational) benefits are mostly intended to adjust income maintenance as much as possible to the lost real earnings.

The specific form of federalism, established in the constitution of 1978, has led to a very complicated division of powers between the central government and the autonomous communities.
On the grounds of article 149 Constitution, the Spanish State enjoys exclusive authority in respect of the economic regime of social security, as well as the basic legislation on social security, without this detracting from the possibility of entrusting the administration of social security to the autonomous communities (article 149(1)(17) Constitution). Basic legislation includes all legislation that is not concerned purely with administrative organisation. The economic regime of social security includes provisions concerning the resources of the social security system and the territorial and functional division of the means. Article 148 Constitution states that the autonomous communities can be given powers in respect of social assistance, health and hygiene (article 148 (1)(20,21) Constitution). In line with this, the regulations of the autonomous communities contain provisions concerning social security competencies with regard to the statutory implementation of the basic legislation of the State, except for norms which concern the economic regime of social security, as well as to administration of the economic regime. For this purpose the autonomous communities are able to set up and administer all the services which are considered necessary within their territory; they will also exercise control over all the service providing institutions without neglecting the high supervision of the State.
The autonomous communities link the exercise of their powers in the field of social security and health to rules concerning the democratic participation of all the people involved, as well as of the organisation of employers and employees. It thus appears that the extensive, albeit still embryonic, legislation of the autonomous communities gives further contents to the social protection system. The various autonomous communities did not take up the same level of powers. This legislation of the autonomous communities will not be dealt with.

Although, in principle, this book confines itself to giving the actual situation of the social security legislation, it seems appropriate to mention nevertheless that in 1996 the Government and the most representative trade unions reached an agreement on the reform of social security (the 'Toledo-pact'); this pact will be translated into legislative amendments.

2. *Administrative organisation*

With regard to the institutional administration of social security, health and employment policy, there are the following specialised administrative bodies:
- the National Social Security Institute (*Instituto Nacional de la Seguridad Social, I.N.S.S.*), responsible for the administration of all social security schemes which provide benefits in cash, including unemployment benefits, but excluding the scheme for the mariners;
- the National Health Institute (*Instituto Nacional de la Salud INSALUD*), charged with the administration of health care;
- the National Institute for Migrations and Social Services (*Instituto Nacional de Migraciones y Servicios Sociales, IMSERSO*), charged with the administration of social services, in kind as well as in cash, in respect of the migrants and the less able bodied, invalids and the elderly;
- the National Institute for Employment Policy (*Instituto Nacional de Empleo, INEM*), in which employment policy and vocational training are organised;
- the Social Institute for Mariners (*Instituto Social de la Marina I.S.M.*), which is charged with the benefit schemes for mariners; and
- the (General) Treasury of Social Security (*Tesoreria General de la Seguridad Social T.G.S.S.*), charged with the administration of the resources of social security, the collection of contributions and the payment of benefits, except unemployment benefit.

All these administrative bodies have the status of a legal person. They are functionally decentralised bodies of the central government and fall under the authority of the competent minister; this, depending upon the case, is the Minister of Labour and Social Affairs or the Minister of Health. The competent minister is head of the administrative bodies and carries out supervision.

As mentioned before, the constitution gives the autonomous communities certain administrative tasks in respect of social security. Some of these tasks, especially in the field of health care and social services, are already carried out by the autonomous communities. It is expected that in time the autonomous communities will all succeed in taking over the entire administration of social security (as is provided in the Constitution), whilst the central government retains competence in the field of legislation and the fundamental principles of social security policy. Although in principle the administration of social security is attributed to the autonomous communities, the administration of the resources of social security remains with the general treasury of social security.

The administrative organisation of the insurance scheme for industrial injuries has some special features. Enterprises are free to insure industrial injuries either with the public social security institutions or with the industrial injury insurance mutual aid associations of the employers (*Mutuas de Accidentes de*

Trabajo y Enfermedades Profesionales). The latter are non-profit making, private institutions which were originally exclusively charged to insure against industrial injuries. However, the resources of these institutions constitute a part of the social security resources and not of the employer's industrial injuries scheme themselves. Originally, the *mutua's* function was to pay for the benefits for the labour accidents and occupational diseases, to which workers that were employed by the *mutua*'s members employers. Since 1994, their task has been widened: they are now managing the sickness benefits payable to the employees of the *mutua*'s members employers as well as to the workers falling under the special schemes and the self-employed. This extension of the activity radius of the *mutuas* has been considered by some as the beginning of the privatisation of social security.

Article 129 Constitution gives the claimants the right to participation within the administration of social security; this right is to be further implemented by statute. The constitution does not state how intensive the participation should be, nor does it state which representatives will carry out the right to participation.
The participation of the claimant is channelled via the employee and employer organisations as well as via the public administration itself. These three levels participate and are present on the general board of the *I.N.S.S.*, of the *IN-SALUD*, of the *IMSERSO*, of the *INEM* and of the *I.S.M*. The general boards consist of thirteen representatives from the administration, thirteen representatives from the most representative employers' organisations and thirteen representatives from the most representative employees' organisations.
The following competencies are attributed to these participation bodies:
- participation in and control over the administration of the aforementioned social security institutions;
- development of internal regulations of these institutions;
- development of a draft proposal for the budget of these institutions;
- approval of the annual report of these institutions.

However, the activities of the participation bodies get little response from the socially insured people. Indeed, the great majority of employees are not even aware of their existence; this is partly due to the fact that the unions send representatives to the boards without any intermediation from the employees. Moreover, none of the previously mentioned competencies of the participation bodies have a real impact upon the social security institutions concerned; the competencies do not consist of real participation within the administration, but merely of the control thereof.
For the sake of completeness we repeat that some of the regulations of the autonomous communities also establish a right to participation in the administration of social security.

3. Personal scope of application

Since 1985 social security consists of a general system and special systems, the latter being mainly for the self-employed, for the agricultural sector, for mariners, for mineworkers, for domestic servants and for students.

The general system covers all dependent employees who are active in industry and services, except those who, in view of the enterprise for which they work, belong to a special scheme.
However, some wage earners with short-term contracts or training contracts are excluded from the personal scope of some schemes of the general system, such as the sickness benefits and the unemployment benefits.

The special systems for the agricultural sector and for mariners cover both persons who are active on their own account and workers who are active on account of others. The system for the self-employed covers all self-employed persons belonging to the listed professions. Yet there are still self-employed individuals who do not belong to one of these special schemes; for example, this is the case for a number of free professional groups, such as medical doctors. These groups have their own independent systems of social protection which operate within the margins of the public scheme. Some of the previously excluded free professional groups have been integrated within the public system of social protection for the self-employed. This took place as a result of a request from the professional board of the occupational group in question; once incorporated, affiliation to the system of the self-employed becomes compulsory to all members of the profession. Among others, architects and pharmacists have been incorporated in this way.
Other groups of free professionals, such as lawyers, can choose between their independent system and the self-employed system.

Civil servants and military personnel have their own special system, the benefits and financing of which are different from those for persons who are active on their own account or on account of others. However, the civil servants of local administrations were integrated in the general social security system for wage earners.

The separate social protection schemes for certain free occupational groups, as well as those for civil servants, will not be considered further.

The social security non-contributory level covers those people in need who have never contributed or who have not contributed enough time, so as to be entitled to the benefits under the contributory level.

Finally, it should be mentioned that not only the employees who are active on the account of others, the diocesan clergy, pensioners and other people entitled to a periodic benefit from the general system, qualify for health care under the general scheme, but also people who enjoy unemployment benefit on an assistance level, provided they are registered with the labour exchange and have an income below the minimum wage. Since 1989, the law also extended the right to health care to all Spaniards residing in Spain without sufficient financial means. Spaniards who have emigrated yet who have temporarily returned to Spain, also qualify for health care under the general scheme. The following people are also insured for health care provided they live together with, or are dependent upon, a person insured under the general scheme: the spouse, descendants, brothers and sisters under age, ascendants and their spouses and foster children. The joint insurance of the ex-spouse and the descendants is not terminated as a result of a divorce.

4. Risks and benefits

4.1. Old age

Entitlement to an old age pension (*pensión de jubilación*) under the general scheme of social security is subject to the condition that the claimant has paid contributions for a minimum period of 15 years, two years of which must have been during the eight years (which will become ten and thereafter fifteen years) immediately preceding the termination of employment (or the claim for pension). Furthermore, he must be 65 years of age or older. However, exceptions do exist concerning both requirements.

The amount of the old age pension is determined by two factors, i.e. the basis of calculation and the pension rate.
The basis of calculation is related to the insured person's income from work during his active career, in respect of which he has paid contributions. The basis of calculation is equal to the quotient determined by a common denominator of 112 and the contribution bases during the 96 months (Toledo-pact: gradually raised to respectively 210 and 180 months) immediately preceding the materialisation of the insured risk. However, only the real contribution basis of the last 24 of these 96 months is actually taken into account; the above contribution bases are first actualised. This means that they are increased in accordance with the evolution of the index of consumption prices (between the contribution year and the two years preceding the entitlement to a pension). If, during some of these 96 months, the claimant has not paid any contributions, account is taken of the minimum contribution basis for adult employees, applicable for the corresponding period (possibly actualised).

The pension rate is related to the number of years during which a person has made contributions. Whereas until now, the first 15 years counted for 60%, the subsequent years for 2% each, the scale of contribution rates starts with the minimum period of contributions of 15 years; the pension rate will then be 50%. From the 16th year of contribution until the 25th, the pension rate will increase by 3% for each extra contribution year; from the 26th year onwards the pension rate will increase by 2% per additional contribution year. The total pension rate may never exceed 100%, this maximum is thus reached with a contribution record of 35 years.

The minimum pension varies according to whether or not one has a dependent spouse; the amount is lower for those below 65 years of age.

The statute provides the opportunity for people who paid contributions before 1 January 1967 to retire at the age of 60. For each year of early retirement the early retirement pension (*pensión de jubilación anticipada*) is reduced by 8%. Employers have used this formula to discard their surplus employees or to reduce the age of their work force; they offer their employees a benefit from 60 years of age upon early retirement, which compensates for the loss of 8% per year of early retirement.

In principle, old age pension is incompatible with any employment of the pensioner, although activities which are not within the scope of any social security scheme are permitted. If the pensioner nevertheless wishes to carry out some other work, he must give notice of this to the social security institution and request a suspension of his pension.

Nearly all collective labour agreements provide supplements to the old age pension. Firstly, these provide for early retirement benefit, as described above. Furthermore, there are supplementary benefits which aim to bring the income of the retired person as far as possible in line with his income during his active life. As a rule the amount of the supplementary benefit is dependent upon the seniority of the claimant within the enterprise and upon his previous income.
Three further types of early retirement exist.

Early retirement from the age of 64 is possible whilst maintaining 100% of one's pension rights, if provisions for this purpose are adopted within the collective or individual labour agreements. The claimant must fulfil all the conditions of the usual old age pension, except for the age requirement. Also, the job which is made available must be taken immediately by a younger employee or by a person enjoying unemployment benefit at an assistance level.
Benefits from the sectorial industrial conversion are payable to people who are at least 55 years of age and when the enterprise has requested and obtained a statement from the government declaring a crisis situation. Between the ages of 55 and 60 the claimant receives 80% of his average income during the six months preceding the crisis declaration. Between the ages of 60 and 65 he receives 75% of his average wages during the 60 months preceding his early retirement. In some enterprises, part-time retirement is possible from the age of 62. The level of the pension is calculated in the same way as for the normal old age pension. The old age pension is reduced in proportion to the number of hours which the retired person works.

The old age risk is also covered at the non-contributory level. The people entitled to this benefit, are those who are older than 65, who live in Spain, have lived there for at least 10 years, and who do not have enough resources for subsistence. The benefit is due even if they have never paid contributions for social security or they have not paid enough to get a pension at the contributory level. These benefits are flat rate and they are not compatible with those of the Social Assistance Scheme.

4.2. Death

In 1983 the Constitutional Court declared that the existing inequality between men and women with respect to the entitlement condition of survivor's pensions was incompatible with the Constitution. Since this judgement the same conditions for the survivor's pensions apply for both widows and widowers. As a matter of convenience, we shall only refer to widower's pensions as indicating equally a widow's pension and a widower's pension.

Upon their death, employees who are affiliated to the social security system (or who are treated as such), give access to entitlement to a survivor's pension or to other survivor's benefits. It is further required that the deceased must have paid contributions for at least 500 days during the five years preceding his death. The latter requirement does not apply if his death was due to an accident, to a terrorist action or if the deceased was retired. The surviving spouse must normally have lived with the deceased employee, albeit that widower's pension is also granted in case of divorce or separation, i.e. in ratio to the period of cohabitation.

The widower's pension (*pensión de viudedad*) amounts to 45% of the basis of calculation. The basis of calculation is determined in a similar way to the basis of calculation for old age pension. If the deceased already enjoyed a retirement or invalidity pension, the basis of calculation of such a pension is simply taken over, albeit after a revaluation. The minimum widower's pension varies according to whether the survivor is younger or older than 60 years.

Entitlement to widower's pension terminates upon remarriage. If the remarriage takes place before he reaches 60 years of age, the widower receives a lump sum equal to 24 months of widower's pension.

Widower's pension is compatible with all the widower's income from work, just as with retirement or invalidity pension to which he would have been entitled.

Orphan's pension (*pensión de orfandad*) is payable to all children of the insured deceased person, who are under 18 (Pact of Toledo: raised this to 21 or 23 if the orphan has lost both parents) years of age or who are handicapped. Where adopted children or step children concerned, there must be at least two years between the adoption or marriage on the one hand and the death on the other hand. In respect of the deceased the same employment conditions apply as with the entitlement for widower's pension. The level of the orphan's pension is also calculated in the same way as that of the widower's pension, albeit not at a rate of 40%, but at a rate of 20% of the basis of calculation. If there is no surviving spouse who is entitled to widower's pension, the orphan's pension is increased by an amount equal to the (fictitious) widower's pension, which is divided between the number of orphans who are eligible for benefit. The total amount of widower's pension and orphan's pension must in no case exceed the basis of calculation. Orphan's pension is compatible with income from work; a minimum orphan's pension is provided.

If the death was due to an industrial injury or occupational disease, no contribution conditions apply for entitlement to benefit. Widower's pension and orphan's pension are payable at the same level as when death was due to another cause. However, in addition, the widower is entitled to six times the amount of the monthly basis of calculation; for each orphan this additional payment amounts to one times this amount.

Also included within the concept of survivor's pensions are a number of pensions which are payable to family members of the deceased other than his spouse and children, such as his grand children, brothers or sisters, grand parents, as well as the children and brothers or sisters of the survivor entitled to the pension, provided that they are older than 45 years of age. In order to be eligible for such a pension the survivors must have lived with, and been dependent upon, the deceased person. Furthermore, they must be without sufficient means for subsistence after the death of the insured person.

Survivor's pensions are often supplemented by collective labour agreements in which, just as with invalidity and old age pensions, certain supplementary benefits are provided. Frequently the collective labour agreements provide an obligation on the enterprise to conclude life insurance in favour of the family members of the employees who could become victims of an industrial injury.

Under some schemes, which are part of the general scheme (such as survivor's pensions and invalidity pensions), a death benefit is payable. This benefit is flat-rate.

4.3. Incapacity for work

Social protection in respect of incapacity for work consists of three parts:
- Insurance for temporary incapacity (*incapacidad temporal*);
- Insurance for maternity, paternity and adoption ;
- Insurance for permanent invalidity (*invalidez permanente*) .

The risks covered by the insurance for temporary incapacity are:
- common or professional disease;
- industrial or non industrial injuries (i.e. all accidents whether they occur at work or not);
- periods of observation for the prevention of professional diseases when interruption of work is necessary.

The requirements for entitlement and the amount and duration of the benefit will depend upon the risk which is covered.

In case of common disease, the insured person must have paid contributions for at least 180 days in the five years immediately preceding the interruption of work. Entitlement to benefits in case of professional disease or accident does not require any previous contribution period.

The amount of the benefits varies according to the basis of calculation and the cause of the incapacity. The basis of calculation is determined by the average income of the claimant during the month preceding the termination of work. In the case of a common disease or injury, the benefit amounts to 60% of the basis of calculation, from the fourth to the twentieth day, thereafter at a rate of 75%. From the fourth until the fifteenth day of incapacity, payments are to be borne by the employers. In the case of a labour accident or professional disease, the benefit amounts to 75%. In all cases the duration of entitlement is twelve months with the possibility of being extended to eighteen months if certain conditions are met. After this period, the person involved may qualify for a permanent invalidity benefit.

In case of maternity, the beneficiary must have paid contributions for at least 180 days in the five years immediately preceding the termination of work as a result of the pregnancy. Maternity benefits amount to 100% of the contributory basis, i.e. the daily salary of the month preceding the termination of work. The benefit is paid for up to a maximum of 16 weeks (18 weeks in case of multiple birth). Under certain conditions, the father qualifies for paternity benefit. The maternity insurance also includes a right to specialist medical care.

Entitlement to permanent invalidity pension is further subject to the condition that the claimant has sustained severe anatomical or functional health damage, which can be objectively determined and which is assumed to be definitive. This health damage must notably diminish the capacity for work of the claimant.

In order to be entitled to a permanent invalidity pension, the insured person must have paid contributions during a specified period, except when the invalidity was due to an accident (both industrial and common) or a terrorist action in which case there are no contribution requirements.

If, at the moment that invalidity occurs, the claimant is registered with the social security system, the required minimum duration of contribution payments amounts to one fourth of the time between a person's twentieth birthday and the start of the invalidity, subject to a minimum contribution record of five years. Furthermore, it is required that at least one fifth of the minimum period of payment of contributions falls within the last ten years. If the claimant is not registered with the social security system at the moment that the incapacity occurs, the minimum contribution record amounts to 15 years. There are reduced contribution requirements for employees younger than twenty six years of age; for them the minimum period of contributions merely covers half of the time between their sixteenth birthday and the start of the invalidity.

The statute recognises various degrees of invalidity, each with corresponding benefits:
- in case of partial incapacity in respect of the usual occupation, there is a presumed reduction of the capacity for work of at least one third; this degree of incapacity does not give rise to entitlement to pension, but to a compensation of an amount equal to 24 months of the basis of calculation;
- total incapacity in respect of the usual occupation supposes that it is impossible for the employee to carry out all or the most important tasks within his usual occupation, without excluding the possibility that he could carry out another occupation. The corresponding monthly pension is equal to 55% of the basis of calculation. This percentage amounts to 75% if the insured person is older than 55 and does not work. In view of the relatively low level of this pension and the employer's opportunity to dismiss a beneficiary of such a pension, the potential beneficiaries often choose not to claim any benefit and fully exploit their capacity for work in order to claim one of the subsequent benefits at a later stage;

- absolute and permanent incapacity for work, which supposes full incapacity to carry out any occupation or service. The corresponding benefit amounts to 100% of the basis of calculation; and
- severe invalidity. Severe invalidity is acknowledged in respect of those who should not only be recognised as being absolutely and permanently incapable of work, but, also need the help of another person in order to perform the most essential tasks of daily life, such as dressing, moving around and eating. The pension for severe invalidity amounts to 150% of the basis of calculation.

The basis of calculation for the invalidity pensions is calculated in the same way as that for the old age pension. Special rules exist in cases where the required contribution record amounts to less than the normally required minimum.

If the permanent invalidity is the result of an industrial injury or occupational disease, the level of the benefit is calculated in a different way; the real income of the employee during the year preceding the industrial injury is taken as the basis of calculation. If the consequences of an industrial injury or occupational disease do not result in permanent invalidity, yet do cause permanent damage, such damage is compensated by a benefit, the level of which is determined by the degree of severity of the damage and the part of the body where the damage occurred. In contrast with the benefits provided in the case of common diseases or injuries, the invalidity benefits for a labour accident or a professional disease are not automatically adjusted to the raises in the consumer price index; they are normally adjusted once a year.

Invalidity benefits are usually supplemented by employer's benefits. Such benefits are provided for in approximately 50% of the collective labour agreements. The supplementary benefits, which are borne by the enterprise are usually determined by the recognised degree of incapacity for work and by the seniority of the employee within the enterprise. In cases of absolute invalidity, the supplement usually pays up to 100% of the previously earned income; in cases of total incapacity for the usual occupation, up to 75% of the previously earned income is paid. Today, the supplements often do not only consist of a monthly benefit, but also of a capital sum, the amount of which is determined by the previously earned income and the seniority within the enterprise.

Benefits in case of invalidity are also payable at a non-contributory level. People entitled to these benefits are those older than 18 and younger than 65 who at present have legal residence in Spain and who have lived in this country for at least five years. The degree of incapacity has to be at least 65% and their income has to be below a certain (indexed) minimum. The amount of the benefit is flat rate.

4.4. Unemployment

In respect of unemployment, a distinction must be made between two levels of protection, a contributory level and an assistance level. The cash benefits on a contributory level are called *prestación por desempleo*, those on an assistance level *subsidio por desempleo*. On the contributory level the totally or partially unemployed person is granted an income maintenance benefit, related to the loss in the previously earned wages. The assistance scheme provides benefits which are complementary to those of the contributory scheme, in the sense that the duration of the benefit is extended rather than that the amount is supplemented; thus, the level of extended benefit is not related to the previous wages of the unemployed person.

Unemployment benefits are payable to people who are capable and willing to carry out employment but have lost their job or whose duration of employment has been reduced by at least one third.
In order to be entitled to contributory benefit the unemployed person must have paid contributions over a period of twelve months during at least the last six years prior to the unemployment. Furthermore, he must not have reached his normal pensionable age (as a rule 65 years of age).

Entitlement to unemployment benefit can also exist after 65 years of age if the claimant has not paid sufficient contributions to be entitled to the full old age pension.

The duration of the *prestación por desempleo* is dependent upon the contribution record of the employee (within six years preceding the unemployment). Thus, for example, the person who has paid twelve months contributions during the six years preceding the unemployment is entitled to benefit for four months; the person who has paid contributions over a period of 36 months is entitled to benefit for twelve months; and the person who has paid contributions during the complete six year period (72 months) preceding unemployment has the right to a (maximum) benefit of 24 months. During the first six months of unemployment, unemployment benefit amounts to 70% of the average basis of contribution during the six months preceding unemployment. From the seventh month till the termination of payment the amount of the benefit is 60% of the basis of calculation. The amount of unemployment benefit may neither fall below the inter-professional minimum wage nor exceed 170% of this amount, except if the employee has dependent children in which case the maximum amount of unemployment benefit comes to 195% (with one dependent child) or 220% (with two or more dependent children).

Unemployment benefit on an assistance level (*subsidio por desempleo*) is payable to:
- employees who have exhausted their unemployment benefit under the contributory system and are responsible for a family;
- employees older than 45 who have exhausted their unemployment benefit of at least twelve months and do not have the responsibility of a family;
- workers who, when cessation of employment occurs, have not covered the minimum contributory period necessary for the contributory benefit; and
- workers considered as fully capable or partially invalid after a situation of severe invalidity, or total or absolute permanent invalidity in respect of their usual occupation.

Under certain conditions, returned immigrants and ex-prisoners may also receive these benefits. Unemployment benefit on an assistance level is payable for a maximum period of six months. However, this term may be renewed twice, thus to a total of eighteen months. Depending upon certain conditions, workers over 52 years of age, who are unemployed, may receive the benefit until they reach pensionable age. The *subsidio por desempleo* amounts to 75% of the inter-professional minimum income.

In the framework of the employment policy, non-profit private placement offices as well as enterprises for temporary work were authorised. The job integration of young unemployed people and an increase in the amount of part time work are being promoted.

4.5. Health care

In the general system of social security, health care is due from the first to the last day of sickness.

Specialist care is provided free of charge by the doctors who, after a comparative examination, are appointed by the *I.N.S.S.* to the vacant places. The general practitioners and specialists who do not work in hospitals, obtain a fixed amount for each insured person registered with them. In general, hospital physicians are remunerated as employees. People are free to choose their general practitioner, paediatrician and gynaecologist, provided that in the area of their residence there is more than one doctor.
Medical care provided by the hospitals is also free in the institutions of the *I.N.S.S.*, as well as in the other public and private hospitals which have a contract with the *I.N.S.S.* However, non-surgical hospitalisation medical care is only provided free of charge, if the administrative authorities determine that hospitalisation is required in order to make a diagnosis, if a person has a contagious disease, or if the general state and behaviour of the patient require continuous care.

The insured people pay 40% of the price of medicines which are contained in a list based upon price-quality ratios and comparisons. Exclusion from the list is possible. However, medicine is free of charge for pensioners, persons admitted into hospital and conscientious objectors performing social work.

Dental prosthesis, as well as optical, hearing and other special prosthesis may be granted in the form of assistance. Under the social assistance schemes, certain categories of persons (e.g. pensioners, invalids and the mentally handicapped) may also receive home care.

4.6. Family

The children of people insured under the general scheme are entitled to family benefits (*prestaciónes familiares*), until they have reached the age of 18, except

when the child is severely handicapped, in which case the duration of benefit is unlimited. Family benefit consists of a monthly, fixed amount per child, to be increased by a fixed amount per child if the beneficiary is unemployed or retired with a pension, the level of which is below the minimum old age pension for those who are 65 years old. Family benefits are also increased in favour of families with more than two children (15% per each new-born child).
There is a special family allowance for handicapped children. Furthermore, there are a number of benefits covering the specific needs of these children. There is a special education allowance for families with more than three children, one of which is partly invalid.

There are also family benefits in a non-contributory scheme. People entitled to these benefits are those having children younger than eighteen or children who are more than 65% handicapped. Orphans and abandoned children are also entitled. Parents claiming this benefit must not be entitled to any other family benefits and their income should not be greater than a fixed amount. The amount of the benefit is flat-rate, although it varies depending upon the age or the degree of handicap of the child. The same amounts apply as for family benefits at a contributory level.

5. *Financing*

Income maintenance benefits, the level of which are related to the previously earned income from employment, are financed mainly by contributions from the insured people and the enterprises for which they work. Recently, these sources of finance have been supplemented by increasingly important state subsidies.
Within the general scheme, the contributions are levied upon the wages of the insured people. One sixth of these contributions are paid by the employees and five sixths by the employers.
The contribution liability is subject to both upper and lower wage limits; below and above the limits contributions are levied upon the respective minimum and maximum wage. Special rules apply for part-time workers. Here, the lower and the upper limit vary according to the professional category in which a person may be classified. The lower and the upper wage limits are annually adjusted to the development of the inter-professional minimum wage and to the increases of the wages in general.

The special systems for miners, seamen and the self-employed apply the same contribution rate as is applicable for the general scheme; in respect of activities on account of others the ratio of distribution of contributions between employers and employees is the same. Here too there are lower and upper income limits. The system for the self-employed only operates with a lower income limit; if they wish to do so, they are free to pay contributions over a much higher occupational income. For domestic personnel, as well as for the special agricultural system, there are derogating rates and ratios of distribution.

Within the general scheme, there is a special contribution for the unemployment insurance scheme on a contributory level. This contribution is levied mainly upon the employers. Furthermore, there is a separate contribution for the wage guarantee fund exclusively borne by the employers and a special contribution for occupational training which is mainly borne by the employers and, only to a limited extent, by the employees.
The enterprises also pay contributions for industrial injuries and occupational diseases; the level of this contribution depends upon the degree of danger of the activities within the enterprise. The contribution is calculated on the basis of the real wages of the employees.

There is a large number of rules which provide a decreased contribution liability in order to promote employment.
The state bears all the costs of unemployment assistance.

As mentioned before, the state subsidies also constitute an important source of social security financing. Within the last ten years, the state subsidies have increased considerably.
Since 1994, VAT has been introduced as an extra source of financing social security; this has allowed a reduction in the social contribution rates.

One of the basic principles agreed upon in the 'Toledo-pact' was to separate and clarify the way social security is being financed: the non-contributory schemes are to be financed by the state and the contributory ones to be financed out of social security contributions.

The supplementary benefit schemes, as set up by collective labour agreements, are mostly financed by the employers; in exceptional circumstances, the employees also contribute to the financing. However, the latter is not very common and is usually only the case when the supplementary benefits constitute a collective or personal insurance (collective life insurance, hospital insurance, etc.) in respect of which the employee is free to join in or to opt out.

6. Judicial review

The constitution provides a framework for judicial review which protects the citizen's rights, including those related to social security. Article 24 Constitution provides that the law shall assist all people in obtaining protection of their rights and lawful interests from the judges and the courts. Art. 29 Constitution recognises the right of individual petition for each Spaniard. Furthermore, the Constitution provides for the existence of a "protector of the people" (*Defensor del Pueblo*), who is a sort of ombudsman to whom all people may resort with complaints and suggestions concerning the operation of the public administration.

The purest form of judicial review is the one which results in decisions of the administration being challenged before the courts, i.e. the so-called social courts (*Juzgados de lo Social, Sala de lo Social de los Tribunales Superiores de*

Justicia de las Comunidades Autonomas and the Sala de lo Social del Tribunal Supremo). Every *Social Juzgado* (one or more for every province) is composed of a single judge. The Social Chamber of the *Tribunales Superiores de Justicia de las Comunidades Autónomas* (17 courts) and the Social Chamber of the *Tribunal Supremo* are composed of several judges each, according to the legal provisions.

Before a person can appeal to a court, he must first lodge a complaint with the social security institution which has made the contested decision. The applicant can do so within 30 days from the time that the decision has been received. Then the social security institution has 45 days in which it must take a decision on the complaint. If no decision is made, it is assumed that the original contested decision has been confirmed (negative administrative reticence). After this 45-day term, or as soon as the social security institution has responded to the complaint, the applicant has 30 days to start a procedure before the courts.
The case is dealt with by the *Juzgado Social*. The decision of this court is subject to appeal with the competent *Tribunal Superior de Justicia (recurso de suplicación)*. The judgements of the *Tribunales Superiores de Justicia* are subject to a limited appeal in cassation.

If the applicant considers the statutory provision on which the litigious decision was based to be incompatible with the Constitution, he may also appeal to the *Tribunal Constituciónal*.

Chapter Fifteen

SWEDEN

1. Concept and sources

The Swedish social welfare system provides social security for the whole population. The concept of social security is not clear-cut. Social security law is usually characterised as the part of the legal system regulating the support given to individuals by society, either financially or in kind.

The financial social support can be separated into three different types:
i) Social insurance: which provides protection against any loss of income in case of sickness, parenthood, old age, work-injury and unemployment;
ii) Special allowances: these benefits are parts of the family policy. They can be general, such as the child allowance, or means tested, like the housing allowance.
iii) Social assistance: this involves means-tested financial assistance for any individual who cannot support himself.

Besides these different types of financial support, the social security system guarantees health care and provides different kinds of social services for the elderly, families, the handicapped and other individuals in need of special care.

The people's right to protection against the different social risks is laid down by statutory law. There is no explicit constitutional protection of social security benefits. Although the Swedish Constitution imposes social care and social security as some of the main goals for society, as well as protecting private property, there are serious doubts that these provisions can actually be used to prevent cutbacks in benefit-rates and protect the welfare state in a wider perspective.

The legal material in Swedish social security law differs from other traditional legal sources. At first look it might seem that statutory law is very detailed but in fact it only constitutes a framework, setting up general goals and objectives. As a result, there is extensive room for the administrative authorities to adjust the application and supervision of social security. More detailed regulations are issued by the government or by the responsible administrative authorities. This technique is intended to let legislation provide for goal oriented objectives and to leave specific decisions as to the implementation, and consequently the development of norms, to the level where supervision and application are actually operating.

Outside the general social security system, additional insurances have grown more important. These insurances consist of both labour agreements and a growing private insurance market topping up decreasing benefit rates in public insurance. The tax system gives incentives to private saving through insurances.

2. *Administrative system*

The responsibility for welfare is divided between the state, the counties and the municipalities. They are all governed by bodies elected in general elections and have the right to levy taxes.

All social insurance benefits, except for unemployment benefits, are administered by the local social insurance offices and the National Social Insurance Board. In each county, there is a social insurance office with a number of local offices. These insurance offices are not part of any municipality but are legally constituted entities with public administrative tasks. However, in most legal matters, the insurance offices are to be considered as being public authorities. The National Social Insurance Board is a public supervisory authority with overall responsibility for the administration of the system and for a just and uniform application of social insurance law. For this reason, the National Social Insurance Board has been given the power to issue regulations and general recommendations concerning the application of social insurance law. The decentralisation of administrative legislative tasks is complimentary to the responsibility for legislative and budgetary issues of the Ministry of Social Affairs. The local offices have no funds of their own and are obliged to execute the law and regulations given by the parliament, government and central authority, in this case the latter being the National Social Insurance Board. The National Social Insurance Board cannot, however, impose an interpretation of the rules in a specific case concerning an individual.

Issues concerning unemployment benefits come within the responsibility of the Ministry of Labour. The unemployment insurance is voluntary and is administered by special Approved Unemployment Insurance Funds (*A-Kassas*) acting under the supervision of the Labour Market Board. Their activities are usually closely connected to the trade unions, even though they are also open to non-union members. The approval of and registration with the Labour Market Board entitles the funds to state subsidies. A basic insurance, with the character of a cash benefit, is paid to people who do not fulfil the requirements to receive benefits from the voluntary insurance or who are simply not members of an unemployment fund. The basic insurance is also under the responsibility of the Labour Market Board and administered by the Approved Unemployment Insurance Funds.

The tax authorities are responsible for the collection of contributions. The link between contributions and benefits is very weak in the sense that the responsibility for raising contributions lies within the Ministry of Finance and the National Tax Board. The fees paid by members in the *A-kassa* are however paid directly to the unemployment insurance fund.

Health care is under the responsibility of the county councils. The county councils are appointed by general election and have the right to levy taxes in order to finance their activities, of which health care forms the largest part.

The Social Services Act places the responsibility for all social services for people staying in the municipality with the respective municipality. The level of social assistance is also determined at a municipal level. The local body which takes all the decisions concerning social assistance is called the Local Social Welfare Board. Hierarchically, it comes under the local government but its activities are regulated in the Social Services Act and controlled by both the county governing board and the National Health and Social Welfare Board. The National Health and Social Welfare Board also has the legislative power to issue recommendations concerning the application of the Social Services Act. The county governing board supports the county administrative courts and provides both counselling and information to individuals.

3. *Personal scope of application*

The national social insurance system is extensive in the sense that all Swedish citizens, no matter where they live, and all non-citizens legally resident in Sweden are insured. All individuals falling within these two categories are obligatorily insured in the national social insurance, which means that the system has a universal character. There is no possibility to stay outside the insurance. However, a person's status as insured does not mean that this person is actually entitled to a benefit under the national insurance schemes.

From the day an insured person turns 16, he has to be registered with the local insurance office where he is domiciled. In addition, a non-citizen living and working or studying in Sweden with a residence permit for at least one year, will be registered with a social insurance office. Registration is a precondition for entitlement to many benefits, e.g. the sickness insurance, parental insurance and the maternity benefit. The general rule is accordingly that residence is a prerequisite for entitlement to social security benefits.

The basic old age pension is based upon a residency rule where each year of residency between the ages of 16 and 65 entitles the claimant to 1/40 of a full pension; alternatively the number of years that the insured has had income giving entitlement to supplementary pension (*ATP*) may be taken into account. The residence requirement also applies for basic pension in case of early retirement. Survivor's pension is paid out to a surviving spouse or child under the precondition that he is resident in Sweden.

Every person residing in Sweden is entitled to medical care. An additional general condition is that the medical care is offered in Sweden.

Everyone who is a member of an unemployment insurance fund is insured against unemployment. Membership in an unemployment fund is open to everyone who fulfils the fund's conditions concerning work in its field of action. Self-employed persons in different fields have special funds and some funds admit both employed and the self-employed to become members. The unemployment insurance does not involve any residence or citizenship requirements.

Everybody working in Sweden is insured against occupational injuries and diseases, however, residence is required from the self-employed. If an employee is sent away by a Swedish employer in order to work in another country for a maximum period of one year, he is insured during that period. A worker that is sent to Sweden by a foreign employer in order to work for less than one year is not insured.

Child allowance is paid for children domiciled in Sweden and who are Swedish citizens. It is also paid if the child is not a Swedish citizen but brought up by someone who is legally domiciled and registered in Sweden. If the parents have joint custody, the allowance is paid to the mother and in other cases to the person who is the legal guardian or has custody of the child.

Social assistance is offered to all individuals with the right to stay in the country, being unable to provide for their own living and who are not in receipt of benefits under the normal social insurance schemes.

4. *Risks and benefits*

Swedish social insurance introduced the concept of the 'base amount'. Today, it is widely used and recognised both in the private and the public sector. The concept was invented to provide for the calculation of benefits and incomes to be smoothly adjusted to changes in living costs. Each year the amount is determined by the government according to a calculation established by law. In social security legislation many of the benefits are expressed in a percentage of the base amount. However, the base amount is purely mathematical and statistical; it does not represent any minimum level of living standard or any other such level.

4.1. Old age

The first tier of the pension system is a public social insurance with two co-ordinated pension schemes, one flat-rate national basic pension scheme (*folkpension*) for all persons who are 65 or older, and one earnings-related national supplementary pension scheme (*ATP*). The retirement age is 65, but this is optional. One can start to draw a reduced pension at 60 or wait until the age of 70 and receive a higher pension as compensation. At the age of 61, both workers and self-employed persons also have the option to draw a part-time pension, if they can show a decrease in working hours of at least five hours per week. The self-employed claimant has to show an actual decrease in working hours, e.g. by a lower business turn-over which is a sign that he is actually working fewer hours. The purpose of this possibility is to offer a smooth shift from worker to pensioner. On top of the state schemes you have collectively bargained insurance schemes of which there are four main schemes: one for those employed by central government, one for those employed by local government, one for blue-collar workers in the private sector and, finally, one for white-collar workers in the private sector. The first tier (both components) guarantees a pension of about 65% of the lost income and with the second tier this percentage rises to about 75%.

The national basic pension scheme is of classic Beveridge-type and is aiming to guarantee everyone a basic security. The pension amount is 96% of the base amount per year for unmarried pensioners and 78,5% for married pensioners, irrespective of whether the spouse receives a pension or not. However, if the married pensioners live apart they receive the higher benefit. Each year of residence entitles the claimant to 1/40 of a full pension. Insurance for fewer than three years does not confer any right to pension, whilst 40 years of insurance leads to a full pension. An alternative way is to have 30 years of earnings amounting to a minimum of one base amount per year, which is the lowest pensionable income. If the requirements for a full pension are not met, the pension is reduced proportionally.

The *ATP* has become the most important of the two public pension schemes. *ATP* is earned by all Swedish residents between 16 and 65 having income from work amounting to more than one base amount per year. To get a full *ATP*, 30 years of earnings are required and the pension is then based on the average of the 15 years of the highest real income earnings. *ATP* is payable at 2% of the average income for these best-earning years multiplied by the number of years in which income was earned. Earnings over a ceiling of 7,5 base amounts do not influence the size of the pension. If a person has less than 30 years of earnings the pension amount is reduced proportionally.

People who are not entitled to a supplementary pension can receive an additional pension supplement, that is not means-tested, in order to boost their basic pension. Together they constitute a guaranteed minimum pension. There is also a possibility to obtain a means-tested housing supplement for pensioners. If a pensioner only receives the guaranteed minimum pension this housing supplement covers about 85% of the housing costs.

The pension system is in the final stage of reform and by the beginning of the next century pensions in the new system will start to be paid. The main ideas behind the reform is, first of all, to guarantee a basic income for everyone in old age, secondly the state is trying to create a more viable pension system by using insurance rather than redistribution principles.

In the reformed system, pensions will be based on earnings in every year from 16 until retirement. The contribution will be 18,5% of each year's earnings and that amount also constitutes the accrued pension credits. This means a significant change from the former system where the best 15 years are the base for the *ATP*. The size of pensions will be totally dependent upon the contributions paid by the persons retiring and their expected remaining lifetime. Pension credits will also be indexed to average national earnings instead of the base amount.

For those with low or no earnings there will be a guaranteed pension of 2,1 base amount for an unmarried pensioner and 1,87 for married pensioners. To qualify for the guaranteed pension, one has to have resided in Sweden for 40 years between the ages of 16 and 65. If the pensioner receives a total pension of more than 3,0 base amounts for unmarried, or 2,655 for married, only the earnings related pension will be paid out. The guaranteed pension will be price indexed.

4.2. Death

Survivor's pension can be paid as Child Pension, Adjustment Pension and Special Survivor's Pension. After a reform in 1990, the weight of the survivor's pensions was placed on the Child Pension. This reform took place due to changes on the labour market. The basic idea behind the reform was to remove the differences between the sexes concerning the right to a survivor's pension since the number of women in active employment has increased.

Child Pension from the *folkpension* and the *ATP* is paid to a child until the age of 18 if one or both of his parents are deceased. A child that has reached the age of 18 can be entitled to Extended Child Pension until the age of 20, if he is still in school and is entitled to Extended Child Benefit or study assistance.

The Child Pension is always at least 25% of the base amount if one parent has died and 50 % if both parents have died. This constitutes the basic level and is paid to each child from the *folkpension*. In addition, the children share the parent's right to *ATP*. The total Child Pension paid from the *ATP* and the *folkpension* together has to reach a guaranteed level of at least 40% of the base amount. This amount is paid irrespective of whether the child has a right to *ATP* or not. If both parents die this guaranteed level is 80% of the base amount.

A surviving spouse has the right to an Adjustment Pension from the *folkpension* and the *ATP*. The Adjustment Pension is payable for a period of six months under the conditions that the surviving spouse is under 65 years old and at the time has the custody of and is permanently living with a child under the age of twelve years, or has been living together with the deceased without interruption for a minimum period of five years prior to death. If the child is still under the age of twelve when the pension terminates, the Adjustment Pension can be granted for another six-months period. This extension can be done more than once and will continue until the child reaches the age of twelve.

Other surviving spouses that cannot support themselves by working and do not receive a retirement pension may be entitled to a Special Survivor's pension. This pension is paid out when the right to an Adjustment Pension expires. The

Special Survivor's Pension can be limited in time and in any case it will be reviewed every three years. It is not means-tested, the deciding factor is whether the surviving spouse is able, or should be able, to support himself by working.

4.3. Incapacity for work

A person, earning more than a certain amount per annum, who looses his capacity to work due to sickness or injury and thus loses his income from employment or self-employment, is entitled to sickness benefits. One has the right to sickness benefit when the incapacity for work is at least 25%. The incapacity to work due to sickness can be either 100%, 75%, 50% or 25%.

When one is sick notification is made to the employer who is responsible for paying sick pay for the first 28 days. From the 29th day, sickness allowance is received from the local insurance office. Sickness benefit is not given the first day of sickness but from day two at a rate of 80% of the salary. There is a ceiling of income conferring entitlement at 7,5 base amounts. For people with a documented high risk of falling sick no waiting period is required. There is also a general exception stating that the total amount of waiting days is limited to ten days per person per year. Self-employed people can choose a waiting period of either 3 or 30 days. The contribution is lower if the longer waiting period is chosen. To make it easier for individuals who have been sick for a long time to come back to work, there is a rehabilitation benefit. This rehabilitation can take the form of e.g. work training, where the individual can try out his former work to see if he is ready to go back, or education in order to get another job.

The pregnancy benefit is part of the sickness insurance even if pregnancy is not leading to incapacity for work. It was introduced for women with strenuous work and women whose working environment puts the foetus at risk. In the case of strenuous work, the pregnant woman is obliged to try to change her working situation with the full co-operation of her employer. An evaluation of the type of work and the ability to work is done in each case. If an alternative job is not available, she is entitled to 50 days of pregnancy benefit which can be drawn, at the earliest, from 60 days before expected delivery. If the working environment causes risks, the pregnant woman receives pregnancy benefits if she is proscribed from continuing her work due to regulations in the Working Environment Act. Only women in gainful employment are eligible to receive pregnancy benefits.

For people who are disabled or suffering from chronic illness and so are unable to work, a disability pension within the *folkpension* and the *ATP* is provided. The concept of invalidity within the disability pension can be described as an estimation of the invalidity based on medical factors. The assessment of the invalidity is also given with respect to the preconditions and social situation in the individual case. Disability pension can be obtained as a full, three-quarter, half or quarter pension, meaning that the reduction in working capacity must be at least 25%. If the working capacity is not permanently reduced but expected to last for a limited period of time, one may obtain a temporary disability pension. The pension amount corresponds to what the person becoming invalid would have received at the normal retirement age.

Occupational injury or disease are covered by a special scheme. Economic compensation for sickness or injury caused by accidents at work is more generous than compensation from the other social security schemes. The scope of the scheme is wide since it encompasses all accidents and diseases caused by working conditions. The insurance is supplementary only, meaning that in the event of injury at work or invalidity, the general benefits are paid first and then they are usually supplemented by benefits from the occupational insurance. The scheme provides, within certain limits, for full compensation of loss of income resulting from injury at work. If short term incapacity for work is caused by injury from work and sickness benefit is payable, no supplement is paid; but for lasting injury and complete incapacity, in principle a life annuity of 100% of the lost income is payable up to retirement age. However, there is a ceiling of 7,5 base amounts.

4.4. Unemployment

Support for the unemployed is provided through the unemployment insurance. Before a reform in 1997, the unemployment insurance was split up into two different but complimentary schemes that were also administered by different bodies. One of the schemes provided an assistance benefit for unemployed people who did not qualify for the voluntary insurance benefit; the other provided a voluntary social insurance benefit. The reform brought these two schemes of different characters together under one statute. However, the insurance is still split up into two parts. One basic insurance with an assistance character and one voluntary insurance against loss of income.

In order to be entitled for benefits it is required that, during a period of twelve months before unemployment, the applicant has worked at least 70 hours a month for six months, or at least 450 hours over a period of 180 days on condition that the work took place during six periods of 30 days with a working time of at least 45 hours in each period. This last condition is created to adapt the unemployment insurance to a more flexible labour market. There are numerous exceptions from the working requirement, e.g. recently graduated students qualify after a waiting period of 90 days for the basic insurance benefit without fulfilling the working conditions. The right to unemployment benefit is also subject to certain general conditions; the unemployed claimant must be capable of work, willing to accept suitable employment, registered at the public unemployment office and unable to find work. There must also be a total reduction of income from work which means that someone who has been granted a 'golden handshake' will not be considered as an unemployed person immediately after losing his job.

A person can also be partially unemployed. In this case, unemployment benefit is given to them for the time that they are actually available on the labour market. The size of this benefit depends on how much the person worked before unemployment, the extent of current employment and how much he wants to work.

If an unemployed person fulfils the stated conditions, he is entitled to the basic insurance benefit of a fixed sum per day. In order to be entitled to the income-related benefit, it is required that the unemployed person has been a member of an insurance fund for a minimum of twelve months. In that case he is paid 80% of his previous income. However, there is a maximum amount of about 240% of the basic benefit per day. Unemployment benefit is paid after a waiting period of five days. The maximum period of payments is 300 days if the unemployed recipient is under the age of 57, and 450 days if the unemployed beneficiary is at least 57 years old.

There are possibilities for the unemployed claimants to qualify for another 300 days or 450 days of payments. The work-related qualifying conditions can be replaced by, for instance, participation in vocational advancement, special job training or other activities that are classified as work at the discretion of the government.

4.5. Health care

Health insurance includes, next to income replacement benefits, the right to financial compensation, limiting every individual's costs for medical and dental treatment. The Health and Medical Care Act defines health and medical care as 'measures to medically prevent, diagnose and treat illness and injuries'. As a concept, health care also includes measures of illness prevention, abortion, childbirth and sterilisation. The health care system is primarily public and of a universal character. All citizens are compulsory insured.

Each county is responsible for ensuring that its residents have access to good health care. The county operates hospitals, dental services and other health care facilities. It also employs most of the staff occupied in the health care sector. Doctors with independent practices may be included in the universal system and remunerated by the county. This means that there is very little financial difference for the patient whether he goes to a public institution or a private practitioner.

In order to finance health care, the counties levy income tax on their residents. Additionally, when consulting medical staff, patients have to pay a charge which is not reimbursed but works as a user's charge. This charge depends on what kind of medical service is used and varies from county to county but ranges between SEK 100-350 per visit. Hospital care is also subject to a charge at a maximum rate of SEK 80 per day. For pensioners the cost for hospital care is charged through a pension deduction.

Drugs given on prescription are covered by the general insurance system and not by the counties' responsibility for health care. Certain drugs for people suffering from chronic diseases and severe illnesses are 100% reimbursed. Other

drugs given on prescription are reimbursed in accordance with a discount-system. The individual pays:
- the total cost up to a sum of SEK 400
- 50 % of the cost between SEK 400 and 1200
- 25 % of the cost between SEK 1200 and 2800
- 10 % of the cost between SEK 2800 and 3800.

Nothing is paid for the cost over SEK 3800 which means that the total cost never exceeds SEK 1300 per year. Pharmacies are directly reimbursed from national insurance.

Dental care is also part of the general national insurance. Up to the age of twenty dental care is free of charge. Other people pay:
- the total cost up to a sum of SEK 700
- 65 % of the cost between SEK 700 and 13500
- 30 % of the cost between SEK 13500 and the actual cost

4.6. Family

The parental insurance has evolved from a classic maternity insurance to a parental insurance for loss of income, giving, in all essentials, the same benefit to both parents. Parental support benefit gives a right to compensation for loss of income when a child is born or adopted. The benefit can also be temporary if a parent has to stay home from work in order to take care of the child or e.g. visit the child's school.

Parental support benefit in connection with childbirth is payable for a maximum of 450 days for each child. The father and the mother are both obliged to take one month each (a total of 60 days), the remaining period (390 days) can be divided between the mother and the father as they see fit. The mother can start claiming the benefit 60 days before expected delivery and it may be drawn at any time until the child has reached the age of eight or completed his first year in school. During the first 360 days the parent is compensated with 80% of the lost income estimated in the same manner as in cases of sickness. A condition for receiving payment higher than a guaranteed rate at SEK 60 a day for the first 180 days is that the parent has been insured for at least 240 days before the child was born. For the last 90 days, the benefit is payable at the guaranteed rate of SEK 60 a day.

The temporary parental benefit is paid to parents with children who are no older than 12 years of age, this age-limit can be extended to 16 for children with special needs. Normally, the benefit is payable up to 60 days per child annually. Another temporary parental benefit is paid to the father for 10 days in conjunction with child birth. The compensation is 80% of the lost income estimated in the same manner as in case of sickness.

For children under 16 a general child allowance is payable. This allowance is universal and paid to all parents with children residing in Sweden. The allowance is tax-free and independent of the family's income. Families with three or more children are entitled to a large-family supplement. When a child reaches the age of 16, the child allowance is replaced by extended child allowance on the condition that the child is attending the nine-year compulsory school. Child care allowance is paid to parents taking care of a child under the age of 16 who, as a result of illness or handicap, requires special care or assistance.

Another financial support for families is the housing allowance. This allowance is means-tested and given to all persons with low wages, not only families, in order to provide for a certain standard of living.

4.7. Need

Social assistance is given to individuals who are unable to support themselves and whose needs cannot be met in any other way. The assistance is a form of last resort safety net and guarantees a reasonable standard of living for every individual. The Social Services Act is a target oriented law giving municipalities freedom to decide for themselves what kind of services and particular activities they want to provide for their citizens. This also means that each municipality is responsible for providing this assistance to people living in their geographical jurisdiction.

The right to assistance is a subjective right and non-discretionary. The allowance is means-tested and paid out according to norms given in each municipality, meaning that the amount might differ substantially between different municipalities. However, the National Board of Health and Welfare gives recommendations for monthly amounts. Additional allowances are paid in respect of dependants and supplements can also be paid for special or exceptional needs. A decision in an individual matter may be challenged before a court. The administrative courts are not bound by the norm set by the municipality and the recommendations given by the National Board of Health and Welfare is seen as a minimum level. If the assistance set by the municipality is considered too low to provide for a reasonable standard of living, it may be changed by the court.

5. *Financing*

The Swedish social security system is financed through taxation and contributions from both employers and employees.

Social assistance, health care and family allowances are financed through general taxation even though different public bodies have the financial responsibility for each scheme. Social assistance is financed mainly by taxes levied by the municipalities and health care is financed by taxes paid to the county councils. A small part of the health care system is, however, financed by patient fees. Family allowances are totally financed by the state and the state also gives substantial subsidies to most parts of the social insurance system.

The social insurance system was originally financed through contributions with a strong link to the benefits. When creating the extensive Swedish welfare state, this link between contributions and benefits vanished to a large extent, thus giving the contributions a character similar to taxes. Today, the contributions are very important for the general stability of the public economy, meaning that a large part of the general public revenue comes from the system of collecting contributions. In addition, the tax authorities have the responsibility for collecting both taxes and contributions, and the Ministry of Finance is also the ministry responsible for all funds collected. However, contributions are still, to some extent, assigned to specific social security purposes meaning that the term contributions is not an entirely inappropriate term. The unemployment insurance is, apart from employer's contributions and state subsidies, also financed by a membership fee paid directly to the unemployment insurance fund.

Social contributions have traditionally been levied on employers and the self-employed according to the principle that employers should take the responsibility for the welfare of their employees. The contributions are around 30% of the total sum of wages and in the case of self-employed people, around 30% of their income from work. This means that the contributions are not levied individually but through a collective system on a company's total wage cost.

The 30%-contribution is split up in percentages earmarked for the different social insurance schemes. This earmarking, however, is only the legal situation and not the de facto one. Instead, the extent to which contributions actually finance social insurance varies, e.g. the health insurance is over financed while the basic pension is a pay-as-you-go scheme (current income financing) financed from the State budget plus a small pay-roll-contribution, in addition the *ATP* is financed through partial funding from the employer's and the self employed's contributions.

In the 1990s employee contributions have been introduced in the form a General Individual Contribution and a General Wage Contribution. These contributions are paid by both employees and the self-employed. The General Individual Contribution is paid at 1% of the individual's income from work to the pension system and 3,95% is paid to the sickness insurance. The General Wage Contribution is 1,5% of the income from work and the money collected is only general public revenue. So far, the contributions only cover a minor part of the insurance cost but the change is important. The major reason for shifting to employee contributions is to make the costs of social insurance more visible to each citizen and to strengthen the link between contributions and benefits.

6. Judicial review

Disputes concerning social security follow the general administrative procedure which consists of the formal procedural rules for dealing with administrative matters and review which concern administrative authorities and the administrative courts.

The possibility to demand the reconsideration of a decision made by the decision making body is an important principle of administrative procedure. The reason is, of course, to facilitate a quick and inexpensive way of dealing with cases. This first step in administrative procedure is applied when an authority considers an appeal internally. A decision taken by an adjudication officer cannot be appealed before the decision has been re-considered.

Appeals are made to the general Administrative Courts where all judges are professional lawyers. The administrative court system has three instances: the County Administrative Court, the Administrative Court of Appeal and the Supreme Administrative Court. Only cases of special significance are tried by the Administrative Court of Appeal and the Administrative Supreme Court.

If an individual is not satisfied with a decision taken by the Approved Unemployment Funds, an appeal can be made to the Labour Market Board. However, the decisions taken by the Approved Unemployment Funds have to be reconsidered before they are handed over to the Labour Market Board. The Labour Market Board can also review a decision made by an Approved Unemployment Fund ex officio. Decisions taken by the Labour Market Board can be appealed through the general administrative court system.

It is the local social welfare board that determines if an application for social assistance is to be granted or not. If an application is denied, procedural rules oblige the decision making body to provide the applicant with explanation of both the outcome of the decision and how to make an appeal. A negative decision regarding social assistance can be appealed to the County Administrative Court as an administrative appeal (*förvaltningsbesvär*), or as a communal appeal (*kommunalbesvär*). The difference is that an administrative appeal can only be made by the parties and that the decision can be both quashed and changed or replaced. The communal appeal is an appeal that can be made by any member of the community, the court only taking a decision based upon whether the decision taken by the administrative body is lawful or not.

One should also mention the importance of the office of the Parliamentary Ombudsman. The Ombudsman can undertake supervisory action either through his own initiative or after a complaint has been filed. Although the office of the Ombudsman cannot change a decision, its criticism of an administrative body and recommendations are taken very seriously.